One God in Three Persons

One God in Three Persons

Unity of Essence, Distinction of Persons, Implications for Life

Edited by
BRUCE A. WARE AND JOHN STARKE

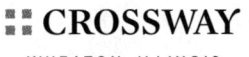

WHEATON, ILLINOIS

One God in Three Persons: Unity of Essence, Distinction of Persons, Implications for Life

Copyright © 2015 by Bruce A. Ware and John B. Starke

Published by Crossway
    1300 Crescent Street
    Wheaton, Illinois 60187

All rights reserved. No part of this publication may be reproduced, stored in a retrieval system, or transmitted in any form by any means, electronic, mechanical, photocopy, recording, or otherwise, without the prior permission of the publisher, except as provided for by USA copyright law.

Cover design: Dual Identity, inc.

First printing 2015

Printed in the United States of America

Unless otherwise indicated, Scripture quotations are from the ESV® Bible (The Holy Bible, English Standard Version®), copyright © 2001 by Crossway, a publishing ministry of Good News Publishers. Used by permission. All rights reserved.

Scripture quotations marked KJV are from the King James Version of the Bible.

Scripture references marked NIV are taken from The Holy Bible, New International Version®, NIV®. Copyright © 1973, 1978, 1984 by Biblica, Inc.™ Used by permission. All rights reserved worldwide.

Scripture references marked NRSV are from *The New Revised Standard Version*. Copyright © 1989 by the Division of Christian Education of the National Council of the Churches of Christ in the U.S.A. Published by Thomas Nelson, Inc. Used by permission of the National Council of the Churches of Christ in the U.S.A.

All emphases in Scripture quotations have been added by the authors.

Trade paperback ISBN: 978-1-4335-2842-2
ePub ISBN: 978-1-4335-2845-3
PDF ISBN: 978-1-4335-2843-9
Mobipocket ISBN: 978-1-4335-2844-6

Library of Congress Cataloging-in-Publication Data

One God in three persons: unity of essence, distinction of persons, implications for life / edited by Bruce A. Ware and John Starke.
    pages cm
Includes bibliographical references and index.
ISBN 978-1-4335-2842-2 (tp)
1. Trinity. I. Ware, Bruce A., 1953– II. Starke, John, 1981–
BT111.3.O54   2015
231'.044—dc23   2014034078

Crossway is a publishing ministry of Good News Publishers.

VP		25	24	23	22	21	20	19	18	17	16	15
15	14	13	12	11	10	9	8	7	6	5	4	3	2	1

To our wives

Jodi
who is my (Bruce's) faithful companion
in life and ministry

Jena
who supports me (John) in my weaknesses
and encourages me to pray

Contents

Abbreviations — 9

Preface — 11

1 Doctrinal Deviations in Evangelical-Feminist Arguments about the Trinity — 17
  WAYNE GRUDEM

2 "I Always Do What Pleases Him" — 47
  The Father and Son in the Gospel of John
  CHRISTOPHER W. COWAN

3 God Is the Head of Christ — 65
  Does 1 Corinthians 11:3 Ground Gender Complementarity in the Immanent Trinity?
  KYLE CLAUNCH

4 "That God May Be All in All" — 95
  The Trinity in 1 Corinthians 15
  JAMES M. HAMILTON JR.

5 Eternal Generation in the Church Fathers — 109
  ROBERT LETHAM

6 True Sonship—Where Dignity and Submission Meet — 127
  A Fourth-Century Discussion
  MICHAEL J. OVEY

7 Augustine and His Interpreters — 155
  JOHN STARKE

8	"To Devote Ourselves to the Blessed Trinity" *Eighteenth-Century Particular Baptists, Andrew Fuller, and the Defense of "Trinitarian Communities"* MICHAEL A. G. HAYKIN	173
9	An Examination of Three Recent Philosophical Arguments against Hierarchy in the Immanent Trinity PHILIP R. GONS AND ANDREW DAVID NASELLI	195
10	Simplicity, Triunity, and the Incomprehensibility of God K. SCOTT OLIPHINT	215
11	Does Affirming an Eternal Authority-Submission Relationship in the Trinity Entail a Denial of *Homoousios*? *A Response to Millard Erickson and Tom McCall* BRUCE A. WARE	237
Contributors		249
General Index		251
Scripture Index		259

Abbreviations

ANF	*The Ante-Nicene Fathers*. Edited by Alexander Roberts and James Donaldson. 10 vols. 1885–1887. Reprint, Edinburgh: T&T Clark, 1993.
ATJ	*Ashland Theological Journal*
BDAG	Bauer, W., F. W. Danker, W. F. Arndt, and F. W. Gingrich. *Greek-English Lexicon of the New Testament and Other Early Christian Literature*. 3d ed. Chicago, 1999.
EFE	Eternal functional equality
EFS	Eternal functional subordination
ERAS	Eternal relational authority-submission
JBMW	*Journal for Biblical Manhood and Womanhood*
JETS	*Journal of the Evangelical Theological Society*
JTS	*Journal of Theological Studies*
NICNT	New International Commentary on the New Testament
NPNF	*Nicene and Post-Nicene Fathers of the Christian Church*. Edited by Philip Schaff and Henry Wace. Edinburgh: T&T Clark, 1886–1900.
PG	*Patrologia Graeca*. Edited by J. P. Migne et al. Paris, 1857–1866.
PL	*Patrologia Latina*. Edited by J. P. Migne et al. Paris, 1878–1890.
TDNT	*Theological Dictionary of the New Testament*. Edited by G. Kittel and G. Friedrich. Translated by G. W. Bromiley. 10 vols. Grand Rapids, 1964–1976.
TrinJ	*Trinity Journal*
WAF	*The Complete Works of the Rev. Andrew Fuller*. Edited by Joseph Belcher. 3 vols. 1845. Reprint, Harrisonburg, VA: Sprinkle, 1988.

WJP *The Theological and Miscellaneous Works of Joseph Priestley.* Edited by J. T. Rutt. 25 vols. London, 1817–1832. Reprint, New York: Klaus, 1972.

WTJ *Westminster Theological Journal*

Preface

The concern of this volume is the doctrine of God and, in particular, a debate among evangelicals concerning how the persons of our Trinitarian God relate to one another. This is not a debate concerning *being* among the persons of the Godhead, nor *status*, but concerning *relation*. The points among orthodox Christians are clear: the Father, Son, and Holy Spirit are identical in *being* and equal in *status*. But the matter before us concerns *relations* among the persons of the Father, Son, and Holy Spirit.

What often becomes central in the debate is how the Son relates to the Father, not because the Holy Spirit is inconsequential, but because in the New Testament the incarnation of the Son dramatically forces us to ask questions about the relationship of the persons of the Trinity in a way Pentecost does not. Therefore, much of the debate before us answers the question, Does the human obedience of Christ to the Father have a basis in the eternal Son of God, or is it restricted to his humanity and incarnate state?

One side of the debate argues that we must restrict Christ's obedience to the Father to his incarnate state, and to affirm otherwise gets us dangerously close to dissolving the deity of Christ. The other side affirms that, indeed, the human obedience of Christ has a basis in the eternal Son of God, and to affirm otherwise would threaten the integrity of the human and divine nature of the Son or lead to a modalistic error of a "Christ whose proper being remains hidden behind an improper being."[1]

The essays in this volume argue for the latter position.

---

[1] Robert Letham, *The Holy Trinity: In Scripture, History, Theology, and Worship* (Phillipsburg, NJ: P&R, 2004), 398. Letham makes this point from Karl Barth, *Church Dogmatics*, IV/1: 198–200.

The Debate in Context

Debates over the nature of God never exist in a vacuum. Theological controversies throughout the church's history have arisen from particular cultural moments. This controversy is no different. While trying to find the source is a bit like peeling back an onion with no center, just layers upon layers, the cultural *moment* was the rise of feminism and an increasingly feminized doctrine of God within Protestant denominations in North America, Europe, and Australia. Feminist theologians like Elizabeth Schüssler Fiorenza and Catherine LaCugna, and those sympathetic to feminism like Jürgen Moltmann, along with some evangelicals, labored to eliminate anything appearing to give credence to the Son's submitting to the Father from eternity. They thereby gave ontological reinforcement to a completely egalitarian relationship between male and female.[2]

In response, conservative evangelicals countered the rise of feminism in the church primarily by arguing for a complementarian structure to gender and the local church, but also by appealing to the Trinity.[3] In response to complementarian appeals to the Trinity, a more concerted opposition came from *evangelical* egalitarians,[4] which has, in turn, produced a response of entire (or large portions of) volumes on both sides aimed entirely at this debate,[5] along with any number of journal articles and theological society papers.

Since this debate carries with it not only historical questions about the doctrine of God and the Trinity, but also cultural baggage of modern feminism and gender debates, emotive language and heresy charges tend

---

[2] See Elisabeth Schüssler Fiorenza, *Discipleship of Equals: A Critical Feminist Ekklesia-logy of Liberation* (New York: Crossroad, 1993); Fiorenza, *Jesus: Miriam's Child, Sophia's Prophet: Critical Issues in Feminist Christology* (New York: Continuum, 1994); Catherine Mowry LaCugna, *God for Us: The Trinity and Christian Life* (San Francisco: HarperSanFrancisco, 1991); Jürgen Moltmann, *The Trinity and the Kingdom: The Doctrine of God* (London: SCM, 1991).
[3] See John Piper and Wayne Grudem, eds., *Recovering Biblical Manhood and Womanhood* (Wheaton, IL: Crossway, 1991); Robert Letham, "The Man-Woman Debate: Theological Comment," *WTJ* 52 (1991): 65–78.
[4] See Gilbert Bilezikian, "Hermeneutical Bungee-Jumping: Subordination in the Trinity," *JETS* 40 (1997): 57–68; Kevin Giles, *The Trinity and Subordinationism: The Doctrine of God and the Contemporary Gender Debate* (Downers Grove, IL: InterVarsity, 2002).
[5] See Bruce A. Ware, *Father, Son, and Holy Spirit: Relationships, Roles, and Relevance* (Wheaton, IL: Crossway, 2005); Wayne Grudem, *Evangelical Feminism and Biblical Truth: An Analysis of More than 100 Disputed Questions* (Colorado Springs: Multnomah, 2004; repr., Wheaton, IL: Crossway, 2012); Millard J. Erickson, *Who's Tampering with the Trinity? An Assessment of the Subordination Debate* (Grand Rapids: Kregel, 2009); Thomas H. McCall, *Which Trinity? Whose Monotheism? Philosophical and Systematic Theologians on the Metaphysics of Trinitarian Theology* (Grand Rapids: Eerdmans, 2010).

to cloud the matter—even trivialize it. However, our cultural moment does not trivialize the question, nor should our emotional impulses from gender debates cloud the matter. What is at stake is larger than our cultural moment since it concerns the nature of God and the doctrine of the Trinity.

Finally, some argue that we should be slow to use or should cease from using Trinitarian arguments to support a particular view of human relations.[6] Some even find these discussions to be useless and needless speculation. But such conclusions fall short of proper Christian devotion. Take, for example, the call for Christians to follow in the humility of Christ (Phil. 2:1–11). Our call is not just to follow the Christ of the incarnate state who ate and drank with sinners (though indeed it is that), but also to follow the Christ who "was in the form of God" and then took "the form of a servant" (2:6, 7), humbling himself in order for the Father to exalt him (2:9–11). And we are to follow Christ not only into humility, but also into exaltation *from* the Father. Not that *we* will be worshiped, or that every tongue will confess that *we* are Lord; but if you "humble yourselves before the Lord, . . . he will exalt you" (James 4:10). And how will we understand true humility in hopes of true exaltation if we do not adequately understand the Son as the Servant of the Lord (see Isaiah 42) humbling himself in order to be exalted by the Father? For it is not the example of the Father's humility that we should follow, but the Son's, and it is not the Son who will exalt us, but the Father.

Is it not obvious, though, that the humility we learn from the Son has strong implications for human relations? And is it not reasonable that Paul may then want husbands and wives to consider the relationship of the Father and Son when considering how they relate to one another (1 Cor. 11:3; see also 15:28)? Is it not pastoral of Paul to present not only the sacrificial and self-giving relationship of Christ and his church, but also the union of love that the Father has with the Son and the Son with the Father to guide Christian marriage, rather than an arbitrary cultural norm, whether a traditional hierarchicalism or modern egalitarianism?

---

[6] Michael F. Bird, "Subordination in the Trinity and Gender Roles: A Response to Recent Discussion," *TrinJ* 29 (2008): 267–83.

Worse, calling for Christians to cease reflecting on the relationship of the Father with the Son is like asking Christians to cease reflecting on heaven. The Son prays to the Father that we might in fact be brought into the relationship of the Father and the Son. Jesus prays "that they may all be one, just as you, Father, are in me, and I in you, that *they also may be in us* . . . . The glory that you have given me I have given to them, that they may be one even as we are one, *I in them and you in me*, that they may become perfectly one" (John 17:21–23). The intra-trinitarian relationship in question is also filled with a kind of love and glory and joy that Christians can look forward to participating in. Not that we will be brought into God's proper being, but we will be brought into the joy and delight the Father has in the Son and the Son in the Father. So then, the result of all contemplation of God should finally develop into praise, and with praise, joy.

Toward a Comprehensive Approach

Most volumes noted above have labored, in some measure, to approach this debate through matters of biblical interpretation, church history, theological perspective, and philosophy. But no one author can hope to be comprehensive in this matter. Yet that is the aim of this volume with its multiple contributors: to seek to be comprehensive in matters of Scripture, history, theological perspective, and philosophy.

Certainly there will be overlap among chapters, since each discipline is interdependent upon the others. However, our essays on *Scripture* aim to show that modern interpreters who argue that the New Testament authors, more specifically the apostles John and Paul, never intended to communicate an eternal submission of the Son of God to the Father are out of step with not only the meaning of the text, but also its implications for Christian discipleship.

Our essays concerning church history show that while this debate was not the center of many of the early-to-medieval church controversies, it was certainly addressed, and to hold that the Son's submission to the Father is restricted to the incarnate state puts one at odds with orthodox christologies or forfeits important safeguards against heterodoxy.

Finally, the essays that concern theological and philosophical perspectives maintain that when we understand the relationship of the eternal Father and Son as one of authority and submission, we rightly think God's thoughts after him as creatures contemplating his nature.

It is our hope that this volume will bring praise to God the Father, God the Son, and God the Holy Spirit, while adorning the church with wisdom and clarity. With this, then, let us persevere toward the reward of knowing God.

> O Lord God Almighty,
> eternal, immortal, invisible, the mysteries of whose being are unsearchable:
> Accept our praises for the revelation you have given of yourself,
> Father, Son, and Holy Spirit,
> three persons in one God,
> and mercifully grant that in holding fast this faith
> we may magnify your glorious name,
> for you live and reign, one God, world without end. Amen.[7]

Bruce A. Ware
John Starke

---

[7] Prayers of Adoration on Trinity Sunday, *The Worship Sourcebook* (Grand Rapids: Baker, 2004).

1

Doctrinal Deviations in Evangelical-Feminist Arguments about the Trinity

WAYNE GRUDEM

Several evangelical-feminist authors have denied that the Son is eternally subject to the authority of the Father within the Trinity. These authors include Gilbert Bilezikian, Rebecca Groothuis, Kevin Giles, and Millard Erickson.[1] More recently, some additional essays have supported this view, especially essays by Phillip Cary, Linda Belleville, Kevin Giles (again), and Dennis Jowers.[2]

In reading these arguments, I noticed that they contained important doctrinal deviations either in what was said or in what was implied by the form of argument used. The arguments either deviated from the

---

[1] See Gilbert Bilezikian, *Community 101: Reclaiming the Local Church as Community of Oneness* (Grand Rapids: Zondervan, 1997), 190–91; Rebecca Merrill Groothuis, *Good News for Women: A Biblical Picture of Gender Equality* (Grand Rapids: Baker, 1997), 57; Kevin Giles, *The Trinity and Subordinationism: The Doctrine of God and the Contemporary Gender Debate* (Downers Grove, IL: InterVarsity, 2002); Giles, *Jesus and the Father: Modern Evangelicals Reinvent the Doctrine of the Trinity* (Grand Rapids: Zondervan, 2006); Millard J. Erickson, *Who's Tampering with the Trinity? An Assessment of the Subordination Debate* (Grand Rapids: Kregel, 2009).

[2] See the essays in Dennis Jowers and H. Wayne House, eds., *The New Evangelical Subordinationism? Perspectives on the Equality of God the Father and God the Son* (Eugene, OR: Pickwick, 2012): Phillip Cary, "The New Evangelical Subordinationism: Reading Inequality into the Trinity" (1–12); Linda Belleville, "'Son' Christology" (59–81); Kevin Giles, "The Trinity without Tiers" (262–87); and Dennis Jowers, "The Inconceivability of Subordination within a Simple God" (375–410).

orthodox doctrine of the Trinity, or rejected the authority of Scripture. The following essay explains those deviations.[3]

Arguments That Deviate from the Orthodox Doctrine of the Trinity

Denying the Trinity by Denying Any Eternal Distinctions between Father, Son, and Holy Spirit

Essential to the doctrine of the Trinity, as taught in the Bible, is the idea that there is a distinction between the persons of the Trinity. The Father is not the Son; the Father is not the Holy Spirit; and the Son is not the Holy Spirit. They are three distinct persons. They are equal in deity, so that each person is fully God. And there is only one God. Yet within the one being of God himself, there are three distinct persons.

But several recent evangelical-feminist writers are *unwilling to specify any distinctions between the persons.* This is a significant deviation. For example, rather than agreeing that the names "Father" and "Son" indicate a distinction between the persons, several evangelical feminists argue that these names show *only* that the Son is *like* the Father, not that he is distinct from the Father in any way. Millard Erickson writes, "There is considerable biblical evidence, however, that the primary meaning of the biblical term *Son* as applied to Jesus is likeness rather than subordinate authority. So, for example, the Jews saw Jesus' self-designation as the Son of God as a claim to deity or equality with God (e.g., John 5:18)."[4]

Similarly, Kevin Giles objects that the names "Father" and "Son" "are not used in the New Testament to suggest that the divine Father always has authority over the Son. They speak rather of an eternal correlated relationship marked by intimacy, unity, equality, and identical authority."[5]

---

[3] I understand my argument in this essay to be supplemental to the basic biblical argument for the eternal submission of the Son to the Father that I made in Wayne Grudem, "Biblical Evidence for the Eternal Submission of the Son to the Father," in Jowers and House, *The New Evangelical Subordinationism?*, 235–42.
[4] Erickson, *Who's Tampering with the Trinity?*, 116.
[5] Giles, *Jesus and the Father*, 127. Giles also objects that arguing for the Father's authority by analogy to human father-son relationships is "exactly like" the Arian error of speaking of the Son as "begotten," and therefore it is the same as arguing that the Son was created, just as human children are begotten by their fathers (66–67). In response: the rest of Scripture prohibits the idea of the Son as a created being. So that aspect of an earthly father-son relationship cannot be true of God. But the rest of Scripture does not prohibit the idea of authority and submission in a father-son relationship. It rather confirms it. The issues are different.

But if "intimacy" and "identical authority" were all that Jesus wanted to indicate by calling himself Son and calling God his Father, he could have spoken of "my friend in heaven" or "my brother in heaven" or even "my twin in heaven." Those images were ready at hand. But he did not. He spoke of "my Father in heaven." Emphasizing likeness in deity only, while failing to specify any distinction between the persons of the Trinity, is a failure to affirm any distinction between the three persons, which is one important aspect of the doctrine of the Trinity. This failure alone is a significant doctrinal deviation.

Denying the Trinity by Claiming That an Act of Any One Person Is Actually an Act of All Three Persons

Even more troubling is the tendency of evangelical feminists to claim that any action taken by any person in the Trinity is an action of all three persons in the Trinity. When faced with many biblical texts that show that the Son is always subject to the Father (see list under "Ignoring Verses That Contradict Your Position" below), and not the Father to the Son, Millard Erickson proposes a different solution. He suggests that *an act of any one person in the Trinity is actually an act of all three persons*: Erickson says that "an overall principle can be formulated." He states it this way:

> Although one person of the Trinity may occupy a more prominent part in a given divine action, the action is actually that of the entire Godhead, and the one person is acting on behalf of the three. This means that those passages that speak of the Father predestining, sending, commanding, and so on should not be taken as applying to the Father alone but to all members of the Trinity. Thus they do not count as evidence in support of an eternal supremacy of the Father and an eternal subordination of the Son.[6]

But the way Erickson argues this is to point out that *some* of the actions of the Father, Son, and Holy Spirit are done by more than one person. For example, he shows that both the Father and the Son are involved in *sending the Holy Spirit* into the world after Pentecost (p. 125).

---
[6] Erickson, *Who's Tampering with the Trinity?*, 137–38.

He shows that both the Son and the Father are involved in *judging the world* (p. 126). Both the Son and the Holy Spirit *intercede before the Father* (p. 126). The Father, Son, and Holy Spirit all *indwell those who believe* in Christ (pp. 126–27). The Father, Son, and Holy Spirit all *give gifts* (pp. 128–30). The Father and Son *love the world* (pp. 130–31). Both the Father and the Son *receive prayer* (pp. 131–32).

Erickson concludes, "The various works attributed to the different persons of the Trinity are in fact works of the Triune God. One member of the Godhead may in fact do this work on behalf of the three and be mentioned as the one who does that work, but all participate in what is done" (p. 135).

But these verses hardly prove Erickson's point. Yes, it is true that both the Father and the Son send the Holy Spirit into the world. But the Holy Spirit does not send the Holy Spirit into the world. And yes, both the Son and the Holy Spirit intercede before the Father, but the Father does not intercede before the Father.

As for actions that are directed toward people in the world, such as loving the world, judging the world, and indwelling believers, it is true that all three persons are involved in some way. But that does not prove Erickson's point, because the real issue is the relationship between the Father and the Son within the Trinity. And on that issue the testimony of Scripture is clear that the Son consistently, throughout eternity, submits to the authority of the Father.

This is manifest even in some of the passages that Erickson appeals to. At one point he says that it is not only the Father who predestines some to be saved, but Jesus also elects some to salvation. This is because Jesus said, "The Son gives life to whom he will" (John 5:21), and, "No one knows the Father except the Son and anyone to whom the Son chooses to reveal him" (Matt. 11: 27). Erickson concludes, "It appears that Jesus chooses those to whom he reveals the Father."[7]

It is remarkable that Erickson mentions these texts, because in the very context of both of them, Jesus attributes superior authority to the Father, authority by which he carries out this activity of choosing as the Father has directed. Just before John 5:21, Jesus says, "The Son can do nothing of his own accord, but *only what he sees the Father*

---

[7] Ibid., 124.

doing. For whatever the Father does, that the Son does likewise. For the Father loves the Son and shows him all that he himself is doing" (vv. 19–20). A few verses later Jesus says, "*I can do nothing on my own*. As I hear, I judge, and my judgment is just because I seek not my own will but the will of him who sent me" (v. 30). Erickson does not mention these verses, which occur in the same context.

And then in the next chapter, Jesus also says that those who come to him are the ones the Father has chosen:

> *All that the Father gives me will come to me*, and whoever comes to me I will never cast out. For I have come down from heaven, not to do my own will but the will of him who sent me. And this is the will of him who sent me, that I should lose nothing of all that he has given me, but raise it up on the last day. (John 6:37–39; see also vv. 44, 65; 8:28)

Therefore the Son only "chooses" in conjunction with what he has been shown of the will of the Father. As for Erickson's other passage, Matthew 11:27, the beginning of the verse (which Erickson does not quote) says, "All things have been handed over to me *by my Father*."

Therefore the testimony of Scripture on this matter is consistent. When the Son chooses people for salvation, he is simply following the directives of the Father. He is not acting independently of the Father's authority. Yes, both Father and Son participate in choosing, yet their actions are not identical but distinct. The Father chooses; the Father shows the Son who has been chosen, and the Son chooses those who have been given to him by the Father (John 6:37).

What is even more troubling about Erickson's argument is that he seems to deny any difference between the persons of the Trinity. In this section he is arguing against the idea that the Son has eternally been subject to the authority of the Father. Erickson is trying to nullify that by denying that some things done by the Son are not also done by the Father and the Spirit. Erickson wants to make any such discussion impossible.

But in order to make his point, he is apparently saying that the actions of any one person of the Trinity are the actions *not just of the whole being of God*, but *of every person in the Trinity*. And to say this is to deny what is taught by literally hundreds of passages of Scripture that speak of different actions carried out by different members of the Trinity.

For example, at the baptism of Jesus at the river Jordan, God the Father was speaking from heaven, saying, "This is my beloved Son, with whom I am well pleased" (Matt. 3:17). God the *Son* was not speaking from heaven saying those words. Nor was the *Holy Spirit* speaking those words. In fact, God the Son was being baptized in the person of Jesus (v. 16), and the Holy Spirit was "descending like a dove and coming to rest on him" (v. 16). God the *Father* was not being baptized, nor was the *Holy Spirit* being baptized. The *Son* was not descending like a dove, nor was the *Father* descending like a dove. It simply confuses the teaching of Scripture to say (or imply) that all three persons of the Trinity are doing each particular action. But this is what Erickson seems to be saying.

Of course, Erickson is able to show some passages in which more than one member of the Trinity participates in a certain action. Certainly it is true that Father, Son, and Holy Spirit all come to live within a believer. Of course it is true that both the Father and the Son are somehow involved in sending the Spirit into the world and in judging the world. But this simply proves that *some* activities are done by more than one person. It does not prove that all activities are done by all the persons at the same time.

More significantly, none of Erickson's examples of the persons acting together show the one-directional kind of activity between two members of the Trinity where one person initiates the activity and the other person receives the activity. For example, the Father *sends* the Son into the world. But this is not an activity done by all three persons. It would be contrary to the biblical texts to say that the Son sends the Father into the world, or that the Son sends the Son into the world, or that the Holy Spirit sends the Father into the world, or that the whole Trinity sends the whole Trinity into the world. This is simply not the way Scripture speaks, and it is contrary to what Scripture teaches. When Erickson begins to speak in this way, he strays into speculation that seriously conflicts with the teaching of Scripture.

Similarly, God the Son took on human nature and, in the person of

Christ, died for our sins. The Father did not die for our sins. The Holy Spirit did not die for our sins. It was the Father who gave the Son to die for our sins. And it was the Father who put on the Son the penalty that we deserved for our sins.

Erickson is aware that in attributing an action of any person of the Trinity to "the entire Godhead," so that "those passages that speak of the Father predestining, sending, commanding, and so on should not be taken as applying to the Father alone but to all members of the Trinity,"[8] he is coming very close to an ancient heresy called "patripassianism." This heresy said that the Father also suffered for our sins on the cross. The ancient church condemned this view because it obliterated the differences among the members of the Trinity.

So Erickson attempts to guard himself against the same mistake. He says, first, "It was the Son who died on the cross, but in a very real sense, the Father and the Spirit also suffered."[9] But then Erickson immediately says, "This is not the ancient teaching of patripassianism. This is referring to the other persons' sympathetic suffering and the Son's actual suffering on the cross. Probably most parents have experienced this in seeing the pain of their child and in a very real sense feeling that pain themselves."[10]

But as Erickson attempts to escape from patripassianism, he has to admit that the Son was suffering on the cross in a way that the Father and Spirit were not suffering. It was the Son who bore the penalty for our sins, not the Father and not the Spirit. It was the Son who bore the wrath of God the Father that we deserved against our sins, not the Father and not the Holy Spirit.

If this is true, it means that in order to avoid this ancient heresy, Erickson actually shows that the specific suffering of Christ on the cross was an action that he undertook *himself*, not an action that the Father and Spirit carried out in the same way. What is troubling is that Erickson will not explicitly acknowledge a difference in the actions of the Father and the Son; he only points out a similarity, speaking of sympathetic suffering. What Erickson gives with the right hand he takes back

---
[8] Ibid., 138.
[9] Ibid., 135.
[10] Ibid.

with the left. In the end he still insists that the actions of any one person are the actions of all three persons: "Those passages that speak of the Father predestining, sending, commanding, and so on should not be taken as applying to the Father alone but to all members of the Trinity. Thus they do not count as evidence in support of an eternal supremacy of the Father and an eternal subordination of the Son."[11]

To say this is actually to obliterate the differences among the members of the Trinity. Although Erickson disavows patripassianism, he does not escape from but rather affirms the same kind of error with regard to all other actions of any person of the Trinity. And at this point it is hard to distinguish what Erickson says from the ancient heresy of modalism, the view that there is only one person in God who manifests himself in different ways or "modes" of action.

Erickson's view here is certainly inconsistent with hundreds of texts that show unique activities carried out by the individual persons of the Trinity. So, as with patripassianism, we are back to asking, how does Millard Erickson avoid modalism in his explanation? The answer is not clear. If all three persons do *every action* in the *same way*, then there is no difference at all between the persons. And if there is no difference between the persons, then we no longer have the doctrine of the Trinity. Such a significant doctrinal deviation coming from a widely respected evangelical theologian is very troubling.

At this point someone may object that the *whole being* of God has to be involved in every action of each person of the Trinity. I agree with this, because each person of the Trinity is fully God, and part of the deep mystery of the Trinity is that the very being (or substance) of each person of the Trinity is equal to the whole being of God. So when one person of the Trinity is acting, it is also true, in some sense that we only understand very faintly, that the entire being of God is acting. This is because of what is sometimes called "perichoresis," the idea that each of the persons of the Trinity is somehow present "in" the other two persons. Jesus said, "the Father is in me and I am in the Father" (John 10:38).

But this truth is not what Erickson means, because he is arguing not that the *whole being of God* is somehow involved in every action, but that the action of any one person is also in the same way *an action of the*

---
[11] Ibid., 137–38.

other two persons, so that any action done by one person is also done by the other two persons. This is something Scripture never teaches and the church has never held. And it is something that means we no longer have the doctrine of the Trinity. We have modalism.

Another evangelical-feminist author to go this direction is Sarah Sumner. She at first seems to affirm the orthodox doctrine of the subordination of the Son to the Father,[12] but then modifies it with a novel proposal: "So then, to whom is Christ finally subjected? God. Christ the Son is subject to the triune God of three persons. The Son is subjected to 'the God and Father.' And in that sense, the Son is subjected to himself. This is the doctrine of the Trinity."[13]

But this is *not* the doctrine of the Trinity. To say that "the Son is subjected to himself" is the ancient heresy of modalism.[14] If we are to maintain the doctrine of the Trinity, we may not erase the distinctions between the persons or preclude that one person in the Trinity does something the others do not.

The Bible simply does not speak the way Sumner does. The Father did not send *himself* into the world to become man and die for our sins; he sent the Son. The Father did not *himself* bear the penalty for our sins (which is patripassianism), nor did the Holy Spirit, but the Son did. The Son did not pray to *himself*; he prayed to the Father. The Son sits not at the right hand of *himself* but at the right hand of the Father. And the Son is not subjected to *himself*; he is subjected to the Father. To deny these distinctions is to deny that there are different persons in the Trinity, and thus it is to deny the Trinity.

Sumner's misunderstanding carries over into a statement about

---

[12] Sarah Sumner, *Men and Women in the Church: Building Consensus on Christian Leadership* (Downers Grove, IL: InterVarsity, 2003), 177.
[13] Ibid., 178. Sumner returns to a similar theme later when she appeals to the doctrine of perichoresis or *circumincession* and says, "Circumincession also affirms that the action of one of the persons of the Trinity is also fully the action of the other two persons" (289n10). But she misunderstands this doctrine. The term refers to the mutual indwelling of the persons of the Trinity in one another, and it may be used to affirm that the action of one person is the action of the being of God, but it should never be understood to deny that there are some things that one person of the Trinity does that the other persons do not do. Sumner refers to Miroslav Volf, *After Our Likeness* (Grand Rapids: Eerdmans, 1998), to support her understanding of perichoresis, but Volf, unlike Sumner, is careful not to blur the distinctness of the persons: "Perichoresis refers to the reciprocal *interiority* of the Trinitarian persons . . . though . . . they do not cease to be distinct persons. . . . Perichoresis is 'co-inherence in one another without any coalescence or commixture'" (209). (The quotations from Augustine that Sumner gives on p. 178 should not be understood to deny the distinctness of the persons in the Trinity.)
[14] Modalism is also called modalistic monarchianism. See Craig A. Blaising, "Monarchianism," in *Evangelical Dictionary of Theology*, ed. Walter A. Elwell (Grand Rapids: Baker, 1984), 727; also Wayne Grudem, *Systematic Theology: An Introduction to Biblical Doctrine* (Grand Rapids: Zondervan, 1994), 242.

wives' submitting to their husbands: She says, "The paradox of their oneness means that in submitting to her husband (with whom she is one), the wife ends up submitting to herself." She claims this is parallel to "Christ's submission to himself."[15]

But Paul says that husbands should love their wives "*as* their own bodies" (that is, in the same way as they love their own bodies—Eph. 5:28),[16] not because a husband's wife is identical with his own physical body, which would be nonsense.[17] If in submitting to her husband a wife is really just submitting to herself and not to a different person, then her husband has no distinct existence as a person. This also would be nonsense. Would Sumner say that when a wife disagrees with her husband, she should simply give in to him, since this is just giving in to herself?[18] Sumner would not say this, of course, but such an argument would show the same kind of nonsense.

Linda Belleville makes a similar mistake. Regarding the teaching of Philippians 2 that Christ "did not count equality with God a thing to be grasped, but emptied himself, by taking the form of a servant, being born in the likeness of men" (vv. 6–7), Belleville seeks to demonstrate that the Son was acting in a way different from God the Father, or in a way that implies that the Son was being subject to the Father. She says, "The language of God the Son is absent. Instead it is God himself who

---

[15] Sarah Sumner, *Men and Women in the Church*, 198.
[16] Greek *hōs* here is best understood to tell the manner in which husbands should love their wives. When Paul says in the next sentence, "He who loves his wife loves himself," he does not mean, "He who loves himself loves himself." He means that he who loves his wife will *also* bring good to himself as a result.
[17] Sumner several times wrongly says that the wife *is* the husband's body (*Men and Women in the Church*, 161, 167, 184). She derives this idea by drawing unjustified deductions from the metaphor of the husband's being the "head" of the wife, but Scripture never says "the wife is the body of the husband." If the wife *is* the husband's body, then either he himself has two bodies, or he has no body and his wife is his body, and neither of these ideas can be true. Someone could draw all sorts of weird deductions from the metaphor of the husband as the head of the wife (she has no eyes, she can't see, she can't eat because she has no mouth; he can't walk, she is his feet and must walk for him, and so forth), but none of these are intended by the metaphor, which conveys the idea of authority and leadership but none of these other ideas. (See additional discussion of Sumner's understanding of *kephalē*, "head," in Wayne Grudem, *Evangelical Feminism and Biblical Truth: An Analysis of More than 100 Disputed Questions* [Colorado Springs: Multnomah, 2004; repr., Wheaton, IL: Crossway, 2012], 208–9.)
[18] Another novel theological concept of Sumner's is that "Mary was so human that Jesus got his male humanity from her. . . . Jesus received his humanity from Mary and his divinity from the Holy Spirit" (67). This is surely wrong, because Jesus did not "receive . . . his divinity" from anyone. He has eternally been the fully divine Son of God. Nor should we say that Jesus got his "male humanity" from Mary. If Jesus's human nature had been derived solely from Mary's physical body, he would have been her clone, and therefore he would have been a woman. The doctrine of the virgin birth must be understood in a way consistent with Matt. 1:20, which says, "*That which is conceived in her* is from the Holy Spirit." What was conceived in Mary's womb was a human baby, and it was "from the Holy Spirit," which suggests that half of the genetic material that Jesus received was miraculously created by the Holy Spirit, and half was from Mary.

takes on human form: 'He who existed in the form of God . . . emptied himself by taking on the form of a servant . . .' (Phil. 2:6–7)."[19]

But in Belleville's rush to deny that the Son of God is in view in verse 6, she fails to note the subject of the first part of the sentence, which is found in verse 5: "Have this mind among yourselves, *which is yours in Christ Jesus*, who, though he was in the form of God, did not count equality with God a thing to be grasped, but emptied himself" (Phil. 2:5–6). It is not the whole Trinity but God the Son who took on a human form and lived among us. In her haste to disallow any eternal difference in authority between the Father and the Son, Belleville is simply confusing the persons of the Trinity.

Similarly, Belleville says:

> When Jesus is addressed as "Son of God" in the Gospel narrative, the monotheism of both the Old Testament and of Second Temple Judaism precludes a Trinitarian understanding. . . . Elsewhere in the New Testament, Son of God as a title is rare. . . . This suggests that "Son" was not primary in the early churches' understanding and certainly not Trinitarian.[20]

But then what shall we make of Jesus's own statement, "baptizing them in the name of the Father and of the Son and of the Holy Spirit" (Matt. 28:19)? Is this not a Trinitarian statement? Belleville gives no explanation.

And what shall we do with John 3:16: "For God so loved the world, that he gave his only Son"? If "Son" is not a Trinitarian title here, then in what sense can Jesus be called God's "only Son"? Surely this indicates that Jesus is "Son" in a way that no other human being is son. He is God's only Son, his unique Son—that is, his eternal, fully divine Son.

Belleville reaches a similarly remarkable conclusion regarding 1 Corinthians 15:28. The verse says, "When all things are subjected to him, then the Son himself will also be subjected to him who put all things in subjection under him, that God may be all in all." Belleville says of this verse, "The end result will not however be the subjection of

---
[19] Belleville, "'Son' Christology," 71.
[20] Ibid., 68.

all things (including God the Son) so that the Father may be 'all in all' but that GOD may be such."[21]

Once again, Belleville fails to pay attention to the context. "God" in this context is clearly not the entire Trinity, but God the Father only. Paul begins this section of verses by saying, "Then comes the end, when he delivers the kingdom to *God the Father* after destroying every rule and every authority and power" (1 Cor. 15:24). As very often in the New Testament, the name "God" (Greek: θεός/*theos*) refers not to the entire Trinity but to the Father. This is why Paul says, "The Son himself will also be subjected to him who put all things in subjection under him" (1 Cor. 15:28). This means the Son will be subjected to the Father. No other person than the Father can be the referent of "him who put all things in subjection under him." Therefore in the very next phrase, "that God may be all in all," the name "God" refers to God the Father, not to the entire Trinity. Belleville again confuses the persons of the Trinity, thereby denying any eternal distinctions between Father, Son, and Holy Spirit. This is a significant deviation from the historic doctrine of the Trinity.

Denying the Trinity by Denying That God the Son Was Eternally God the Son

Throughout the entire history of the Christian church, to my knowledge, no significant and doctrinally orthodox church leader or teacher ever denied that God the Son was eternally God the Son, until several modern evangelical feminists attempted to obliterate all differences between the persons of the Trinity.

In fact, no teacher who did not accept the Nicene Creed (AD 325) or the Chalcedonian Creed (AD 451) would have been allowed to continue in a teaching position in any orthodox church. The Nicene Creed confesses belief "in one Lord Jesus Christ, the only-begotten Son of God, *begotten of the Father before all worlds*, God of God, Light of Light, Very God of Very God, begotten, not made." If he was eternally "begotten of the Father," then he was eternally the Son of God. And he was eternally "the only-begotten Son of God."[22]

---
[21] Ibid., 66.
[22] I realize that there are differences of interpretation in the meaning of the phrase "only begotten" and the phrase "begotten of the Father." I myself have written about this in some detail (see appendix 6 of my

Similarly the Chalcedonian Creed confesses belief in "one and the same Son, our Lord Jesus Christ. . . . *begotten before all ages of the Father* according to the Godhead." To deny that the Son was eternally Son would be to deny both the Nicene and the Chalcedonian Creeds. But now, contrary to the entire history of the church, evangelical feminists have begun to deny that the Son of God was eternally God the Son. For example, Millard Erickson objects that the names "Father" and "Son" might not be eternal names because, he says, "The references to the names may be those used at the time of writing but may not indicate that the persons actually had those names at the time to which the writing refers."[23]

If Erickson is indeed saying that the Father and Son might not have eternally had those names, his view is hardly consistent with Scripture. Several passages indicate that the names "Father" and "Son" applied to those persons eternally. Before creation, God the Father "predestined" us "to be conformed to the image of his Son" (Rom. 8:29); and the author of Hebrews says, "In these last days he has spoken to us by his Son, whom he appointed the heir of all things, *through whom also he created the world*" (Heb. 1:2). These actions of predestining and creating occurred long before Christ came to earth as a man, and in these actions the Son is indeed called "Son." When we recall the importance that the Bible attaches to personal names in describing someone's nature or character, it becomes clear that nothing in these passages suggests merely that the person who would *later* be called "Father" predestined us to be conformed to the image of the person who would *later* be called "Son."

When Jesus came to earth, he didn't suddenly become Son, but he revealed to us what the glory of the Son was already like. John says, "We have seen his glory, *glory as of the only Son from the Father*" (John 1:14). The best-known verse in the Bible also indicates this: "For God so loved the world, that he gave his only Son . . ." (John 3:16). In order for the Father to *give* the Son, the two had to first be in a Father-Son relationship before the Son came into the world. Therefore, there is good reason to believe that the Father did not suddenly become Father when

---

Systematic Theology [added in 2000], 1233–34). But what is not controversial is that, whatever the phrase meant, it always meant that the Son was eternally the Son from the Father.
[23] Erickson, *Who's Tampering with the Trinity?*, 221.

he created the world, or when he sent his Son into the world, but that the persons of the Trinity have eternally been Father, Son, and Holy Spirit.

Bruce Ware perceptively argues that in Psalm 2, "the LORD" (God the Father) and "his Anointed" (the Messiah to come) are two distinct persons (see Ps. 2:2), and that "the LORD" declares, "I have set my King on Zion, my holy hill" (v. 6), and that this coming king will rule "the nations" (v. 8) at the direction of God the Father. Who is this coming King and Messiah? He is the one whom the Lord calls "my Son" in verse 7.[24] This messianic prophecy, cited in the New Testament to refer to Christ (see Acts 13:33; Heb. 1:5; 5:5), shows another preincarnation application of the title "Son" to Christ.

In another place, Erickson lists Psalm 2:7, "You are my son; today I have become your father" (NIV), and deems this as "in connection with a reference to Jesus' resurrection (Acts 13:33)." He says that these verses "seem to suggest that Sonship had a point of temporal, rather than eternal, beginning."[25]

But an alternative explanation for these verses appears often in the commentaries: at Jesus's baptism (Mark 1:11) and again at Jesus's transfiguration (Mark 9:7), then again at the resurrection (Acts 13:33), God declared that a new aspect of sonship had begun, one in which Jesus *as the God-man* was now relating to God as his Father. This does not mean that the eternal Son of God was *not* Son prior to this time (see verses under "Denying the Trinity by Denying Any Eternal Distinctions" above, including the discussion of Psalm 2), and it does not mean that God first became Jesus's Father upon Jesus's baptism at about age thirty (for he proclaimed that God was his father at age twelve, in Luke 2:49); but it simply means that *a new aspect of the Father-Son relationship began when Jesus's earthly ministry began.*

A related argument shows Belleville's determination to deny the New Testament view of Jesus as God's eternal Son. She says of John's Gospel, "The Gospel starts, 'In the beginning was the Word, and the Word was with God, and the Word was God' (John 1:1). There is no 'In the beginning was the Son'; it is the Word that became flesh, not

---

[24] See Bruce Ware, "Christ's Atonement: A Work of the Trinity," in *Jesus in Trinitarian Perspective*, ed. Fred Sanders and Klaus Issler (Nashville: B&H, 2007), 161–62. Note also the phrase "kiss the Son" in Ps. 2:12.
[25] Erickson, *Who's Tampering with the Trinity?*, 118.

the Son" (1:14).[26] Belleville is curiously oblivious to the fact that in this very passage John proclaims that the "Word" who "became flesh and dwelt among us" was revealed in his glory to be "the only *Son* from the Father," the eternal, Trinitarian Son of God: "And the Word became flesh and dwelt among us, and we have seen his glory, *glory as of the only Son from the Father*, full of grace and truth" (John 1:14).

Does Belleville actually think that the "Word" who was "in the beginning with God" was someone other than the eternal Son of God? Her appeal to this passage is remarkable. Once again, Belleville's view deviates sharply from orthodox Trinitarian thinking and orthodox Christian doctrine. Nor is it faithful to the very words of John's Gospel.

Belleville also says that, at the end of John's Gospel, "When Thomas makes his profession of faith, it is not to God's Son or to the Father's Son but to 'My Lord and my God' (John 20:28)." But in saying this, she misses the point of the passage, which John makes explicit two verses later. He wrote his Gospel specifically so that readers who had not seen Jesus with their own eyes, as Thomas had, would have the same kind of faith Thomas had; because Jesus responded to Thomas, "Blessed are those who have not seen and yet have believed" (v. 29). Immediately after this comes John's reason for writing his entire Gospel: "Now Jesus did many other signs in the presence of the disciples, which are not written in this book; but these are written so that you may believe that Jesus is the Christ, *the Son of God*, and that by believing you may have life in his name" (vv. 30–31). John was not writing so that readers would believe that Jesus is Lord and God but not the Son of God. He was writing so that readers would believe he is all those things.

In another place, Belleville writes: "For as the Father has life in himself, so he has granted the Son also to have life in himself (John 5:26). This 'son' is not divine; only God grants life and only God's creation receives life."[27]

It is surprising that Belleville can say that "only God grants life" and miss the fact that just five verses earlier, in the same discourse, Jesus declares, "The Son gives life to whom he will" (John 5:21). Does this not then prove that this "Son" is the divine Son of God? This is the same Son

---
[26] Belleville, "'Son' Christology," 75.
[27] Ibid., 74.

of whom Jesus speaks two verses later when he speaks of the Father's intention "that all may honor the Son, just as they honor the Father" (v. 23). But if the Father is God and the Son is honored in the same way as the Father, then surely this Son must also be honored as God.

In this same context, Jesus says that an hour is coming "when the dead will hear the voice of the Son of God, and those who hear will live" (John 5:25). How can this be anyone other than the fully divine Son of God, whose voice has power to raise the dead to life? This is the same Son, in the next verse, of whom it is said, "For as the Father has life in himself, so he has granted the Son also to have life in himself" (v. 26). It is troubling that Belleville denies that this Son of God is the eternal, divine Son of God.

In another place, Belleville says, "'Father' is found on the lips of Jesus in Acts 1, but as 'the Father' rather than 'my Father.' The Father's authority is mentioned but not in relationship to Jesus."[28] But this is simply not true of the entire context. In the very next chapter Peter explains what happened at Pentecost by saying this, "Being therefore exalted at the right hand of God, and *having received from the Father* the promise of the Holy Spirit, he has poured out this that you yourselves are seeing and hearing" (Acts 2:33).

All of these egalitarian arguments labor so strenuously to falsify the eternal submission of the Son to the Father that they stray into the serious doctrinal deviation of denying that the Son of God was eternally God the Son. No respected theological leader in the history of the church, before modern evangelical feminism, has made this claim, so far as I know.[29] It is something of a surprise to me that writers who deny that the Son has eternally been the Son of God are still accepted as legitimate representatives for orthodox, evangelical Christianity.

Arguments That Reject the Authority of Scripture
Implying That Things the New Testament Teaches Less Often Are Not True

Millard Erickson says that the title "Son of Man" occurs seventy-eight times in the Gospels with reference to Jesus, but the title "Son of God"

---
[28] Ibid., 77.
[29] Of course, the Arians denied that the Son eternally existed, but that was a different kind of argument.

is used of Jesus only twenty-three times.[30] It is not clear how this is an argument for the position that Erickson favors, the "temporary submission" view. If the New Testament says that Jesus is the "Son of God" twenty-three times, is that not enough to convince us? Is Erickson implying that something the New Testament says seventy-eight times should qualify as reliable evidence, but not something it says twenty-three times? Surely Erickson cannot mean this, but it is unclear why he brings this up as an argument against the eternal submission of the Son to the Father.

Erickson also argues that the New Testament often uses other names for members of the Trinity. He says, "This is especially true of Paul, who uses the names, God, Lord, and Spirit, even more frequently than the father-son terminology."[31]

This is the same kind of argument as the argument about the titles "Son of Man" and "Son of God." The Bible teaches many things about God and uses many different names for God. Is Erickson suggesting that only what is taught by the names "God" and "Lord" is true, and what the New Testament teaches by the names "Father" and "Son" is not true? Are only the most frequent New Testament teachings true? Surely Erickson cannot mean this. But then what is the point of bringing up the greater-frequency argument?

The question before us is not, What things are taught most often in the New Testament? but rather, What does the New Testament teach about the eternal relationship between the Father and the Son? To that question, the New Testament teaches in at least seven places (see list under "Ignoring Verses That Contradict Your Position" below) that the Father had authority over the Son and the Son submitted to that authority *even before the world was made*. And Erickson so far has given us nothing to disprove that teaching.

Linda Belleville takes a similar approach. She says:

> Elsewhere in the New Testament [i.e., outside the Gospels], Son of God as a title is rare compared with other titles such as "Lord." This suggests that "Son" was not primary in the early church's understanding and certainly not Trinitarian. Paul rarely uses "God's

---

[30] Erickson, *Who's Tampering with the Trinity?*, 116.
[31] Ibid., 117.

Son" or "Son" of Jesus and not in a father-son relationship. He does speak of "the God and Father of our Lord Jesus Christ." But it is *God* who sends his son (Rom. 8:32) and *God* who did not spare his own son (Rom. 8:3; Gal. 4:4)—not the Father.[32]

But what can the point of Belleville's argument be? She seems to suggest that the New Testament does not teach that Jesus is the Son of God, because that title is "rare compared with other titles" in the New Testament. But is a title used forty-three times in the New Testament not true? May we disbelieve something the New Testament teaches "only" forty-three times? Or should we disbelieve that Jesus is the Son of God because he is called that only sixteen times in the New Testament Epistles?

And what can Belleville mean by saying that it is "God" who sends his son, "not the Father," and "God" who did not spare his own son, "not the Father." By definition, someone who sends *his* son is, of course, the father of that son.

We can hardly say that Paul denies the Father-Son relationship in the Trinity. He speaks of "the God and Father of our Lord Jesus Christ" (Rom. 15:6; also 2 Cor. 1:3), and "the God and Father of the Lord Jesus" (2 Cor. 11:31; see also Eph. 1:3; Col. 1:3). Paul could hardly address Christian churches and speak of "God, the Father of *our son Jesus Christ*," because Jesus is not our son—he is our Lord. But when Belleville uses Paul's expression "our Lord Jesus Christ" to minimize the importance of the Father-Son relationship in the Trinity and to imply that Paul's less frequent reference to Christ as God's "Son" precludes this idea, it seems that she is again implying that things the New Testament teaches less often are not true. This kind of argument is a rejection of the authority of "all Scripture" as "breathed out by God" (2 Tim. 3:16).

Affirming Things about Scripture That Are Not True

A different kind of rejection of the authority of Scripture occurs when an author affirms something about Scripture that is in fact not true. This is misleading to readers (many of whom will not have the time to

---
[32] Belleville, "'Son' Christology," 68.

check and verify what the author claims about Scripture), and, even more importantly, it also shows a failure to adequately respect what the Scripture actually says.

For instance, Belleville says that "no title or task is applied to God the Father that is not equally applied to God the Son." But this statement is simply false. The Father frequently is said to "send" the Son into the world, but the Son is nowhere said to send the Father into the world (see John 3:16; Gal. 4:4; 1 John 4:9–10; and many other verses).[33]

In addition, the Father is said to choose us and predestine us for salvation *in his Son* (see Rom. 8:29; Eph. 1:3–5; 3:9–11; 2 Tim. 1:2, 9–10).

God the Father is always represented as having the task of hearing the prayers of Jesus Christ, the Son of God, but the Son is *never* shown as hearing the prayers of the Father (or of himself! see Matt. 11:25; 26:39; Luke 10:21; John 11:41).

The Father is always pictured as the one who delegates authority to the Son, and this task is never reversed. The Son never delegates authority to the Father (see Acts 2:32; Rev. 1:1; 2:26; and with respect to final judgment, John 5:22, 26–27; Acts 10:42; 17:31).

The Father is always the one who creates through the Son, but the Son does not create through the Father (see John 1:1; 1 Cor. 8:6; Heb. 1:1–2).

Therefore, when Belleville says that "no title or task is applied to God the Father that is not equally applied to God the Son," she is saying something false about the New Testament.[34]

Belleville also says, "In the final analysis, Father-Son language is specific to the Johannine materials."[35] But is Father-Son language found only in John's writings in the New Testament? What about "No one knows the Son except the Father" (Matt. 11:27)? What about "Not even the angels in heaven, nor the Son, but only the Father" (Mark 13:32)? Or this: "All things have been handed over to me by my Father,

---

[33] In fact, Millard Erickson himself mentions a long list of texts in which Jesus speaks of the Father who sent him: Matt. 15:24; Mark 9:37; Luke 4:18, 43; 9:48; 10:16; John 4:34; 5:23–24, 30, 36–38; 6:29, 38–39, 44, 57; 7:16, 18, 28–29, 33; 8:16, 18, 26, 29, 42; 10:36; 11:42; 12:44–45, 49; 13:20; 14:24; 15:21; 16:5; 17:3, 8, 18, 21, 23, 25; 20:21 (Erickson, *Who's Tampering with the Trinity?*, 111).

[34] In this same section, Belleville makes a false statement about the modern business world as well. She says, "Businesses today typically have a CEO, a CFO, and a COO. . . . All three are Cs or 'chiefs' and thereby equal (albeit different) in authority and responsibility" ("'Son' Christology," 61). This is simply not true in the modern corporate world, since the CEO has ultimate authority.

[35] Ibid., 70.

and no one knows who the Son is except the Father, or who the Father is except the Son and anyone to whom the Son chooses to reveal him" (Luke 10:22)? Matthew, Mark, and Luke are all outside the writings of John. Or what about Peter's writing: "For when he received honor and glory from God the Father, and the voice was borne to him by the Majestic Glory, 'This is my beloved Son, with whom I am well pleased' . . ." (2 Pet. 1:17)? Again, Belleville's statement is false.

Moreover, Belleville says, "Nowhere in the New Testament is 'obedience' predicated of a pre-existing Son of God."[36] But what about the texts where Jesus says that he came to earth in obedience to his Father? If he came to do the Father's will, he came in obedience to his heavenly Father, an obedience that issued from before he came to earth. "For I have come down from heaven, not to do my own will but the will of him who sent me" (John 6:38; see also Heb. 10:7–9). In saying, "I seek not my own will but the will of him who sent me" (John 5:30), Jesus implies that he obeyed when he was sent. He adds, "I have not come of my own accord. He who sent me is true" (John 7:28).

Belleville goes on to make the rather remarkable claim: "When God is referred to as 'Father' it is not as *pater* [Father] of the Son. . . . Indeed, the two are not linked anywhere in Paul."[37] But is it true that God the Father is never seen as the Father of the Son in Paul's writings? Consider the following: "But when the fullness of time had come, *God sent forth his Son*, born of woman, born under the law" (Gal. 4:4). Does Belleville really ask us to believe that when Paul speaks about God's sending "*his Son*," this does not mean that God is the Father of that Son? How can the Son be *his Son* if God is not the Father? Or what about "He who did not spare his own Son but gave him up for us all . . ." (Rom. 8:32)? Does Paul really not consider God to be the Father of "his own Son"?

In addition, Paul speaks of "the God and Father of our Lord Jesus Christ" (Rom. 15:6; 2 Cor. 1:3; Eph. 1:3). Does Belleville actually want us to think that the apostle does not here consider Jesus to be the Son of God, the same person that he calls "the Son of God" elsewhere (Rom. 1:4; 2 Cor. 1:19; Gal. 2:20; Eph. 4:13)? When Belleville says that God

---
[36] Ibid., 72.
[37] Ibid., 74–75.

the Father and God the Son "are not linked anywhere in Paul," her statement is again simply false.

Ignoring Verses That Contradict Your Position

Some evangelical feminists argue that the Son was not eternally subject to the authority of the Father, but they simply ignore verses that contradict this view, and they give no alternative explanation for what these verses could mean.

In the following paragraphs, I mention at least seven passages that show that the Father had a leadership role the Son did not have before creation. These verses contradict the "temporary submission" position, the view of evangelical feminists that the Son's submission to the Father was only during his incarnation. But in several evangelical-feminist arguments that deny the eternal submission of the Son to the Father, there is no treatment of these verses. They are either not mentioned at all or mentioned and then ignored. Consider the following.

THE FATHER CHOOSES US IN THE SON BEFORE CREATION
Ephesians 1:3–5

> Blessed be the God and Father of our Lord Jesus Christ, who has blessed us in Christ with every spiritual blessing in the heavenly places, even as he [the Father] *chose us in him* [the Son] *before the foundation of the world*, that we should be holy and blameless before him. In love he [the Father] *predestined us for adoption as sons through Jesus Christ*, according to the purpose of his [the Father's] will.[38]

This passage speaks of acts of God "before the foundation of the world." Long before the Son's incarnation, the Father is the one who *chooses* and *predestines*, and the Son is already designated as the one who will come in obedience to the Father in order to be our Savior and earn our adoption as God's children.

The passage does not say that "the Father *and Son* chose us." It says that the Father chose us in the Son. It does not say, "The Father

---
[38] This and the next twelve passages are adapted from my essay "Biblical Evidence for the Eternal Submission of the Son to the Father," 223–61.

suggested some people for salvation and the Son agreed on some and disagreed on others." It says that the Father chose us in the Son. This happened before the foundation of the world, and it indicates a unique authority for the Father—an authority to determine the entire history of salvation for all time, for the whole world.

Of course, the Son was in full agreement with the Father regarding this eternal plan of salvation. We should never confuse the idea of the Father's authority with any thought that the Son disagreed with the Father's plan or submitted to it reluctantly. Jesus said, "My food is to do the will of him who sent me and to accomplish his work" (John 4:34). He was the true fulfillment of the words of the psalmist who said,

> I delight to do your will, O my God;
>   your law is within my heart. (Ps. 40:8)

The Son and the Spirit fully agreed with the plans of the Father. But if we are to be faithful to the meaning of Ephesians 1:3–5, we still must say that in the eternal councils of the Trinity, there was a role of planning, directing, initiating, and choosing that belonged specifically to the Father.

Other verses support this:

Romans 8:29

> For those whom he [the Father] foreknew he also *predestined to be conformed to the image of his Son*, in order that he might be the firstborn among many brothers.

Before creation the Father had authority to predestine, and the Son was already designated as the one who would come as our Savior, and to whose image we would be conformed. The Son did not predestine us to be conformed to the image of the Father. The roles of Father and Son were distinct, not identical.

2 Timothy 1:9

> [God] who saved us and called us to a holy calling, not because of our works but because of his own purpose and grace, *which he gave*

us in Christ Jesus before the ages began [πρὸ χρόνων αἰωνίων, literally "before times eternal"] . . .

"Before the ages began," before the creation of the world, when there was nothing except God himself, what happened in the eternal councils of the Trinity? The Father planned to save us *through* his Son and *in* his Son. He planned that his Son would be our Savior, and we would be conformed to his image. Long before the incarnation, the Son was subordinate to the planning of the Father.

Ephesians 1:9–11
> . . . making known to us the mystery of his [the Father's] will, according to his purpose, which he [the Father] set forth in Christ as a plan for the fullness of time, to unite all things in him [the Son], things in heaven and things on earth. In him [the Son] we have obtained an inheritance, *having been predestined according to the purpose of him* [the Father] who works all things according to the counsel of his [the Father's] will.

The role of planning, purposing, and predestining for the entire history of salvation belongs to the Father, according to Scripture. There is no hint of any such authority of the Son over the Father. The Bible speaks of full deity for the Son (John 1:1). It speaks of glory that the Father gave the Son (John 17:5, 24). But the authority to plan salvation and to decide to send the Son is an authority that Scripture attributes to the Father only.

Ephesians 3:9–11
> . . . and to bring to light for everyone what is the plan of the mystery hidden for ages in God who created all things, so that through the church the manifold wisdom of God might now be made known to the rulers and authorities in the heavenly places. This was according to the *eternal purpose* that he [the Father] has realized in Christ Jesus our Lord.

Here is the Father's eternal purpose to include Jews and Gentiles in the church—a purpose to be carried out by the Son. The Father planned this eternally, and his purpose was then realized in the Son's obedience to this plan.

1 Peter 1:19–20
> ... but with the precious blood of Christ, like that of a lamb without blemish or spot. *He was foreknown before the foundation of the world* but was made manifest in the last times for the sake of you.

Here Peter says that Christ was "foreknown" (in this context, this indicates that the Father knew of the Son as the one who would shed his blood, "the precious blood of Christ") as our Savior before the foundation of the world. The Father from eternity knew that the Son would come to save us. (In addition, 1 Pet. 1:1–2 speaks of "the foreknowledge of God the Father" regarding the situation of Peter's readers as "elect exiles of the dispersion.")

Revelation 13:8
> And all who dwell on earth will worship it [the beast], everyone whose name has not been written *before the foundation of the world* in the book of life of the Lamb who was slain.

Here we see that before the foundation of the world, which means in the eternal councils of the Trinity, there already was "the book of life of the Lamb who was slain." It had already been determined within the Trinity that the Son ("the Lamb") would die for our sins, and it had been determined whose names were in the Book of Life.

Therefore at least seven passages of Scripture indicate that prior to creation, the Son was eternally subject to the planning and authority of the Father with regard to our salvation.

What do advocates of the "temporary submission" view say about these verses? In his brief summary of this argument in *Who's Tampering with the Trinity?*, Millard Erickson does not deny what these passages teach.[39] Instead, his method of argument is to bring up several *other verses*[40] that he claims support the temporary submission view (what he also calls the "equivalent-authority view"). Then he concludes that the two sets of verses form a "stalemate." But the verses that Erickson cites to support the equivalent-authority view can readily be understood

---
[39] See Erickson, *Who's Tampering with the Trinity?*, 109–11.
[40] Ibid., 116–21.

in a way that is consistent with the eternal submission of the Son to the Father (as I have argued elsewhere).[41] Significantly, Erickson never explains how any of these verses that I have just mentioned can mean anything other than the submission of the Son to the Father in the eternal past.

Is Erickson implying that Scripture teaches *both* that the Son was subject to the Father before creation and that the Son was not subject to the Father before creation? That Scripture teaches both "A" and "not A," affirming contradictory things, so that we are left with a "stalemate"? Surely that position undermines the authority of Scripture as God's completely trustworthy Word. But Erickson offers no alternative explanation for these seven passages, nor do the other evangelical-feminist authors that I have mentioned.

The Father Creates the World through the Son

Another set of verses is simply ignored by Erickson and other temporary submission advocates. These advocates say that the Son's submission to the leadership of the Father was only for his time on earth, or else it was only with respect to the purpose of becoming a man and earning our salvation.

But this argument fails to account for verses that show this same relationship between the Father and the Son in the creation of the world. This is an activity completely distinct from coming to earth to earn our salvation. Yet in this activity also, the Father is the one who initiates and leads, and the Son is the one who carries out the will of the Father.

John 1:1–3

> In the beginning was the Word [here referring to the Son], and the Word was with God, and the Word was God. He was in the beginning with God. All things were made *through* him, and without him was not any thing made that was made.

Hebrews 1:1–2

> Long ago, at many times and in many ways, God spoke to our fathers by the prophets, but in these last days he has spoken to us by

---

[41] See Grudem, "Biblical Evidence for the Eternal Submission of the Son to the Father," 235–42.

his Son, whom he appointed the heir of all things, *through* whom also *he created* the world.

In the process of creating the universe, the role of initiating, of leading, belongs not to all three members of the Trinity equally, but to the Father. The Father created *through* the Son. This cannot be a submission limited to the incarnation, as the temporary submission view holds, for it was in place at the first moment of creation. The Son did not create through the Father, nor would that have been appropriate to the personal differences signified by the names "Father" and "Son."

1 Corinthians 8:6

> Yet for us there is one God, the Father, *from* whom are all things and for whom we exist, and one Lord, Jesus Christ, *through* whom are all things and through whom we exist.

Here is the same pattern: all things (that is, the entire universe) come "from" the Father (who directs and initiates) and "through" the Son (who carries out the will of the Father). This was the pattern in the planning of salvation prior to creation, and this is also the pattern in the process of creating the world.

As far as I can determine, Erickson does not even discuss these creation passages. Yet they directly contradict the temporary submission view.

THE SON'S SUBMISSION TO THE FATHER CONTINUES AFTER HIS EARTHLY MINISTRY AND HIS COMPLETED REDEMPTIVE WORK ON EARTH

The submission of the Son to the Father did not end with his return to heaven. It continued then and it continues still today in his ongoing ministry as Great High Priest.

Hebrews 7:23–26

> The former priests were many in number, because they were prevented by death from continuing in office, but he holds his priesthood permanently, because he continues forever. Consequently, he is able to save to the uttermost those who draw near to God through

him, since he always lives *to make intercession for them* [εἰς τὸ ἐντυγχάνειν ὑπὲρ αὐτῶν].

For it was indeed fitting that we should have such a high priest, holy, innocent, unstained, separated from sinners, and exalted above the heavens.

Romans 8:34

Who is to condemn? Christ Jesus is the one who died—more than that, who was raised—who is at the right hand of God, who indeed is *interceding* for us [ὃς καὶ ἐντυγχάνει ὑπὲρ ἡμῶν].

The verb that both passages use is significant. To "intercede" (ἐντυγχάνω/*entynchanō*) for someone means to bring requests and appeals on behalf of that person *to a higher authority*, such as a governor, king, or emperor (cf. Acts 25:24, which uses the same verb to say that the Jews "petitioned" the Roman ruler Festus). Thus Jesus continually, even today, is our Great High Priest who *brings requests* to the Father, who is greater in authority. Jesus's high priestly ministry indicates an ongoing submission to the authority of the Father.

This is not a "temporary submission," only for the time that Jesus is on earth. It continues while he is now in heaven. Similarly, even in the eternal kingdom, Jesus will not have authority to decide who sits at his right hand and at his left, for that will be something that has been determined by God the Father. Jesus says this explicitly:

Matthew 20:23

. . . but to sit at my right hand and at my left is not mine to grant, but it is for those for whom it has been prepared by my Father.

Many more passages than these thirteen could be considered,[42] but these should be sufficient to show a consistent pattern of teaching in Scripture regarding the eternal submission of the Son to the Father.

Evangelical Feminists' Refusals to Consider These Verses

Even though I brought up many of these verses in the section on the Trinity in my 2004 book *Evangelical Feminism and Biblical Truth*,[43]

---

[42] See my discussion of thirty-one passages in ibid.
[43] Grudem, *Evangelical Feminism and Biblical Truth*, chap. 10.

evangelical feminists generally just ignore them in their discussion of the issues. Even in the recent set of essays edited by Jowers and House, *The New Evangelical Subordinationism?* (2012), proponents of temporary submission fail to treat these key verses. They are significant verses that contradict the temporary submission view. To refuse even to consider these significant challenges to their position seems to me to indicate a rejection of the authority of these scriptural passages. Temporary submission advocates give the impression that they will hold to their view despite express biblical testimony to the contrary.

Kevin Giles has another method of ignoring such verses. He minimizes them by calling them "isolated texts" and "problematic isolated verses."[44] This is why, Giles explains, "simply opening our Bibles cannot settle the debate as to what should be believed about the Trinity."[45]

Thus, Giles has a convenient way of dismissing verses that are uncomfortable for his temporary submission viewpoint. Without even quoting them he just says that they must be understood in light of "the overall perspective and primary message of Scripture. This is not found by appeal to one or more texts but by an ongoing reading of the whole of Scripture."[46] He is sure, of course, that the "overall perspective" and "primary message" is that the Son is eternally equal to the Father and therefore cannot be subject to the Father's authority. But this is simply begging the question, assuming the conclusion at the outset of the argument.

Giles's approach reveals a refusal to submit to the overall authority of Scripture. Accordingly, if a number of verses disagree with your premises, you need not even discuss them. You can just declare them "isolated" (which means they don't count), irrelevant anomalies that must be interpreted in light of the "primary message" (by which you mean your own position). But this way of neutralizing verses is really a refusal to be subject to the authority of Scripture in one's theology.

---

[44] Giles, "The Trinity without Tiers," 271.
[45] Ibid., 272. I might add that I am not sure what Giles means by "isolated verses." I have not been able to locate any isolated verses in my Bible. They all seem to occur in contexts that connect them with other verses.
[46] Ibid., 273.

Conclusion

Recent evangelical-feminist arguments about the Trinity display serious departures from the orthodox doctrine of the Trinity and implicitly reject the authority of Scripture. These are troubling and highly significant doctrinal deviations in evangelical feminists' arguments about the Trinity.

2

"I Always Do What Pleases Him"

The Father and Son in the Gospel of John

CHRISTOPHER W. COWAN

"θεὸς . . . is predicative and describes the nature of the Word. The absence of the article indicates that the Word is God, but is not the only being of whom this is true. . . . The deeds and words of Jesus are the deeds and words of God; if this be not true the book is blasphemous."[1] So writes the late C. K. Barrett on John 1:1. Such a view rightly understands John to ascribe deity to Jesus, though not as a challenge to Jewish monotheism. Likewise, numerous modern Johannine commentators interpret the Fourth Evangelist as portraying the Father and Son—who are distinct—as having the same divine "nature," "essence," or "being."[2]

---

[1] C. K. Barrett, *The Gospel according to St. John: An Introduction with Commentary and Notes on the Greek Text*, 2nd ed. (Philadelphia: Westminster Press, 1978), 156.
[2] E.g., B. F. Westcott, *The Gospel according to St. John: The Authorized Version with Introduction and Notes* (Grand Rapids: Eerdmans, 1951), 3; F. F. Bruce, *The Gospel of John: Introduction, Exposition, and Notes* (Grand Rapids: Eerdmans, 1983), 31; George R. Beasley-Murray, *John*, Word Biblical Commentary (Waco, TX: Word, 1987), 11; Rudolf Schnackenburg, *The Gospel according to St. John*, trans. Cecily Hastings et al., 3 vols. (New York: Crossroad, 1990), 2:177, 3:333. Commentators who may not use the terminology "nature," "essence," or "being," but who nonetheless interpret the texts in a similar manner, include, e.g., J. H. Bernard, *A Critical and Exegetical Commentary on the Gospel according to St. John*, 2 vols., International Critical Commentary (Edinburgh: T&T Clark, 1928), 1:cxlv, 2; G. H. C. Macgregor, *The Gospel of John*, Moffatt New Testament Commentary (London: Hodder & Stoughton, 1928), 4; Barnabas Lindars, *The Gospel of John* (London: Oliphants, 1972), 84; D. A. Carson, *The Gospel according to John*, Pelican New Testament Commentaries (Grand Rapids: Eerdmans, 1991), 117; Leon Morris, *The*

Yet, this equality of divine nature between Father and Son exists alongside John's ubiquitous depiction of a hierarchical relationship between the two, in which the Son is perfectly obedient to his Father. Recently, however, some scholars have questioned the legitimacy of seeing the Son in a subordinate role to the Father in the Fourth Gospel, or they have offered alternative interpretations so that the concept no longer applies. Others acknowledge that Jesus assumes a *temporary* subordinate role during his earthly ministry, but they argue that such is not descriptive of the Son's relationship to the Father in either eternity past or eternity future.

In this chapter I will argue that John presents the Son's functional subordination to the Father as a major theme in his Gospel and will respond to critics of this view. Before concluding, I will present evidence from the Fourth Gospel that indicates that John presents this hierarchical relationship as eternal and not merely limited to the Son's incarnation.[3]

The Son's Subordinate Role to the Father in John

The Son as "Sent" by the Father

Three interrelated themes in John show that Jesus assumes a subordinate role to his Father. The first is John's presentation of the Son as "sent" by the Father. The Father's purpose in sending the Son is that the world might be saved through him (John 3:17), and Jesus repeatedly describes God as "the Father who sent me" or "him who sent me" (e.g. 4:34; 5:23; 6:38; 7:28; 8:29; 12:44; 14:24).[4] His testimony to the Jews is "I have not come of myself," but the Father "sent me" (7:28–29; 8:42). In this way, the Evangelist presents the Son as being sent on a mission initiated by the Father (3:16–17; 7:28–29; 8:42; 17:3).[5] Therefore, he is

---

Gospel according to John, rev. ed., NICNT (Grand Rapids: Eerdmans, 1995), 68–69; Craig S. Keener, *The Gospel of John: A Commentary*, 2 vols. (Peabody, MA: Hendrickson, 2003), 1:374; Andreas J. Köstenberger, *John*, Baker Exegetical Commentary of the New Testament (Grand Rapids: Baker, 2004), 27–29.

[3] This chapter is based on and reproduces portions of my article "The Father and Son in the Fourth Gospel: Johannine Subordination Revisited," *JETS* 49 (2006): 115–35. It is used with permission. In that article, I did address whether or not the Son's subordination to the Father was *eternal*, despite the erroneous claim of Kevin Giles, "The Father and the Son Divided or Undivided in Power and Authority?," 4 and note 27; accessed 28 April 2012, http://www.cbeinternational.org/?q=content/father-and-son-divided-or-undivided-power-and-authority.

[4] Scripture quotations in this chapter are my own translations.

[5] Leon Morris writes, "The very concept of mission, of being 'sent,' contains within it the thought of doing what the Sender wills" (*New Testament Theology* [Grand Rapids: Zondervan, 1986], 251).

accountable to the Father for all he does. As the "sent Son," Jesus seeks the will and glory of the one who sent him, not his own (5:30; 6:38; 7:18). He speaks only the words and teaching that he has received from his Father (7:16; 8:26; 12:49; 14:24). An individual must honor, receive, and believe in the Son, for the very reason that he has been sent from the Father (5:23; 6:29; 13:20). Then when his mission is complete, the Son returns to his sender (7:33; 16:5).

Many have interpreted John against a background of religious and cultural messenger practices, particularly the Jewish institution of "agency" (*shaliach*).[6] Dealing with the agent was considered the same as dealing with the sender. The agent would carry out his mission in obedience to the sender and then return to the sender.[7] According to Jewish midrash, "the sender is greater than the sent" (Genesis Rabbah 78:1). Similarly, Jesus affirms the sent one's subordination to the sender, telling his disciples, "A slave is not greater than his master, nor is one sent greater than the one who sent him" (John 13:16). Yet, as John makes clear in the Fourth Gospel, the Father has sent not just any agent but his only Son. He alone could be relied on absolutely to promote his Father's interests (cf. Mark 12:6).[8]

In the end, whether or not the Jewish concept of agency forms the background for the sending of the Son, the Gospel's language of sending and the accompanying actions of the one sent clearly seem to imply the Son's subordination to his Father who sent him.[9] A comparison to others who were "sent"—in which John uses the same terminology— reveals their obvious subordination to their sender(s): John the Baptist, who was sent by God (John 1:6, 33); the priests and Levites who were

---

[6] See, e.g., Peder Borgen, "God's Agent in the Fourth Gospel," in *Religions in Antiquity: Essays in Memory of Erwin Ramsdell Goodenough*, ed. Jacob Neusner (Leiden: Brill, 1968), 137–48; Anthony E. Harvey, "Christ as Agent," in *The Glory of Christ in the New Testament: Studies in Christology in Memory of George Bradford Caird*, ed. L. D. Hurst and N. T. Wright (Oxford: Clarendon, 1987), 239–50; Helen S. Friend, "Like Father, Like Son: A Discussion of the Concept of Agency in Halakah and John," *ATJ* 21 (1990): 18–28; John Ashton, *Understanding the Fourth Gospel* (Oxford: Clarendon, 1991), 312–17; Calvin Mercer, "Jesus the Apostle: 'Sending' and the Theology of John," *JETS* 35 (1992): 457–62.
[7] Borgen, "God's Agent in the Fourth Gospel," 138–44. Mercer notes that the sending in rabbinical agency implies subordination ("Jesus the Apostle," 462).
[8] Harvey, "Christ as Agent," 243. Of course, these parallels do not necessarily imply dependence, and the rabbinic sources in their final written form postdate the Gospel. However, Craig Keener observes, "While we cannot determine the date at which some aspects of the custom of agency became law, the custom's practice in other cultures suggests that the Jewish custom is older than the rabbinic sources which comment on it" (*The Gospel of John*, 1:311).
[9] Keener writes, "This 'sending' Christology emphasizes the subordinationist aspect (the Son subordinate to the Father) of John's Christology" (Ibid., 1:317).

sent by the Jews/Pharisees to question John (1:19, 22, 24); and the officers who were sent by the chief priests and Pharisees to arrest Jesus (7:32; cf. 7:45). So, it seems only natural to see Jesus's relationship to his sender in the same way.

The Son as Dependent on and Obedient to the Father

A second way John highlights the Son's subordination to his Father is by portraying him as dependent on and obedient to him. While this is clearly tied to the Son's being sent, it warrants a separate evaluation. His total dependence on his Father is expressed through what the Father "gives" (δίδωμι) to him. The Father has given him the Spirit (3:34), to have life in himself (5:26), authority to judge (5:22, 27), works to accomplish (5:36; 17:4), words to speak (12:49; 17:8), and a cup to drink (18:11). Because of man's moral inability to come to Jesus (6:44, 65), he is dependent on the Father to give people to him (6:37, 39; cf. 10:29; 17:2). The Son acknowledges to the Father that his disciples "were yours, and you gave them to me" (17:6; cf. 17:9). Indeed, because of his love for his Son, the Father has given "all things into his hand" (3:35; cf. 13:3). Moreover, Jesus repeatedly tells the Jews that he can do nothing on his own initiative,[10] but only as directed by the Father (5:19, 30; cf. 8:28). Neither his coming (7:28; 8:42) nor his speaking (8:28; 12:49; 14:10) is at his own initiative. Rather, Jesus speaks only those things which he has heard from (8:26; cf. 8:40), seen with (8:38), or been taught by (8:28) the Father.

A passage that places particular emphasis on the Son's dependence on his Father is John 5:19–30. Here, Jesus elaborates on his statement in 5:17, in which he justifies his healing of a man on the Sabbath: "My Father is working until now, and I am working." For this claim, the Jews sought to kill him "since he was not only breaking the Sabbath, but also calling God his own Father, making himself equal with God" (5:18). But far from implying any independence from the Father, Jesus

---

[10] Ποιεῖν ἀφ᾽ ἑαυτοῦ [or ἀπ᾽ ἐμαυτοῦ] οὐδὲν—a common Johannine idiom. See Barrett, *The Gospel according to St. John*, 259 ("without prompting"); Raymond E. Brown, *The Gospel according to John*, 2 vols., Anchor Bible (New York: Doubleday, 1966–1970), 1:218 ("by himself"); Beasley-Murray, *John*, 68 ("by himself"); Rudolf Bultmann, *The Gospel of John*, trans. G. R. Beasley-Murray (Philadelphia: Westminster Press, 1971), 249 ("on his own authority"); Schnackenburg, *The Gospel according to St. John*, 2:103 ("of his own accord"); Carson, *The Gospel according to John*, 250 ("on his own initiative").

insists that "the Son can do nothing of himself, unless it is something he sees the Father doing"; for (γὰρ) the Son does whatever the Father does (5:19). Out of his love for the Son, the Father "shows him all things he himself is doing" (5:20). The Son will execute judgment and grant life to others, because the Father has given him authority to judge and to have life in himself (5:21–29). As a result, the Son does nothing of himself but judges as he hears from the Father, because he does not seek his own will but that of his sender (5:30).

Not only is the Son dependent on his Father, but he also demonstrates total obedience. The Son has come not to do his own will but the will of the one who sent him (John 5:30; 6:38). To do the Father's will and accomplish his work is the Son's food (4:34). During a confrontation with the Jews, Jesus repeatedly tells them that he speaks what he has heard from the Father (8:26, 38, 40) and also that he always does the things that are pleasing to the Father (8:29). The Son has received commandments from the Father regarding what to speak (12:49) and the laying down of his life (10:18). According to Jesus, he does just as the Father has commanded as an expression of his love for him (14:31), and, by keeping his commandments, he also abides in the Father's love (15:10). As the hour for his glorification arrives, the Son declares to his Father, "I glorified you on the earth, accomplishing the work which you have given me to do" (17:4). Then, when his work on the cross is done, he breathes his last words as recorded in the Fourth Gospel, "It is accomplished!" (19:30), signifying the completion of his mission, which he has carried out in perfect obedience to the Father.[11]

The Use of "Father" and "Son" Terminology

The third way that John's Gospel highlights the Son's subordinate role to his Father involves the very use of Father-Son terminology. What does the Father-Son language in the Fourth Gospel imply regarding the relationship between Jesus and God? More specifically, do these terms necessarily imply a hierarchical relationship between the two? It would seem to be no mere coincidence that the Gospel in which

---

[11] On Jesus accomplishing his mission in obedience to the Father in 19:30, see Bultmann, *The Gospel of John*, 674–75; Schnackenburg, *The Gospel according to St. John*, 3:284; Carson, *The Gospel according to John*, 621; Beasley-Murray, *John* 352.

52   *Christopher W. Cowan*

Jesus characteristically and frequently calls God his Father and himself the Son is the same Gospel in which Jesus emphasizes his submission to God.

How would John's readers have understood a father-son relationship? What relational framework would have come to mind? In the patriarchal culture of first-century Palestine, a father exercised authority over his son. In Old Testament Israel, a father was the head of his family and an authority to be respected and obeyed.[12] "From the official and semi-official secular modes of expression one may indirectly draw the conclusion that predominantly, and sometimes even exclusively, Israel regarded the father relationship as one of authority."[13] The Hebrews did not neglect the importance of the physical bond between father and son, W. F. Lofthouse argues,

> but Father, to the Hebrew, suggests so much more than physical origin.... A father, though he might be less than the progenitor, was also much more. Like the Roman father, he was also the lifelong guardian and master of the boy, expecting obedience, cooperation, affection and confidence to the end.[14]

Johannes Pedersen writes: "To the Israelite the name father always spells authority. Naaman is called father by his servants (2 Kings 5,13). The priest is called father of the cultic community, of which he is the head (Judg. 18,19), and Elijah is called father by his disciple (2 Kings 2,12)."[15] For the Hebrew, the words "like father, like son" would express "an ideal bond, in which the father lived and acted in his son, and the son carried out the father's aims and purposes in proud and joyous submission."[16]

Within this context, John presents Jesus as consistently calling God "Father" when speaking of his actions of dependence and obedience in the relationship. Thus, while the use of Father-Son terminology by itself

---

[12] See O. Hofius, "πατήρ," in *New International Dictionary of New Testament Theology*, 3:617; Gordon J. Wenham, "Family in the Pentateuch," in *Family in the Bible: Exploring Customs, Culture, and Context*, ed. Richard S. Hess and M. Daniel Carroll R. (Grand Rapids: Baker, 2003), 22.
[13] Gottlob Schrenk and Gottfried Quell, "πατήρ," in *TDNT*, 5:971. Commenting on John 14:28, Keener writes, "Ancient Mediterranean culture regarded fathers as greater in rank than sons" (*The Gospel of John*, 2:983).
[14] W. F. Lofthouse, *The Father and the Son: A Study in Johannine Thought* (London: SCM, 1934), 23–24.
[15] Johannes Pedersen, *Israel: Its Life and Culture*, 4 vols. (London: Oxford University Press, 1926–1940), 1:63.
[16] Lofthouse, *The Father and the Son*, 24.

would seem to point to a hierarchical relationship between the two, its presence intertwined with the other themes discussed above seems to solidify this conclusion. The Son can do nothing on his own, but only what he sees the Father doing; as the Father does, so the Son does (John 5:19). The Father taught the Son (8:28), whose obedience is evident because he always does what pleases the Father (8:29) and speaks what he has heard from him (8:38). Jesus honors his Father (8:49; cf. Ex. 20:12) and keeps his word (John 8:55). When Jesus's hour draws near, he tells his disciples that he is going to the Father, "for the Father is greater than I" (14:28). Clearly, the language of "Father" and "Son" reflects an intimate, familial relationship: "the Father loves the Son" (3:35; 5:20). Yet a relationship of loving intimacy does not rule out a relational hierarchy—which the Father-Son terminology conveys in its original context.

Criticisms of This View

Recently, several scholars have argued against seeing the Son and the Father in such a hierarchical relationship in John. One such scholar is Kevin Giles.[17] He agrees that the Jewish *shaliach* ("agency") concept is a plausible background to John's sending language. Contrary to the interpreters cited above, though, Giles insists that this actually highlights the *unity* of Father and Son. According to the Jewish institution, the one sent is invested with the authority of the sender.[18] So, while the sending terminology distinguishes Father (the sender) from Son (the one sent), John's emphasis "falls on the authority of the Son as expressing the authority of the Father."[19]

The problem is that Giles's use of this background is selective. He is certainly correct that the sending language implies the unity of Father and Son. As the sent one, the Son speaks and acts with the Father's authority. According to John, one's response to the Son is considered his response to the Father who sent him, since the Son is the Father's representative (5:23; 12:44–45; 13:20; 15:23). However, this is only

---

[17] Kevin Giles, *The Trinity and Subordinationism: The Doctrine of God and the Contemporary Gender Debate* (Downers Grove, IL: InterVarsity, 2002); Giles, *Jesus and the Father: Modern Evangelicals Reinvent the Doctrine of the Trinity* (Grand Rapids: Zondervan, 2006). Though Giles attempts to address the issue more broadly in terms of historical theology and systematic theology, he also includes some discussion of John's Gospel in the latter volume.
[18] Giles, *Jesus and the Father*, 119–20.
[19] Ibid., 120.

half the story: the Jewish concept of agency also clearly implies subordination.[20] Beyond this, the idea that the sent one is subordinate to the sender is clearly implied in John's Gospel, whether the sent one is Jesus, John the Baptist, or the emissaries of the Pharisees. It will not do for Giles to affirm the unity implied by the sending while simultaneously denying the implied hierarchy in roles, saying that the language merely "distinguishes" the two. For a chief feature of their "distinction" is that Jesus seeks not his own will but the will of the one who sent him (5:30; 6:38)

Another interpreter who denies the Son's unilateral dependence on the Father in John is Royce Gordon Gruenler. Instead, he argues for *mutual* deference and subordination between Father and Son. He repeatedly points to texts that speak of the Father's "giving" to the Son and explains them as clear instances of the Father's "deference" to him.[21] Regarding John 5:19–30, he argues that the Father "defers to the Son in giving him all authority to judge. The Father submits to the good judgment of the Son and trusts his judgment completely."[22] Since the Father grants the Son the right to pass judgment (5:27), Gruenler concludes that the Son is "worthy of executing divine judgment, hence the Father willingly subordinates himself to [him]."[23]

It is difficult, however, to see how Gruenler reaches such conclusions, given the context of the passage and of the Gospel itself. No other major Johannine commentator of whom I am aware has interpreted this text to say that the Father "defers to" or "subordinates himself to" the Son's authority (Gruenler cites none in agreement). Contrasted with Gruenler's conclusions, Barrett's comments on the text are arresting: "In vv. 19–30 the main theme is solemnly, constantly, almost wearisomely, repeated.... There is complete unity of action between the Father and the Son, and complete dependence of the Son on the Father."[24] Elsewhere, Barrett writes, "If [the Son] executes judgment and gives life to the dead, this is because these privileges have been granted him by the Father."[25] Other

---

[20] Mercer, "Jesus the Apostle," 462; and Keener, *The Gospel of John*, 1:316.
[21] Royce Gordon Gruenler, *The Trinity in the Gospel of John: A Thematic Commentary on the Fourth Gospel* (Grand Rapids: Baker, 1986), 33 (3:35), 45 (6:37), 124 (17:6).
[22] Ibid., 37.
[23] Ibid., 38.
[24] Barrett, *The Gospel according to St. John*, 257.
[25] C. K. Barrett, "Christocentric or Theocentric? Observations on the Theocentric Method of the Fourth Gospel," in *Essays on John* (Philadelphia: Westminster Press, 1982), 7. See also Barrett, "'The Father Is

commentators understand it similarly.[26] On 5:19, D. A. Carson insists that though Jesus is the unique Son who may truly be called God, he always submits to the Father and does only what he sees his Father doing. "In this sense the relationship between the Father and the Son is not reciprocal. It is inconceivable that John could say that the Father does only what he sees the Son doing."[27] Gruenler inappropriately substitutes the concept of "deference" for John's description of the Father's *unilaterally* giving the Son authority to judge (5:22, 27). There is no indication in John that by giving things to the Son, the Father is somehow subordinating himself to the Son's authority. Such an argument seems to misunderstand the very concepts of subordination and delegated authority.[28]

Other scholars offer correctives to interpreting the Son's actions in John as "obedience." Paul Meyer contends, "The correspondence of action between Son and Father has been misunderstood as obedience within a patriarchally structured relationship." He then points to 10:18 where Jesus speaks of the "command" he received from his Father to lay down his life: it is "not the surrender of Jesus' own will to yield to God's . . . but the willing act of Jesus' own initiative and authority . . . which is grounded in the relationship of mutual knowledge and love between Jesus and his Father."[29] Both Meyer and Ernst Haenchen note the absence

---

Greater than I,' John 14:28: Subordinationist Christology in the New Testament," in *Essays on John*, 19–36. After citing Gruenler's work with apparent endorsement, Kevin Giles quotes Barrett as saying that John "more than any other writer in the New Testament lays the foundation for a doctrine of a co-equal Trinity" (*The Trinity and Subordinationism*, 34n4; see Barrett, *The Gospel according to St. John*, 92). While Barrett clearly affirms the equality of Father and Son in John (see note 1 above), when one considers the rest of Barrett's commentary and his other writings on the Father and Son in John cited above, it seems equally clear that Barrett affirms the Son's functional subordination to the Father—a point one would not realize based on Giles one-sided quotation.

[26] See Beasley-Murray, *John*, 76; Bernard, *The Gospel according to St. John*, 241; Keener, *The Gospel of John*, 1:648; cf. 1:652.

[27] Carson, *The Gospel according to John*, 250–51. See also C. H. Dodd, *The Interpretation of the Fourth Gospel* (Cambridge: Cambridge University Press, 1953), 255–57; Brown, *The Gospel according to John*, 1:218. Carson describes Gruenler's effort as a "vain attempt to bury under the banner of deference the massive differences in the descriptions of the roles of the Father and the Son as depicted in the Fourth Gospel." He adds, "Because I 'defer' to my son's request to pick him up at the soccer pitch does not mean he commands me in the way I command him or that my love for him is displayed in obedience to him" (*The Difficult Doctrine of the Love of God* [Wheaton, IL: Crossway, 2000], 86).

[28] J. Ernest Davey's comments are a stark contrast: "There is no more remarkable element in the Fourth Gospel than the consistent and universal presentation of Christ . . . as dependent upon the Father at every point" (*The Jesus of St. John: Historical and Christological Studies in the Fourth Gospel* [London: Lutterworth, 1958], 90). For a lengthy discussion of "the dependence of Christ as presented in John," see ibid., 90–157. On the significance of this theme in John, see also T. E. Pollard, *Johannine Christology and the Early Church* (Cambridge: Cambridge University Press, 1970), 18; and Leon Morris, *Studies in the Fourth Gospel* (Grand Rapids: Eerdmans, 1969), 115.

[29] Paul W. Meyer, "'The Father': The Presentation of God in the Fourth Gospel," in *Exploring the Gospel of John: In Honor of D. Moody Smith*, ed. R. Alan Culpepper and C. Clifton Black (Louisville, KY: Westminster John Knox, 1996), 260–61.

of the noun "obedience" and the verb "obey" in John's Gospel.[30] Jesus is never said to "obey." According to Meyer, the constancy with which Jesus does the Father's will and works "does not *produce* unity with the Father—as would be the case if it were understood as obedience—but is grounded in, and springs from, the prior unity of Jesus with the Father."[31]

Acknowledging that the Son often "does the will/works" of the Father, Marianne Meye Thompson nevertheless similarly calls attention to the absence of the word "obey," remarking that John "stresses rather dramatically the harmony of the Son's will with the Father's, interpreting the Son's obedience as an *enactment* or *expression* of the Father's will, rather than as submission or acquiescence to it." This does not imply, however, "that the Johannine Jesus has no will, rather, that Jesus' will is fully in harmony with that of the Father."[32] Like Meyer, Thompson points to 10:18, finding that it not only speaks of the command Jesus received from his Father but also simultaneously stresses his sovereignty over his life:

> However, the dialectic is resolved in the peculiarity of the Father-Son relationship in John, in which the Father not only gives the Son his life but grants it to him to dispose of it as he will—or, as the Father wills. . . . The Son's obedience to the Father does not establish their unity, nor is it an obedience construed in terms of submission to an alien command. Rather, the Son's "obedience" is the expression of the will of the One who sent him.[33]

Several responses are necessary. First, granting the absence of the actual *words* "obey," "obedience," and "obedient" (ὑπακούω, ὑπακοή, and ὑπήκοος) in John's Gospel, it is hard to see the relevance of this in light of the clear evidence for the presence of the *concept*. Both Meyer and Thompson acknowledge that John speaks of Jesus's "doing the will" (ποιεῖν τὸ θέλημα) of the one who sent him (4:34; 6:38). Yet the same phrase is used with respect to others "doing God's will" (7:17; 9:31; cf. 1 John 2:17) and is clearly intended to refer to their *obedience*

---

[30] Ibid., 261; and Ernst Haenchen, *A Commentary on the Gospel of John*, trans. J. C. B. Mohr (Paul Siebeck), 2 vols., Hermeneia (Philadelphia: Fortress, 1984), 1:250. For this observation, both point to Ernst Käsemann, *The Testament of Jesus: A Study of the Gospel of John in the Light of Chapter 17*, trans. Gerhard Krodel (Philadelphia: Fortress, 1968), 18.
[31] Meyer, "The Father," 261 (emphasis original).
[32] Marianne Meye Thompson, "The Living Father," *Semeia* 85 (1999): 28 (emphasis original).
[33] Marianne Meye Thompson, *The God of the Gospel of John* (Grand Rapids: Eerdmans, 2001), 95.

to God.³⁴ In addition to "doing God's will," Jesus also "keeps" (τηρέω) his Father's word and commandments (John 8:55; 15:10). This word occurs often in the New Testament with the meaning "to obey" and, moreover, is commonly used in the Johannine literature in this manner.³⁵ Followers of Jesus are to "keep (τηρέω) God's word/commandments" (John 14:23–24; 15:10; 1 John 2:3ff.; 3:22, 24; 5:3). Particularly illuminating is John 15:10, in which Jesus compares his disciples' behavior to his own: "If you keep my commandments, you will abide in my love; just as I have kept my Father's commandments and abide in his love." Here, the obedience of the disciples is to be patterned after the *obedience* of Jesus.³⁶ In actuality, one does not find ὑπακούω, ὑπακοή, or ὑπήκοος in *any* Johannine writings, *even with respect to believers.* Thus, arguments that point to the lack of these words in the Gospel to describe Jesus's actions hardly seem persuasive when one realizes that they are not even a part of John's vocabulary. To "do God's will" and "keep God's word/commandments" are simply the Johannine formulas for expressing obedience to God.

Second, the fact that Jesus speaks of the authority and sovereignty he has over his own life in John 10:18 is not inconsistent with the commandment he has received from his Father to lay it down. The Son willingly submits to the Father's will and lays down his life. In declaring that no one takes his life from him but that he lays it down of his own accord, Jesus is saying that the cross is not a tragic accident of fate or merely a scheme concocted by wicked men—it is the Father's plan.³⁷ John wants his readers to know ahead of time that, while the perpetrators are morally culpable, what is about to happen is directed by divine sovereignty (cf. 13:18–19; 18:8–9; 19:11, 24).³⁸

---

[34] Note under the entry for "ποιέω" in BDAG: "To carry out an obligation of a moral or social nature . . . *do*, *keep* the will or law obediently τὸ θέλημα τοῦ θεοῦ."
[35] John 8:51, 52; 14:15, 21, 23, 24; 15:10, 20; 17:6; 1 John 2:3f.; 3:24; 5:3; Rev. 3:8; 12:17; 14:12. Johannes P. Louw and Eugene A. Nida place this usage of τηρέω in the same semantic domain as (among other words) ὑπακούω, ὑπακοή, and ὑπήκοος, under the heading "Obey, Disobey." (*Greek-English Lexicon of the New Testament Based on Semantic Domains*, 2nd ed. [New York: United Bible Societies, 1989], s.v. "τηρέω." See also BDAG, s.v. "τηρέω."
[36] See Westcott, *The Gospel according to St. John*, 219; Barrett, *The Gospel according to St. John*, 475–66; Carson, *The Gospel according to John*, 520; Morris, *The Gospel according to John*, 597; Herman N. Ridderbos, *The Gospel according to John: A Theological Commentary*, trans. John Vriend (Grand Rapids: Eerdmans, 1997), 519.
[37] See Carson, *The Gospel according to John*, 389.
[38] For these themes in John, see D. A. Carson, *Divine Sovereignty and Human Responsibility: Biblical Perspectives in Tension* (Atlanta: John Knox, 1981), esp. 125–98.

Third, it is a false dichotomy to set Jesus's unity of will with the Father in opposition to his obedience to his Father. To speak of one's "obedience" or "submission" to God's command does not imply any necessary lack of unity of will between the two—as if the one obeying God does so only under protest![39] In the Old Testament, the "delight" of the psalmist "is in the law of Yahweh" (Ps 1:2; cf. 119:14, 16, 24, 35, 70, 77), and God's testimonies are the "joy of [his] heart" (119:111). Psalm 40:8 testifies, "I delight to do your will, O my God." Submission to God's will by the Old Testament saint is described in terms of delight and, thus, harmony of will—not mere acquiescence of his will to yield to God's. If such could be said by the faithful Old Testament believer, how much more is this true of the Son who considers it his very food "to do the will" of his Father who sent him (John 4:34)? Thompson claims that John interprets the Son's "obedience" as "an *enactment* or *expression* of the Father's will."[40] But while this is certainly true, it is not *merely* that. Such emphasis on their unity runs the risk of swallowing up any distinction between the two. Jesus's will is in harmony with the Father's, but he obeys him nonetheless. The oneness of their wills should not be used to trump John's presentation of the Son's loving, willing obedience to his Father's commands (14:31).

When it comes to the use of "Father" and "Son" terminology in John, Thompson insists, "the primary understanding of God as Father in John comes to expression in John 5:26: 'Just as the Father has life in himself, so he has granted the Son also to have life in himself.'" What shapes understanding of God as Father is "the fundamental reality that a father's relationship to his children consists first in terms simply of giving them life. What it means to be a father is to be the origin or source of the life of one's children."[41] John 6:57, which speaks of God as "the living Father," and the above statement from 5:26 "are essential to understanding John's delineation of God as Father and Jesus as Son."[42] So, Thompson argues, "when Jesus calls God 'Father,' he points first to the Father as the source or origin of life, and to the relationship

---

[39] Giles insists, "This story does not depict a battle of wills where the Father prevails over the Son" (*Jesus and the Father*, 121). Of course not! This is a straw man. Language such as "battle of wills" and "prevailing over" simply distorts the view Giles opposes.
[40] Thompson, "The Living Father," 28.
[41] Ibid., 20.
[42] Thompson, *The God of the Gospel of John*, 72.

established through the life-giving activity of the Father."[43] "Precisely in holding together the affirmation that the Son has 'life in himself' with the affirmation that he has 'been *given*' such life by the Father, we find the uniquely Johannine characterization of the relationship of the Father and the Son."[44] So, to label Jesus's words in John 14:28 ("The Father is greater than I") an example of John's "subordinationism" is misleading, says Thompson, "inasmuch as it conceives of the relationship of Father and Son primarily in hierarchical terms." Such statements "ought not to be read against a backdrop of patriarchal hierarchy. The Father is the source of the Son's life; it is as the origin of the Son's very being that 'the Father is greater than I.'"[45]

This understanding of the Father-Son relationship in John, however, seems to result from a very selective use of the evidence. Consider three responses: First, two texts (5:26; 6:57) have become the hermeneutical grid by which the relationship is interpreted. But in their contexts, John 5:26 and 6:57 serve to justify Jesus's ability to mediate eternal life to others. While Thompson would clearly agree with this, what appears unjustified is her assertion that such giving of life represents "the uniquely Johannine characterization" of the Father-Son relationship. As the foregoing discussion has attempted to demonstrate, John in numerous texts throughout his Gospel describes Jesus as the dependent and obedient Son sent on a mission from the Father. How then do *two* verses stand as "essential to understanding John's delineation of God as Father and Jesus as Son"?

Second, in interpreting John 14:28, Thompson asserts that "it is as the origin of the Son's very being that 'the Father is greater than I.'" As evidence, she points to the context, "in which Jesus asserts that he *returns* to the Father, because the Father is greater; that is, he has his origins in the Father."[46] However, this has not been established from the context, but assumed. She has not explained *why* the Father's being greater means that he is the origin of the Son's being. Jesus does speak of "going" to the Father in the context (14:12, 28; 16:5), but he is going back to "him who *sent* me" (16:5). So if Jesus speaks of the Father as

---
[43] Ibid.
[44] Ibid., 79 (emphasis original).
[45] Ibid., 94.
[46] Ibid. (emphasis original).

his "source" or "origin" in this discourse, it seems best to see the Father as the authoritative source or origin of Jesus's mission, to whom he returns. While contextual clues are lacking for Thompson's view, Jesus's statement in 14:28 is certainly consistent with the evidence cited thus far supporting the subordination theme.[47]

Third, clearly the Evangelist does not intend his readers to understand the Father's granting the Son to have life in himself (5:26) in the same manner as God's giving life to human beings or as his creating Israel as a nation. Nor does he intend this to be understood in terms of the Father's superiority to the Son in his essential being.[48] If John intended the Father-Son relationship to be primarily understood in terms of the Father as the origin of the Son's life, this would seem to run not just in tension with but also in sharp contrast to his description of the Son as not a created being but himself God (1:1).

Royce Gruenler also denies the obvious implications of the Father-Son language. He asserts, "The dynamics of the divine Family are relational and symmetrical."[49] But would the first readers of the Fourth Gospel have understood a father-son relationship as "symmetrical"? Could the Son have sent the Father into the world? Could the Father as equally have said, "I do exactly as the Son commanded me"? It is extremely difficult to imagine John writing this. Instead it seems the burden of proof lies with those who would deny that such language necessarily implies a hierarchical relationship.

An Eternal Relationship

Based on the foregoing discussion (and the views of many Johannine interpreters), it seems clear that John intends his readers to view the Son in a subordinate role to his Father—*right alongside* the view that the Son equally shares the same divine essence of the Father. But is the

---

[47] Most major commentators interpret the Father's being "greater" than Jesus either as referring to the Father as the Son's sender or as describing the difference between the Father in his glory and the Son in his present humiliation. See Brown, *The Gospel according to John*, 2:654–55; Schnackenburg, *The Gospel according to St. John*, 3:86; Haenchen, *A Commentary on the Gospel of John*, 2:128; Beasley-Murray, *John*, 262; Carson, *The Gospel according to John*, 507–8; Morris, *The Gospel according to John*, 584–85; and Keener, *The Gospel of John*, 2:983.

[48] For this potential problem with Thompson's interpretation (the Father's ontological superiority), see the review of *The God of the Gospel of John* by Andreas Köstenberger in *JETS* 45 (2002): 522.

[49] Gruenler, *The Trinity in the Gospel of John*, 40. Note his comments elsewhere: "Submission within the divine Family does not run in one direction only, that is, only from Son to Father, but is reciprocal and symmetrical" (33); and on 8:18, "[Jesus] says that the relationship is mutual and symmetrical" (59).

former view merely a function of Jesus's incarnation and earthly ministry? Millard Erickson, for example, concludes, "The texts that speak of the Father commanding and the Son obeying are to be understood as referring to the time of the Son's earthly ministry."[50] Giles concurs: "To suggest that from this earthly story set unambiguously in the time of the Son's humiliation we learn something of the eternal heavenly relationship of the Father and the Son is a mistake."[51]

Does John indicate that this hierarchical relationship of the divine Father and Son is limited to the period between the Word being made flesh and his return to the Father? Or, instead, is there evidence in the Fourth Gospel to suggest that the Son's subordinate role is an aspect of his eternal relationship with the Father—unaffected by his incarnation? I believe John's Gospel presents evidence that allows us to answer yes to the second question. In the final portion of this chapter, I offer the following seven points to substantiate this.[52]

(1) At the outset, one should note the *absence* of evidence to support the view that the Son's subordinate role is temporary. As the discussion above has demonstrated, the submission of the Son to his Father is a major theme that is woven throughout the Gospel. While John clearly emphasizes Jesus's equality of divine essence with the Father—his activity in creation, his sovereignty over his death, and his glorious preexistence—he presents *no* testimony to counter the subordination theme and lead one to believe that there was a time when it did not apply. One would think that if Jesus's submission to his Father's authority held only during his earthly ministry, the apostle would want to make sure his readers clearly understood this.

(2) John asserts that God sent his Son "into the world" (3:17), which would appear to be a sending that occurred prior to the Son's incarnation—that is, an entrance from *outside* the world. Of course, one might argue that the Father's sending of the Son refers solely to his earthly ministry. After all, Jesus has similarly sent the disciples "into

---

[50] Millard J. Erickson, *Who's Tampering with the Trinity? An Assessment of the Subordination Debate* (Grand Rapids: Kregel, 2009), 248.
[51] Giles, *Jesus and the Father*, 121. See also 311.
[52] For major Johannine interpreters who see the Son's subordination to the Father as eternal and *not* limited to his incarnation, see, e.g., Barrett, "Subordinationist Christology in the New Testament," 19–36; Morris, *The Gospel according to John*, 584; Beasley-Murray, *John*, 262; Carson, *The Gospel according to John*, 554–55; Köstenberger, *John*, 445; Köstenberger, *Encountering John: The Gospel in Historical, Literary, and Theological Perspective* (Grand Rapids: Baker, 1999), 160.

the world" (17:18), and this clearly does not refer to entrance from outside the world. However, John indicates that Jesus's entrance "into the world" is from heaven (13:1, 3; 16:28), and his having "come from" God/heaven is set alongside being "sent" from God (6:38; 8:42; 17:8). Thus, *heaven* is the location from which he was "sent." Furthermore, when Jesus says he will return to "the one who sent me" (7:33), he demonstrates that the sending originated *outside* of this world. Therefore, the sending language implies a subordinate role for Jesus not only during his incarnation but prior to it as well. The Father's sending of the Son occurred prior to his being made flesh.

(3) The Father-Son language points to the Son as eternally subordinate to the authority of his Father. As argued above, the use of this language seems to imply a hierarchical relationship. That Jesus is the "Son" not merely during his incarnation is evident. The one sent into the world was the Son (John 3:17). In addition, Carson argues that the "life-in-himself" which the Father granted to the Son must mean the same as the "life-in-himself" which the Father has in the same verse (5:26). The most natural understanding of the phrase is that it refers to the Father's self-existence. Thus, Carson interprets this as an "eternal grant" from Father to Son establishing the eternal nature of their Father-Son relationship.[53] This, combined with Jesus's consistent use of "Father" for God and "Son" for himself throughout John, with nothing to restrict this language to the incarnation, favors his eternal submission to the Father.

(4) The Father's granting to the Son authority to judge (John 5:22, 27–29) is another pointer in this same direction. Jesus says that those who are in the tombs will hear his voice and come forth to a resurrection of life or judgment. One may rightly argue that John's emphasis on the present aspect of his inaugurated eschatology brings judgment into the "now." As people refuse to believe in the Son, they stand already judged (3:18; cf. 3:36). However, John also clearly sees judgment as "not yet." In 5:29, the language of resurrection implies the future eschatological final judgment. So, the Father has given the Son authority to render judgment—a judgment that lies outside of the sphere of his earthly ministry. Therefore, even at the consummation, the Son's role

---

[53] Carson, *The Difficult Doctrine of the Love of God*, 37–38.

as judge will be one that has been delegated to him by his Father (cf. 1 Cor. 15:22–28).

(5) Another text that extends the Son's dependence on the Father into his exaltation occurs during his farewell discourse to his disciples.[54] Jesus tells his disciples that he will ask the Father to send the Holy Spirit to be with them (John 14:16, 26). But, the giving of the Holy Spirit occurs *after* Jesus's resurrection.[55] This promise to ask the Father seems to imply a continued dependence on him after his resurrection (and, most likely, after his ascension; cf. Acts 2:1–4). While Father and Son are equally senders of the Spirit (John 14:26; 15:26), according to John, the Spirit's coming involves Jesus's making a request of his Father.

(6) Jesus's dependence on the Father reaches back into his preexistence in John 17:24.[56] Here, Jesus prays to the Father that his disciples might be with him, so that they might behold his glory, "which you have given me because you loved me before the foundation of the world" (cf. 17:5: "the glory I had with you before the world existed"). The glory which the Father had given to the Son was a result of his love for him prior to creation. Thus, the Son's dependence on his Father for his glory reaches into eternity past before the incarnation.

(7) Commenting on John 20:17, commentators often note that Jesus applies the fatherhood of God to his disciples, while still maintaining a distinction between his relationship with God and theirs. In this postresurrection statement, he says, "I am ascending to my Father and your Father, to my God and your God." God is now the "Father" of the disciples, but not in the same way as he is Jesus's Father. Jesus does not say that he is ascending to "our" Father, but to "my" Father and "your" Father. However, this is not all he says. Barrett observes that Jesus speaks not only of "my Father" but also of "my God"—"still, after the resurrection, recognizing the divine being as one to whom he owes obligation. As Son he has a Father; may we add, as man he has a God?"[57] It is hard to understand why the one whom John calls "God"

---

[54] Noted by Davey, *The Jesus of St. John*, 79.
[55] Even if one wants to contend for a "Johannine Pentecost" in 20:22, the Holy Spirit is still not given until after Jesus's resurrection.
[56] Also noted by Davey, *The Jesus of St. John*, 79.
[57] Barrett, "Subordinationist Christology in the New Testament," 22–23. Of course, Barrett's scholarship on John in general and his quotation at the beginning of this chapter in particular clearly demonstrate that his statement above in no way implies any sort of ditheism.

(1:1, 18) would, after the resurrection, continue to refer to the Father as *his* God unless the hierarchical Father-Son relationship between them continued to exist.

Conclusion

In the same way that the Fourth Gospel presents other combinations of seemingly opposed themes, it also displays a tension in its portrayal of Jesus's relationship to God.[58] John not only depicts Jesus as equal to God in his essential nature, but also displays him as the Son who fulfills a subordinate role to his Father's authority. Though some have denied this, I have attempted to argue that these efforts have fallen short. Not only do they depart sharply from the majority of Johannine scholarship, but they also fail to provide an adequate explanation of John's portrayal of the Son's relationship to his Father based on the data of the Gospel. Given the Fourth Gospel's emphasis on such elements as the deity, preexistence, and sovereignty of Jesus, combined with statements like "I and the Father are one" (10:30), one can perhaps sympathize with a reticence to understand this same Jesus as functionally subordinate to God. However, one need not—indeed must not—choose between the two truths, if evidence for both exists within the text.[59]

The reader of the Fourth Gospel can hardly miss the fact, though, that this relational hierarchy is set in the context of perfect divine love. For it is *because* the Father loves the Son that he shows him all that he is doing (5:20), and it is *so that* the world may know that the Son loves the Father, that he does as he is commanded (14:31). It is this divine love between Father and Son—expressed through the Father sending and the Son obeying—that makes possible the manifestation of the love of God for the world (3:16).

---

[58] Oscar Cullmann writes, "We must allow this paradox of all Christology to stand. The New Testament does not resolve it, but sets the two statements alongside each other: on the one hand the Logos *was* God; on the other hand, he was *with* God. The same paradox occurs again in the Gospel of John with regard to the 'Son of God' concept. We hear on the one hand, 'I and the Father are one' (John 10.30); and on the other hand, 'the Father is greater than I' (John 14.28)" (*The Christology of the New Testament*, trans. Shirley C. Guthrie and Charles A. M. Hall, rev. ed. [Philadelphia: Westminster Press, 1963], 266).

[59] Craig Keener writes, "Although the Fourth Gospel highlights Jesus' deity more than the other gospels, it also highlights Jesus' subordination to the Father more than the others" (*The Gospel of John*, 1:310).

3

God Is the Head of Christ

Does 1 Corinthians 11:3 Ground Gender Complementarity in the Immanent Trinity?

KYLE CLAUNCH

Scholarly exegetical treatments of 1 Corinthians 11:2–16 are legion. In his highly respected commentary on 1 Corinthians, Anthony Thiselton identifies "some eighty publications that invite attention in addition to commentaries and other standard works regularly cited."[1] If one adds to this already daunting list the scholarly treatments of the social and theological issues raised or implied by this text of Scripture, the result is overwhelming. As such, it is paramount to be clear from the outset what I am attempting here and how this chapter fits into the larger body of literature pertaining to 1 Corinthians 11:2–16. It is not the purpose of this essay to contribute yet another exhaustive exegetical analysis of this notoriously difficult passage. Rather, standing on the shoulders of the fine exegetical work of others, I will attempt to answer the following theological question: Does 1 Corinthians 11:3 ground gender complementarity in the immanent Trinity? This question has been elevated to a level of great importance as a result of recent and

---
[1] Anthony Thiselton, *The First Epistle to the Corinthians*, New International Greek Testament Commentary, ed. I. Howard Marshall and Donald A. Hagner (Grand Rapids: Eerdmans, 2000), 800.

ongoing debates concerning the legitimacy of appealing to Trinitarian relations as a model for social relationships. In evangelical circles, the debate has centered especially on the issue of male authority and female submission in both the home and the church.

Some theologians have made sustained appeals to Trinitarian relations as a model for *ontologically* equal parties existing in a relationship of *functional* authority and submission. God the Father and God the Son, it is argued, are ontologically equal—both fully divine—and functionally distinct with respect to roles of authority and submission—the Son submits eternally to the will of the Father. In a similar way, men and women are said to be ontologically equal—both are fully human and created in the image of God—and functionally distinct with respect to roles of authority and submission—the husband is the head of the wife, and the wife submits to her husband.[2] Others have argued forcefully that the analogy between male-female role relationships and Trinitarian relations is illegitimate for a number of reasons.

Some suggest that a functional distinction necessarily entails an ontological disparity. Thus, an eternal functional subordination of the Son to the Father is tantamount to a kind of Arianism.[3] Others have simply argued that an appeal to the Trinity as a model for social relationships is illegitimate because the immanent Trinity is to be adored and worshiped, not imitated in social institutions.[4] It is not difficult to see why 1 Corinthians 11:3, especially the statement "God is the head of Christ,"[5] is of

---

[2] This position has been articulated at length by theologians Bruce Ware and Wayne Grudem. See Bruce A. Ware, *Father, Son, and Holy Spirit: Relationships, Roles, and Relevance* (Wheaton, IL: Crossway, 2005); and "Tampering with the Trinity: Does the Son Submit to His Father?," in *Biblical Foundations for Manhood and Womanhood*, ed. Wayne Grudem (Wheaton, IL: Crossway, 2002), 233–55. See also Grudem, *Systematic Theology: An Introduction to Christian Doctrine* (Grand Rapids: Zondervan, 1994), 257; and *Evangelical Feminism and Biblical Truth: An Analysis of More than 100 Disputed Questions* (Colorado Springs: Multnomah, 2004; repr., Wheaton, IL: Crossway, 2012), 45–49.
[3] This is the basic thrust of Kevin Giles's argument in "The Doctrine of the Trinity and Subordinationism," *Evangelical Review of Theology* 28 (2004): 270–84. Gilbert Bilezikian rehearses a similar argument in "Hermeneutical Bungee Jumping," *JETS* 40 (1997): 57–68. Thomas McCall is even more forceful in his accusation, saying that those who contend for an eternal functional submission of the Son to the Father have denied the *homoousion* of Nicene orthodoxy. See *Which Trinity? Whose Monotheism? Philosophical and Systematic Theologians on the Metaphysics of Trinitarian Theology* (Grand Rapids: Eerdmans, 2010), 175–88.
[4] See Keith Johnson, "Trinitarian Agency and the Eternal Subordination of the Son: An Augustinian Perspective," *Themelios* 36 (2011): 22–24. Fred Hammond argues along these lines in "The Trinity Is Not Our Social Program," in *Trinitarian Theology for the Church: Scripture, Community, and Worship*, ed. Daniel J. Treier and David Lauber (Downers Grove, IL: InterVarsity, 2009). Hammond does not deal specifically with the gender issue. Rather, his contention is with the whole enterprise of appealing to the immanent Trinity as a model for human social relationships and institutions.
[5] Scripture quotations in this chapter are from *The New American Standard Bible®*. Copyright © The Lockman Foundation 1960, 1962, 1963, 1968, 1971, 1972, 1973, 1975, 1977, 1995. Used by permission.

great consequence in this debate, as the entire context of that statement pertains to appropriate expressions of gender roles in the context of corporate worship.[6]

This essay will argue that 1 Corinthians 11:3 does indeed ground gender complementarity in the immanent Trinity, albeit indirectly. The argument will proceed in three stages. First, a limited exegetical analysis of some of the key features of 1 Corinthians 11:2–16 is necessary. Special attention will be given to the metaphorical meaning of "head" (κεφαλή/*kephalē*) in 11:3 and the relationship of the three "head" clauses[7] of 11:3 to the passage as a whole. We will see that the statement "God is the head of Christ" does serve as a ground for the gender complementarity prescribed in that passage.

The second stage of the argument will address the important question of whether the statement "God is the head of Christ" pertains to the eternal relations between Father and Son (the immanent Trinity) or only to the relationship between the Father and the Son in the Son's incarnate state. I will argue that the statement pertains to the Son in his incarnate state *directly*. However, the relationship between the immanent and economic Trinity is such that it is reasonable to conclude, by good and necessary inference, that the statement "God is the head of Christ" pertains to the immanent Trinity *indirectly*.

The third stage of the argument will consider the implications of this study for the larger debate concerning the Trinity and gender roles. In particular, if gender complementarity is grounded in the immanent Trinity, does this entail a commitment to a social model of the Trinity?[8] While many have taken this route, this essay will propose an alternative. I will argue, instead, that the immanent Trinitarian order of subsistence entails a Trinitarian *taxis* (order) of the one divine will, which finds analogical expression in created relationships of authority and submission.

---

[6] Michael Reeves, interestingly, seems to see the relationship of man to woman in 1 Cor. 11:3 as grounded in the immanent Trinity, but he frames his discussion of the analogy between Father/Son and man/woman in terms of giving and receiving love rather than in terms of authority and submission (Reeves, *Delighting in the Trinity: An Introduction to the Christian Faith* [Downers Grove, IL: IVP Academic, 2012], 28–29).
[7] (1) "Christ is the head of every man," (2) "The man is the head of a woman," and (3) "God is the head of Christ."
[8] The terminology of social Trinitarianism is problematic, as there are very wide-ranging models of Trinitarian theology that utilize that label. Furthermore, some who embrace some social elements of Trinitarian theology have avoided the label. For these reasons, I will only use the terminology sparingly in this chapter.

A Brief Exegetical Analysis of 1 Corinthians 11:2–16

Thomas Schreiner is certainly correct when he calls 1 Corinthians 11:2–16 "one of the most difficult and controversial passages in the Bible."[9] Gordon Fee strikes a similar tone as he notes that "this passage is full of notorious exegetical difficulties."[10] These difficulties include the occasion for the instructions; the meaning and usage of the word "head" (*kephalē*) in verse 3 and throughout the passage; whether the Greek words *anēr* (ἀνήρ) and *gunē* (γυνή) in verse 3 should be translated generically as man and woman or as husband and wife, respectively; whether the head covering referred to in the passage is a shawl or hair; in what sense the woman is the "glory of man" (v. 7); the meaning of the "authority" (ἐξουσία/*exousia*), which is to be on the head of the woman (v. 10); the significance of the phrase "because of the angels" (v. 10); and in what way "nature itself" teaches Paul or the Corinthians about appropriate hair lengths for men and women (vv. 14–15). While it is well beyond the scope of this essay to engage all of these difficulties, neither is it necessary to do so in pursuit of this thesis. In spite of the difficulties and voluminous debates, I agree with Schreiner that "the central thrust of the passage is clear."[11]

So, what exactly is the "central thrust" of 1 Corinthians 11:2–16? This passage has featured prominently in the egalitarian versus complementarian debates over gender roles. Scholars on both sides of the debate agree that the passage addresses the question of the appropriate external attire (whether hair, a shawl, or both are in view) to be worn or not worn on the physical heads of men and women in the corporate worship of the church. For Paul, the question of external attire is of great importance because attire communicates the God-ordained distinction between the genders.[12] In other words, the blurring of the lines of gender distinction with respect to outward attire entails a blurring of

---

[9] Thomas R. Schreiner, "Head Coverings, Prophecies, and the Trinity: 1 Corinthians 11:2–16," in *Recovering Biblical Manhood and Womanhood: A Response to Evangelical Feminism*, ed. John Piper and Wayne Grudem (Wheaton, IL: Crossway, 1991), 124.
[10] Gordon D. Fee, *The First Epistle to the Corinthians*, NICNT (Grand Rapids: Eerdmans, 1987), 492.
[11] Schreiner, "Head Coverings," 125.
[12] Some have argued that this passage is a non-Pauline interpolation and is therefore not a reliable guide to Paul's actual apostolic instructions for the church. However, as Gordon Fee demonstrates, this is a fool's errand. There is no strong textual evidence for such a conclusion. The real debate is over the meaning of the passage and its application to the church today, not over the legitimacy of the passage as Pauline and apostolic. See Fee, *The First Epistle to the Corinthians*, 492n3.

the lines of gender distinction that God has woven into the very fabric of the created order.

However, beyond this basic agreement, complementarians and egalitarians offer radically different interpretations of the passage. For complementarians, the word "head" (*kephalē*) connotes "authority over." Complementarians argue that the head coverings required for women while praying or prophesying in corporate worship are intended to demonstrate the God-ordained role of women as submissive to men in the home and the church because "man is the head of a woman" (v. 3). Furthermore, by not wearing head coverings, men are portrayed as loving leaders in the church, as they are also in the home. For most egalitarians, on the other hand, the word "head" in verse 3 connotes "source" rather than "authority over." Egalitarians argue that there is no intended structure of authority and submission in this passage. Rather, by permitting women to pray and prophesy in the church, Paul is making it clear that women can have positions of leadership in corporate worship. The head covering is a symbol demonstrating the fact that now, in Christ, women have the right to lead, just as men do.

Before answering the primary question posed by this essay—Does 1 Corinthians 11:3 ground gender complementarity in the immanent Trinity?—we must ask whether 1 Corinthians 11:2–16 is rightly understood in complementarian terms. In order to demonstrate that the complementarian reading is most convincing, it is sufficient to show that the metaphorical use of the word "head" (*kephalē*) in verse 3 connotes the sense of "authority over," even if the meaning of "source" is not altogether ruled out. Once the complementarian interpretation of the passage is established based on the meaning of *kephalē*, it will be important, for the purposes of this essay, to consider what role the statement "God is the head of Christ" plays in the overall instruction of verses 2–16.

The Metaphorical Meaning of Kephalē

A Review of the Debate

The voluminous debate over the meaning of the Greek word *kephalē* is well documented[13] and need only be rehearsed briefly here. While the

---

[13] For a thorough survey of the most significant literature on the meaning of the word "head," see Alan F. Johnson, "A Review of the Scholarly Debate on the Meaning of 'Head' (Κεφαλή) in Paul's Writings," *ATJ*

literal meaning of *kephalē* as one's physical head is not in question, the metaphorical meaning and usage in Pauline literature is hotly contested. Some prominent New Testament scholars, following Stephen Bedale,[14] have argued that *kephalē* means "source" or "origin."[15] Wayne Grudem has forcefully challenged the legitimacy of "source" as a possible meaning for the word through a painstaking analysis of more than 2,300 occurrences of the word in ancient Greek literature.[16] Grudem's seminal study opened a new chapter in the debate, spawning what Alan Johnson has called "the battle of the lexicons."[17] As a result of this "battle" both sides have been forced to recognize that both meanings, "source" and "authority over," have some attestation in ancient Greek literature, while the meaning "authority over" has the lion's share of definitive examples. Since both meanings are apparently lexically possible, the debate has become a matter of attempting to prove which meaning is more likely in the Pauline texts. The tendency has been to argue that Paul had in mind one meaning *over against* the other.

There is, however, another approach to the question, one that is taken up by Thiselton[18] and later embraced by Alan Johnson.[19] This approach forms somewhat of a via media in the debate over the exact metaphorical meaning of *kephalē* in Pauline literature. Because it is a method, not a position, it could be employed by either a complementarian or an egalitarian. Both Thiselton and Johnson arrive at an egalitarian understanding of 1 Corinthians 11:2–16. In this chapter, I utilize their method while arriving at a complementarian understanding of the passage. The method proposed here, while benefitting from the care-

---

(2009): 35–57. While I do not agree with Johnson's conclusions, his review of the relevant contributions provides a very helpful introduction to the extensive literature in this debate. See also the survey of the debate given by Anthony Thiselton (*The First Epistle to the Corinthians*, 812–22).

[14] Stephen Bedale, "The Meaning of *kephalē* in the Pauline Epistles," *JTS*, n.s., 5 (1954): 211–16.

[15] See Leon Morris, *1 Corinthians*, 2nd ed., ed. Canon Leon Morris, Tyndale New Testament Commentary (Grand Rapids: Eerdmans, 1985); C. K. Barrett, *The First Epistle to the Corinthians*, Black's New Testament Commentary (Peabody, MA: Hendrickson, 1968); and Jerome Murphy-O'Connor, *1 Corinthians*, vol. 10 of *New Testament Message: A Biblical-Theological Commentary*, ed. Wilfrid Harrington, OP, and Donald Senior, CP (Wilmington, DE: Michael Glazier, 1979).

[16] Wayne Grudem, "Does Κεφαλή ("Head") Mean 'Source' or 'Authority Over' in Greek Literature?: A Survey of 2,336 Examples," *TrinJ* 6 (1985): 38–59. After a number of scholarly critiques of the article appeared, Grudem wrote a follow-up: "The Meaning of Κεφαλή ('Head'): A Response to Recent Studies," *TrinJ*, n.s., 11 (1990): 3–72. More critical assessments emerged over the course of the next decade, prompting still a third article by Grudem: "The Meaning of Κεφαλή ('Head'): An Evaluation of New Evidence, Real and Alleged," *JETS* 44 (2001): 25–65.

[17] Johnson, "A Review," 41.

[18] Thiselton, *The First Epistle to the Corinthians*, 820–22.

[19] Johnson, "A Review," 51.

ful lexical research of others, recognizes that lexicography and word counting alone cannot determine the metaphorical meaning of *kephalē* in any specific instance.

Drawing on the work of Gregory Dawes,[20] Thiselton argues that *kephalē* is a living metaphor, rather than a dead metaphor. Thus, any meaning that derives metaphorically from the literal meaning of "head" as the uppermost part of the body should be considered a possible meaning of the metaphorical use of the word in Pauline literature. In other words, in 1 Corinthians 11:3–5, it is unlikely that the semantic parameters for the use of *kephalē* as a metaphor were lexically fixed in Paul's day. Rather, the apostle is likely drawing on the literal meaning of "head" and extending it metaphorically to the relationships that exist with respect to Christ/man, man/woman, and God/Christ. This does not suggest that there were no common metaphorical uses of the word in Paul's day; only that it is likely that Paul did not feel bound to pick between options. In determining the meaning of *kephalē*, Thiselton asks, "In what sense would Paul and his readers use and understand this metaphor which not only elsewhere but specifically in 1 Cor 11:2–16 and in Eph 5:21–33 rests upon the head-body distinction of physiology?"[21] Approaching the question in this way places a high premium on the immediate context of a given use of *kephalē* and on Paul's usage of the word in other contexts.

"Source" and "Authority" as Complementary Meanings

Given this approach to the question, it is not difficult to see how both "authority over" and "source" might be plausible metaphorical senses of *kephalē* in the same context. As a living metaphor, it may have meanings that complement rather than exclude one another. If, taken literally, *kephalē* means "the most prominent part of the body," then the application of *kephalē* as a metaphor to the most prominent, or first, part of a river can yield the meaning "origin" or "source."[22] It is plausible that Paul had a similar use in mind in 1 Corinthians 11:3 because,

---

[20] Gregory W. Dawes, *The Body in Question: Metaphor and Meaning in the Interpretation of Ephesians 5:21–33*, Biblical Interpretation (Leiden: Brill, 1998).
[21] Thiselton, *The First Epistle to the Corinthians*, 816.
[22] Barrett cites Herodotus to this effect and then concludes that the reference to the origin of woman from man in v. 8 strongly suggests that Paul had this idea in mind (Barrett, *The First Epistle to the Corinthians*, 248).

72 Kyle Claunch

with reference to Adam and Eve, it is true that "man is the *source* of woman," as Paul makes explicit in verse 8. And with reference to God the Father and Christ, it is true that "God is the *source* of Christ," in that Christ is sent forth *from* the Father into the world, even if Paul did not have in mind the concept of eternal generation in this passage.

The most difficult statement to reconcile with the meaning "source" is the first one in verse 3. In what sense is it true that "Christ is the *source* of every man"? While this usage is not as patently obvious, it is nevertheless plausible. Fee points out two viable options: "(1) In terms of creation, Christ is the source of every man's life (cf. Col 1:16); (2) in terms of the new creation, Christ is the source of every Christian man."[23] Fee argues convincingly for the second option in that the "new creation" designation in 2 Corinthians 5:17 is given to those who are "in Christ," and in the immediate context, 1 Corinthians 11:4, Paul refers specifically not to men in general, "but to believing men in the Christian assembly."[24] However, contra Fee, while "source" may have been one of the metaphorical senses intended by Paul, the paucity of lexical evidence, the context of the passage, and Paul's use of *kephalē* as a metaphor elsewhere make it clear that "source" is not the only metaphorical sense intended by the apostle.[25]

As the "battle of the lexicons" has demonstrated, the sense of "authority over" is a well-attested meaning for *kephalē* when used metaphorically, far more common in ancient Greek literature than the meaning of "source." This fact alone ought to demonstrate the folly of defining *kephalē* in this passage exclusively as "source." Additionally, given the Pauline usage of *kephalē* elsewhere, coupled with the Pauline theology of gender roles in both the home and the church, the sense of "authority over" as an intended meaning of *kephalē* in 1 Corinthians 11:2–16 must be maintained. Ephesians 5:22–33 is another passage in which Paul uses *kephalē* in the context of gender relations. Here, the

---
[23] Fee, *The First Epistle to the Corinthians*, 504.
[24] Ibid. Barrett, on the other hand, prefers the first option: "As the existence of Christ is given in the existence of God, and as the existence of woman is given in the existence of man, so the existence of man is given in the existence of Christ, who is the ground of humanity" (Barrett, *The First Epistle to the Corinthians*, 249).
[25] Thiselton doubts that Paul intended "source" in this instance at all, although he admits the possibility. While this conclusion is probably too strong, he is surely correct that "source" would be an unfounded "translation" of *kephalē* in 1 Corinthians 11:3 because it would eliminate the possibility of other connotations, which Paul almost certainly intended (Thiselton, *The First Epistle to the Corinthians*, 826).

sense of "authority over" is obvious from the context. In 5:23, Paul says, "For the husband is the head [*kephalē*] of the wife, as Christ also is the head [*kephalē*] of the church." Schreiner rightly points out, "Further support for *head* meaning 'authority' is found in 5:22 and 5:24, for there Paul calls on women *to submit* to their husbands, which accords nicely with the notion that *head* denotes authority."[26] If Paul uses *kephalē* in Ephesians 5:23 to indicate the God-ordained role of men as the loving authority figures over their wives in the home, it is difficult to conceive of him using the same word to refer to the relationship of the man to the woman in 1 Corinthians 11:3 without intending to connote authority in that place as well.

Someone might demur that it is quite reasonable to suppose a difference in meaning because in Ephesians 5:23, Paul is addressing the marriage relationship specifically, while in 1 Corinthians 11:2–16, he is addressing corporate worship. Nevertheless, Paul's theology concerning the authority of men over women is not confined to the marriage relationship but applies to the church as well. This is evident most clearly in 1 Timothy 2:11–13: "A woman must quietly receive instruction with entire submissiveness. But I do not allow a woman to teach or exercise authority over a man, but to remain quiet. For it was Adam who was created first, and then Eve."[27] In this text, Paul commands the same disposition for women in the church that Ephesians 5:22–24 commands for women in the home—submissiveness. Of course, the disposition of submissiveness for women in the church entails a role of authority for men. In the relationship between a husband and wife particularly (Eph. 5:22–33) and in the relationship between men and women in the church generally (1 Tim. 2:11–13), Paul envisions a God-ordained structure of authority and submission. It is, therefore, very difficult to imagine Paul using *kephalē* to describe the man-woman relationship in corporate worship in 1 Corinthians 11:2–16 without intending his readers to understand the notion of the authority of men over women in that context.

---

[26] Schreiner, "Head Coverings," 127.
[27] While many scholars reject the genuine Pauline authorship of 1 Timothy, the text is relevant in this debate for the following reasons. (1) A commitment to biblical inerrancy eliminates the possibility of rejecting the Pauline authorship of 1 Timothy. Thus, no inerrantist who is true to his convictions should be daunted by critical claims concerning authorship. (2) There are convincing arguments put forth by very capable and erudite scholars arguing cogently in defense of the Pauline authorship of 1 Timothy (see Ralph Earle, *1 Timothy*, in vol. 11 of *The Expositor's Bible Commentary*, ed. Frank E. Gaebelein [Grand Rapids: Zondervan, 1981], 341–43).

At this point, one may wonder about the textual warrant for suggesting that Paul may have intended *both* "source" and "authority over" as metaphorical meanings of *kephalē* in 1 Corinthians 11:3ff. However, once again, the immediate context of the passage, coupled with Paul's theology of gender relations, helps to establish the legitimacy of both "source" and "authority over" as intended meanings. It has already been shown that the idea of "source" with respect to man and woman is in the apostle's mind in this discussion, as is made clear by verse 8. Thus, if *kephalē* means "authority over" in this passage, as I have argued, then at the very least, it is clear that the authority of the man over the woman has a parallel in that the man is the "source" of the woman.

Furthermore, consider again 1 Timothy 2:11–13. While the word *kephalē* is not used there, the concept of the authority of men over women is clearly in view. Significantly, in this passage, Paul grounds the ecclesial structure of male authority and female submission in the order in which God created the man and the woman (v. 13). Thus once again, for Paul, the *authority* of man over woman has a parallel in the *origin* of woman from man.

Finally, consider Ephesians 5:22–33 in this light. Schreiner, arguing that "authority over" is to be preferred instead of "source" as the meaning for *kephalē*, has suggested that "source" would make little sense in Ephesians 5:22–33.[28] However, he may have overstated the case. It is true that an individual husband is not the source of his wife. However, it is also true that all marriages are patterned after the first marriage relationship between Adam and Eve. Paul himself makes this clear by his quotation of Genesis 2:24 in Ephesians 5:31. Thus, Paul intends all marriages to reflect the pattern of the first marriage. It does, therefore, seem reasonable to conclude that the authority structure of the marriage relationship in Ephesians 5:22–31 is related to the fact that the man is the source of the woman. In the case of 1 Corinthians 11:3, therefore, it is highly likely that Paul intends his readers to understand both "source" and "authority" as related meanings of the word *kephalē*.[29]

---

[28] Schreiner, "Head Coverings," 127.
[29] Though he never discusses the metaphorical meaning of *kephalē*, Michael Reeves seems to understand the term as connoting "source" in a way that does not rule out a kind of personal primacy of the Father as the one loving the Son and thus eliciting the response of love from the Son. Reeves writes, "There is something about the relationship and difference between the man and the woman, Adam and Eve, that images the being of God—something we saw the apostle Paul pick up on in 1 Corinthians 11:3. Eve is a

In spite of all the exegetical difficulties and uncertainties of 1 Corinthians 11:2–16, the above arguments are sufficient to demonstrate the overall strength of the complementarian interpretation of the passage. For if "head" connotes "authority over," then the head covering worn by women is a symbol of the authority that the woman is under in corporate worship when praying or prophesying (see vv. 4–5, 10) . The ground work is now in place for considering how the particular statement "God is the head of Christ" relates to the gender complementarity of 1 Corinthians 11:2–16.

The Trinitarian Ground of Gender Complementarity in 1 Corinthians 11:3

Verse 3 serves as the theological ground for the instructions given in 1 Corinthians 11:2–16. This is evident from the fact that Paul does not argue *for* the assertions in verse 3. Rather, he wants the Corinthians to "understand" the three "head" clauses in verse 3 so that he can argue *from* them as he instructs men and women concerning the proper external head gear for praying and prophesying in corporate worship.[30]

In order to understand how the three "head" clauses of verse 3 ground the instructions of 1 Corinthians 11:2–16, one needs to consider how the three clauses are related to one another. Calvin argued that Paul's purpose in verse 3 is to remind the Corinthians of "four gradations"[31] of headship. Barrett agrees, suggesting that in verse 3 "a chain of originating and subordinating relationships is set up: God, Christ, man, woman."[32] Having established this fourfold chain of gradations, Barrett argues that Paul then devotes the remainder of the passage to the "practical consequences" of the gradation between men and women.[33] However, while a "chain" of "four gradations" may be

---

person quite distinct from Adam, and yet she has all her life and being from Adam. She comes from his side, is bone of his bones and flesh of his flesh, and is one with him in the flesh (Gen 2:21–24)" (Reeves, *Delighting in the Trinity*, 37; cf. 28–29).

[30] Though proposing an egalitarian understanding of the passage, Fee makes a similar observation with regard to the assertions in verse 3: "What he wants them to know takes the form of a *theologoumenon* (theological statement) that will serve as the point of reference for the response that immediately follows" (Fee, *The First Epistle to the Corinthians*, 501).

[31] Calvin understands the clauses as representing "four gradations," with God in the first place, Christ in the second place, the man in the third, and the woman in the fourth (John Calvin, *First Epistle to the Corinthians*, vol. 20 in *Calvin's Commentaries*, ed. John Pringle [Grand Rapids: Baker, 2003], 353).

[32] Barrett, *The First Epistle to the Corinthians*, 249.

[33] Ibid.

implied by the three "head" clauses, if Paul's primary objective is to establish this, he has written the clauses themselves in a peculiar order.[34]

A better approach is to understand the second "head" clause, "Man is the head of a woman," as the central statement, from which Paul argues for the propriety of head coverings for women and uncovered heads for men in corporate worship. What then of the first and third "head" clauses? Each of these serves a double purpose: (1) to *ground* the second clause in theological principles that transcend gender relations and (2) to *guard* against potential misunderstandings arising from the second clause. The first clause, "Christ is the head of every man," reminds readers that man's headship over woman is a typological reflection of the headship that Christ exercises over men. This is reminiscent of Paul's treatment of the husband's headship over the wife in Ephesians 5:23. In that passage, Paul makes the typological connection explicit: "The husband is the head of the wife, as Christ also is the head of the church." It is, therefore, reasonable that Paul would have a similar idea in mind in 1 Corinthians 11:3.

There is one significant difference, however. In Ephesians 5:23, the role of the husband over his wife is parallel to that of Christ over the church, which is composed of male *and* female. In 1 Corinthians 11:3, Paul says, "Christ is the head of every *man*." The Greek word for "man" is not the generic *anthrōpos* (ἄνθρωπος), which can be understood in reference to the entire human race, but *anēr*, which specifically refers to the male gender. Perhaps Paul mentions Christ's headship over men in particular not to exclude women, but rather to emphasize something specific about men in this context. Even though God has appointed man as the head of woman, man does not exercise his authority in an unaccountable and autonomous fashion. Rather, the duty of men to exercise authority over women in corporate worship is carried out in obedience to Christ. Thus, the exercise of male authority is itself an act of submission, not of men to women, but of men to Christ.

In the Corinthian context, this is properly expressed by head cover-

---

[34] If Calvin is correct, one would expect the statement "God is the head of Christ" to come first, rather than third. Also, the statement "Christ is the head of every man" should be second, rather than first. Finally, the statement "Man is the head of woman" ought to be third, rather than second. Calvin's paraphrase of the three clauses indicates his recognition that his case is better maintained if the order of the clauses is changed: "Christ is subject to God as his head, so is the man subject to Christ, and the woman to the man" (Calvin, *First Epistle to the Corinthians*, 353).

ings for women and uncovered heads for men while praying and prophesying in corporate worship. Thus, the first "head" clause, "Christ is the head of every man," serves as both a ground and a guard to the second and central "head" clause. It is a ground in that male headship is designed by God as a reflection of Christ's headship over men (as in Eph. 5:23). It is a guard against the potential misunderstanding that men are inherently autonomous while women are inherently submissive. Rather, both men and women submit. Men submit to Christ by exercising leadership and authority over women. Women submit to Christ by submitting to the headship of men.

The third "head" clause, "God is the head of Christ," also serves as both a ground and a guard for the second and central "head" clause, "Man is the head of woman." Paul reminds the Corinthians that "God is the head of Christ" in order to show that the headship of the man over the woman is a typological reflection of the headship that God the Father exercises over Christ.[35] The third clause is also a guard against a potential misunderstanding that might arise from the second clause. Just as the first clause guards against a sense of superiority or inherent autonomy on the part of the man because of his role as "head," so the third clause can guard against a sense of inferiority or inherent indignity on the part of the woman because of her role of submission. By submitting to the headship of men in corporate worship, women are reflecting the character, attitude, disposition, and role of Christ. The submission of Christ to the Father's authority during his earthly mission is a testimony to his dignity, not a sign of indignity. The same is true for women who joyfully submit to the authority that God has graciously granted to men in the church.[36] Thus, the statement "God is the head of Christ" serves as both a ground and a guard for the central statement of 1 Corinthians 11:3, "Man is the head of a woman."

This exegetical analysis has demonstrated that the complementar-

---

[35] In fact, in a different way, the third "head" clause also grounds the first clause. For the headship of Christ over every man is the consequence of his faithful completion of the mission for which God the Father sent him into the world. Upon completion of Christ's task as the redeeming Mediator, God "highly exalted him and bestowed upon him the name above every name" (Phil. 2:9).

[36] Consider Eph. 5:22–33 again in this light. In that text, the typological parallel is such that men represent Christ, and women represent the church in the marriage relationship. However, in 1 Cor. 11:3, Paul reminds men and women that, while male headship is a reflection of Christ's headship, female submission is a reflection of Christ's submission. Thus, women also typologically reflect the role and office of the Savior as they submit joyfully to the authority of men in corporate worship.

ian understanding of 1 Corinthians 11:2–16 is the correct one. It has also shown that the three "head" clauses of verse 3 serve to ground the complementarian instruction given in the entire passage (1 Cor. 11:2–16). More to the point of this essay, this analysis has shown that the statement "Man is the head of a woman" is theologically grounded in the headship of Christ over every man and the headship of God the Father over Christ. Therefore, because the statement "God is the head of Christ" serves as a ground for the statement "Man is the head of a woman," it can be safely concluded that verse 3 does indeed ground gender complementarity in Trinitarian relations. What remains to be seen is whether the headship of God the Father over Christ is a strictly economic Trinitarian structural arrangement pertaining only to Christ's incarnation or whether it refers to the immanent Trinity, that is, the eternal relationship between God the Father and God the Son. In other words, does 1 Corinthians 11:3 ground gender complementarity in the *immanent* Trinity?

The Trinity in 1 Corinthians 11:3— Economic or Immanent?

Drawing a distinction between the immanent Trinity and the economic Trinity can be misleading. Of course, there are not two Trinities, but one triune God. Thus the distinction is only a heuristic one.[37] The term "immanent Trinity" refers to God as he is in himself as the one eternally triune God. The one triune God is infinite and eternally immutable, utterly unique, a being for whom there is no parallel or counterpart—in a word, holy. As such, the immanent Trinity is incomprehensible, meaning that the essence and existence of the triune God infinitely transcend the limitations of creaturely understanding. Nevertheless, the consistent affirmation of Christians has always been that the infinite, immutable, holy, and incomprehensible triune God has revealed himself to human beings through creation and redemption. This revelation is indisputably accurate and true because God "cannot lie" (Titus 1:2), but it is neces-

---

[37] The terms "immanent" and "economic" are of relatively recent vintage. However, they roughly correspond to the earlier medieval and Reformed orthodox distinction between the Trinity *ad intra*, referring to God in himself (immanent Trinity) and the Trinity *ad extra*, referring to God in his revelation of himself in the economies of creation and redemption (economic Trinity). Even prior to the use of the terminology of *ad intra* versus *ad extra*, theologians spoke in terms of God *en se* (in himself) and God *pro nobis* (for us).

sarily given in accommodated fashion. That is, revelation must occur at the level of the finite creation. So, while true, the revelation of the triune God given in the economies of creation and redemption is by no means exhaustive. This historical revelation of the triune God is referred to by the term "economic Trinity."

With respect to 1 Corinthians 11:3 and the statement "God is the head of Christ," the pertinent question is, Does the headship of God over Christ refer only to Christ in his incarnate state, or does it also refer to the eternal relationship between the Father and the Son? Even those who would quibble with the complementarian reading of 1 Corinthians 11:3 presented here acknowledge that Christ submitted to the Father for the purpose of his incarnate mission as the Redeemer. In the last two decades, however, a considerable body of literature has developed debating whether it is legitimate to speak of the Son as being *eternally* submissive to the Father functionally, not ontologically. The debate has, at times, been vehement, and the accusation of heresy from both sides has not been uncommon. Obviously, both sides of the debate believe the answer to this question, with respect to 1 Corinthians 11:3, is of great importance.

1 Corinthians 11:3 Refers to the Incarnate State Directly

In 1 Corinthians 11:3, the first and second "head" clauses are best understood in light of the completed work of Christ as the incarnate Savior and the "one mediator between God and men" (1 Tim. 2:5). The first, "Christ is the head of every man," is best understood in reference to Christ's current exalted lordship over the church, for two reasons. First, in every other Pauline instance in which Christ is referred to as the Head of something, the church is the object (cf. Eph. 1:22; 5:23; Col. 1:18). Second, as Fee has observed, the phrase "Christ is the head of every man" is picked up again in 1 Corinthians 11:4 where the men being spoken to are addressed in the context of the corporate worship of the church. Thus, the headship of Christ over every man being spoken of here is his office of exalted Head of the church, which is the direct result of the completion of his mission as the incarnate Mediator.

The second clause, "man is the head of a woman," is also best understood as referring to the current situation in which Christ is reigning as exalted Head of the church. Just as in Ephesians 5:22–33 the man's headship over his wife is patterned after the headship of Christ over the church, so in 1 Corinthians 11:3 the man's headship over woman in the church is patterned after (and guarded by) Christ's headship over every man in the church. With respect to the first and second "head" clauses, therefore, Paul's statements are made with reference to the economy of redemption and the specific office of the Son as the exalted incarnate Mediator and Messiah—in a word, Christ.

It follows, therefore, that the third "head" clause should also be understood with respect to the economy of redemption. While Paul does make some statements that are intended to reflect preincarnational immanent Trinitarian realities, the vast majority of his discourse concerning the Son pertains to his mission as the incarnate Christ and author of our salvation. Thus, it seems likely that by the statement "God is the head of Christ," Paul has in mind that God the Father sent the Son into the world (cf. Gal. 4:4) and that the Son came forth not to do his own will, but the will of the one who sent him (cf. John 6:38). In other words, the headship of God the Father over Christ in 1 Corinthians 11:3 refers directly to the relationship between the incarnate Son of God and God the Father.[38]

So, with respect to the thesis of this essay, it does seem that Paul has in mind economic Trinitarian relations when he says, "God is the head of Christ." However, this conclusion does not tip the scales in favor of an egalitarian reading of this passage or of the rest of the New Testament. Even if economic Trinitarian categories are in view, it has already been demonstrated that the metaphorical meaning of *kephalē* includes the sense of "authority over," and that Paul grounds the headship of man over woman in the (economic) headship of God over Christ. The analogy between man/woman and God/Christ is conceived covenantally, not ontologically. In order to bring about the promise of the new covenant, Christ emptied himself, becoming incarnate and joyfully obedient to

---

[38] While the statement does refer to Christ *as incarnate*, it does not necessarily follow that the headship of God over Christ ends with the exaltation of Christ. Rather the headship of the Father and submission of the Son are permanent features of the incarnation, which do not end with the exaltation. This is evident for several reasons. First, Paul makes the statement in 1 Cor. 11:3 as a present reality that grounds gender relations. So even in his present exalted session at the right hand of the Father, Paul says that God is (presently) the head of Christ. Second, later in this same epistle, Paul points out that even in the *eschaton*, the Son will be subjected to the Father, presumably forever (1 Cor. 15:28). See Schreiner, "Head Coverings," 128.

the point of death (see Phil. 2:5–8). In like manner, women, in order to proclaim the gospel of the new covenant by their roles in the church and the home, joyfully submit to their husbands in marriage and to ordained men in church worship. Thus, a complementarian understanding of 1 Corinthians 11:2–16 stands even if the third "head" clause of verse 3 does not refer *directly* to immanent Trinitarian relations. But more needs to be said. If this verse does directly ground gender complementarity in the economic Trinity, does it preclude the possibility that immanent Trinitarian relations are implied in the passage by good and necessary inference? That is, is it possible that 1 Corinthians 11:3 grounds gender complementarity in the immanent Trinity *indirectly*?

1 Corinthians 11:3 Refers to Eternal Relations Indirectly
Is Headship Rooted in the Nature of God?

It has been common for gender complementarians to appeal to 1 Corinthians 11:3 to show that the functional role distinction between men and women found in the New Testament is grounded in the eternal triune being of God. The importance of this issue in the evangelical gender debate cannot be overstated. Many egalitarians argue that Paul's instructions that women should submit to the authority of men parallel his instructions that slaves should submit to their masters.[39] In order not to upset the social status quo, Paul told slaves to submit to their masters, even though he never enjoined people to own slaves and slavery is antithetical to the *imago dei* and the gospel of Christ. However, if male headship, as conceived by complementarians, is rooted in the very triune being of God, then it cannot be dismissed by a simple appeal to Paul's desire to maintain social customs.

Complementarian theologian Bruce Ware makes the case clearly:

> In 1 Corinthians 11:3 Paul writes, "But I want you to understand that the head of every man is Christ, the head of a wife is her husband, and *the head of Christ is God.*" Without question, the Son stands under the authority, or, if you will, the headship of the Father. In this chapter (1 Corinthians 11) where Paul is about to deal with

---
[39] See Kevin Giles, *The Trinity and Subordinationism: The Doctrine of God and the Contemporary Gender Debate* (Downers Grove, IL: InterVarsity, 2002).

the importance of women acknowledging the headship of men in the community of faith by wearing head coverings, he prefaces his remarks by describing authority and submission in human relations as *a reflection of the authority and submission that exist in the eternal Godhead.*[40]

On the other hand, gender egalitarians have claimed that the idea of an eternal hierarchy of authority in the Godhead is foreign to Scripture and the orthodox tradition. Kevin Giles devotes two full-length books to this contention.[41] In the second of these, Giles writes, "I am more convinced than ever that the *eternal* subordination of the Son is very dangerous teaching standing in direct opposition to how the best of theologians past and present and the creeds and Reformation confessions have understood what the Bible says on the Trinity." He goes on to suggest that both sides cannot be right: "Either the Bible and the best of theologians across the centuries and the creeds and Reformation confessions exclude the idea that the Son of God is *eternally* subordinated to the Father, or they do not."[42]

It is the burden of this essay to demonstrate, contra Giles, that gender complementarity is grounded in the very being of the triune God. However, while Ware seems to see the third "head" clause of 1 Corinthians 11:3 as a direct reference to the immanent Trinity, it is preferable to see the clause as a direct reference to the economic reality of Christ's incarnation and then to articulate carefully the relationship between the economic and immanent Trinity. It can then be shown that the statement "God is the head of Christ" does ground gender complementarity in the immanent Trinity, but it does so *indirectly*, by way of good and necessary inference.

Economic versus Immanent Trinity in Orthodox Theology

The challenging and often theologically dense polemics of the second, third, and early fourth centuries eventually gave rise to a consensus Trini-

---

[40] Ware, *Father, Son, and Holy Spirit*, 72. First italics is original; second italics is emphasis added.
[41] *The Trinity and Subordinationism* and *Jesus and the Father: Modern Evangelicals Reinvent the Doctrine of the Trinity* (Grand Rapids: Zondervan, 2006). He gives considerable space to this issue in a third book on the Trinity as well: *The Eternal Generation of the Son: Maintaining Orthodoxy in Trinitarian Theology* (Downers Grove, IL: InterVarsity, 2012).
[42] Giles, *Jesus and the Father*, 12.

tarian grammar. Rallying around the Creed of Nicaea, orthodox theologians expressed the mystery of the Trinity in terms of one nature/essence and three persons/hypostases. This pro-Nicene Trinitarian grammar set the boundaries for orthodox Trinitarian theology for centuries to come.[43] For many, Augustine of Hippo set the high-water mark of pro-Nicene Trinitarian theology in his famous *De Trinitate*.[44] While scholars on both sides appeal to Augustine, Kevin Giles and Keith Johnson have made the most sustained appeals to his theology with respect to the egalitarian-versus-complementarian debate.[45] Giles argues that Augustine's Trinitarian theology does not allow for any hint of eternal subordination between the Father and the Son. He points to Augustine's first hermeneutical rule for interpreting christological and Trinitarian texts in the New Testament:

> His first rule of interpretation is that all texts that speak of the Son's divinity, majesty, and authority speak of him "in the form of God," and all texts that speak of his dependence on and obedience to the Father, or of his frailty, speak of him "in the form of a servant," in his temporal state as the incarnate Son.[46]

This Augustinian distinction[47] is immensely helpful, even necessary, as one seeks to explain how Jesus Christ can be spoken of in both

---

[43] For thorough scholarly treatments of the development and features of the pro-Nicene Trinitarian theology of the mid-to-late fourth century, see Lewis Ayres, *Nicaea and Its Legacy: An Approach to Fourth-Century Trinitarian Theology* (New York: Oxford University Press, 2004); Ayres, *Augustine and the Trinity* (New York: Cambridge University Press, 2010). Also see Michele René Barnes, "One Nature, One Power: Consensus Doctrine in Pro-Nicene Polemic," in *Theologica et Philosophica, Critica et Philologica, Historica*, in *Studia Patristica* 29, ed. Elizabeth A. Livingstone (Louvain: Peeters, 1997), 5–23.

[44] For nearly a century, Augustine's Trinitarian theology was understood according to a paradigm that pitted his supposedly static, implicitly modalistic thinking against the more relational Trinitarian models of Eastern theologians, such as Gregory of Nyssa and Basil of Caesarea. However, Ayres and Barnes, among others, have successfully proved the fallacy of such a paradigm. They have shown decisively that Augustine's theology belongs in the larger category of pro-Nicene theology, which transcends the East-versus-West divide. For an accessible but detailed treatment of Augustine along these lines, see Michele René Barnes, "Rereading Augustine's Theology of the Trinity," in *The Trinity: An Interdisciplinary Symposium on the Trinity*, ed. Stephen T. Davis; Daniel Kendall, SJ; Gerald O'Collins, SJ (Oxford: Oxford University Press, 1999), 145–76.

[45] See Giles, *Jesus and the Father*, 190–94, and Johnson, "Trinitarian Agency." Johnson's essay follows the same method as does his recent book *Rethinking the Trinity and Religious Pluralism* (Downers Grove, IL: InterVarsity, 2011). In the book, Johnson brings Augustine's Trinitarian theology to bear on religious pluralism. In this essay, he brings the mighty voice of Augustine to bear on the question of the Son's submission to the Father. While I argue in this essay that Johnson has not pursued the implications of Augustine's understanding of Trinitarian *taxis ad intra* far enough, I have benefited tremendously from his learned and well-written treatment of Augustine's theology of the Trinity and its application to current issues in systematic theology.

[46] Giles, *Jesus and the Father*, 190.

[47] Augustine is not the first great theologian to make the distinction. It was a staple of the anti-Arian polemics of the fourth century and can be found in the writings of Athanasius and the Cappadocians, among others. Augustine made perhaps the greatest use of the "rule" in his interpretation of Scripture, and to my knowledge, he is the first to use the terminology from Phil. 2:5–9, "form of a servant" and "form of God."

divine and non-divine terms in Scripture. If Augustine is representative of pro-Nicene orthodoxy on this score, then it seems to follow that the statement "God is the head of Christ" is made with reference to the incarnation only—end of discussion. However, this "first rule of interpretation" must be understood in light of the rest of Augustine's hermeneutical convictions concerning the interpretation of Trinitarian and christological texts in the New Testament. While a full-fledged survey of Augustine's Trinitarian hermeneutic is well beyond the scope of this essay, one important feature is worth considering and appropriating here.[48] For Augustine, the eternal intratrinitarian relations (immanent Trinity) are *revealed* by the economic missions of the Son and the Spirit:

> Just as the Father, then, begot and the Son was begotten, so the Father sent and the Son was sent. But just as the begetter and the begotten are one, so are the sender and the sent, because the Father and the Son are one; so too the Holy Spirit is one with them, because these three are one (1 John 5:7). And just as being born means for the Son his being from the Father, so *his being sent means his being known to be from him*. And just as for the Holy Spirit his being the gift of God means his proceeding from the Father, so *his being sent means his being known to proceed from him*.[49]

Thus, for Augustine there is an inverse relationship between epistemology and ontology in the revelation of the triune God. The immanent Trinity is the ontological ground for the outworking of God's purposes in the economy of redemption. God acts as he does in history in a manner that is consistent with who he is eternally. In terms of epistemology, however, the relationship is inverted. The economic Trinity is the epistemological ground of the immanent Trinity. That is, it is through the economic Trinity that people come to know anything at all about the immanent Trinity. This is what Augustine means when he says that the Son's "being sent means his being known to be from the Father." When Augustine says that the Son is "from" the Father,

---

[48] For a fuller discussion of Augustine's theology of Trinitarian agency, see my essay, "What God Hath Done Together: Defending the Historic Doctrine of the Inseparable Operations of the Trinity," *JETS* 56 (2013): 781–800.

[49] Augustine, *The Trinity (De Trinitate)*, ed. and trans. Edmund Hill, series 1, vol. 5 of *The Works of St. Augustine: A Translation for the 21st Century*, ed. John E. Rotelle (Hyde Park, NY: New City, 1991), 4.5.29, 181–82; hereafter cited in the following form: *The Trinity*, 4.5.29 (181–82). Augustine cites 1 John 5:7 often in *De Trinitate*. Scholars almost unanimously agree that the text is an interpolation into the epistle.

he is referring to the eternal generation of the Son[50] and thus to the immanent Trinity. That the Son is "from" the Father (immanent Trinity) is the reason he is "sent" into the world to be incarnate (economic Trinity). The fact that he is "sent" makes known the fact that he is eternally "from" the Father. Thus, for Augustine, the economic Trinity *reveals* the immanent Trinity. So, even if one must conclude that some feature of the work of the Son pertains directly to the economy of salvation, Christ "in the form of a servant," it must likewise be maintained that this economic reality reveals something fixed and irreversible about the very eternal triune being of God. If this is not the case, then the epistemological void between the economic and immanent Trinity is such that one is left to wonder if there is any correspondence at all.

At this point, a very important caveat must be introduced. To say that the economic Trinity reveals the immanent Trinity is not the same thing as saying that there is strict identification between the economic and immanent Trinity. The best Christian theologians from the Patristic, medieval, Reformation, and post-Reformation eras have always maintained that God's revelation of himself is perfectly true and accurate. However, in order to preserve what Scripture teaches about the utter uniqueness, infinity, and eternity of God, these same theologians have recognized that divine revelation must be accommodated. Finite minds (the objects of revelation) cannot comprehend fully that which is infinite (God, the subject of revelation). For this reason, theologians have often explained that God's revelation and his eternal identity are neither *equivocal* (totally different things) nor *univocal* (totally the same thing) but *analogical* (corresponding to one another in an accommodated way).

For example, if the relationship between God's being and his revelation is *equivocal*, then the Father's sending the Son into the world would not reveal anything about the eternal being of God apart from his creation. It would only reveal that in the economy of salvation,

---

[50] Augustine differentiates between the Trinitarian persons in the immanent Trinity by way of eternal relations of origin. The Son is eternally generated from the Father. The Spirit proceeds eternally from the Father and the Son. Augustine summarizes the eternal relations as follows: "The Father has begotten the Son, and therefore he who is the Son is not the Father; and the Holy Spirit is neither the Father nor the Son, but only the Spirit of the Father and of the Son, himself coequal to the Father and the Son, and belonging to the threefold unity" (*The Trinity*, 1.2.7 [70–71]).

God the Father sent the Son. Indeed, if the relationship is equivocal, it could not even be maintained that Father and Son are eternal categories pertaining to the being of God at all (modalism).

On the other hand, if the relationship between God's being and God's revelation is *univocal*, then a number of consequences follow upon the fact that the Father sends the Son into the world. First, the eternal independence and freedom of God is compromised because inherent to the very being of God is the Father's sending of the Son into the world. Thus, apart from creation and redemption, God would not be God. Furthermore, the very idea that the eternally preexistent Son became incarnate is incoherent because if God's being and God's revelation are univocal, then being sent into the world is eternally inherent to the very identity of the Son of God. Indeed, if revelation is understood in this univocal way, all talk about the immanent and economic Trinity becomes nonsense. The distinction is dissolved entirely.

However, if the relationship between God's being and God's revelation is *analogical*, then the Father's sending the Son into the world reveals something about the eternal relationship of the Father and Son, but the Father would still be the Father and the Son would still be the Son, whether the Son was ever sent into the world or not. For Augustine, the Son's being sent into the world "makes known" (reveals) the eternal truth that the Son is eternally generated from the Father. The sending is economic, and the generation is immanent. The two are not collapsed or identified, but the historical occurrence of the one reveals the eternal reality of the other.

Consider all of this in light of the pertinent clause in 1 Corinthians 11:3, "God is the head of Christ." Egalitarians have argued that the statement is made directly about Christ in the incarnate state submitting his human will to the will of God the Father. Nevertheless, two facts reveal something about the fixed and irreversible being of the triune God from all eternity: it was the Son and not the Father who was sent and became the submissive one; furthermore, it was the Father, not the Son, who sent the Son to become the submissive one. In some mysterious way, God the Son was suited to become the incarnate and submissive one, and God the Father was not so suited. While Paul almost certainly did not have in mind the precise nature of the relationship between the immanent and economic Trinity, if the later Trinitarian grammar of the pro-Nicene tradition in general and Augustine in particular is accurately construed, then any biblical statement about economic Trinitarian relationships bears revelatory correspondence to the immanent triune being of God. The statement "God is the head of Christ," therefore, reveals something about the eternal relationship between the Father and the Son in the immanent Trinity.

Kevin Giles appeals to Augustine's first rule of interpretation to conclude that all language about the Son submitting to the will of the Father is made with reference to Christ "in the form of a servant." He concludes that any attempt to argue that there are submission and authority in the eternal being of God is to read the economic Trinity back into the immanent Trinity and to fail to take into account the unique situation of the incarnation.[51] However, Giles has not dealt adequately with Augustine's conviction that the economic Trinity makes known the immanent Trinity. Contra Giles, to maintain that the economic mission of the Son reveals fixed and eternal truths about the immanent triune being of God is consistent with the Trinitarian theology of Augustine and of the whole pro-Nicene tradition. Giles wishes to affirm some correspondence between the economic and immanent Trinity himself. However, just what is that correspondence, especially as it pertains to the Son's incarnation? This he has left unanswered.

Bruce Ware, on the other hand, assumes that the statement of Christ's submission to the Father in 1 Corinthians 11:3 is made in reference to the immanent Trinity directly. This essays offers a via media, however. With the help of later theological clarification we may conclude, by good and necessary inference, that the revelational correspondence between the immanent and economic Trinity is such that this verse does ground gender complementarity in the immanent Trinity, albeit *indirectly*. It is, therefore, legitimate to appeal to the very triune being of God, by such good and necessary inference from direct statements in Scripture, when explaining the nature of the submission of women to men in the church and in the home.

---
[51] Giles, *Jesus and the Father*, 242–74.

Eternal Authority and Submission in the Godhead?

The burden of this essay has been to answer the question, Does 1 Corinthians 11:3 ground gender complementarity in the immanent Trinity? The question has been answered in the affirmative with some important theological caveats given. What I have not addressed is whether the *terminology* of eternal authority and eternal submission is legitimate with respect to God the Father and God the Son. It has been established that the economic Trinity reveals the immanent Trinity, and that the revelation is to be understood as analogical in nature. But how is the analogical correspondence to be articulated? Can we say that incarnational subordination reveals the fact of immanent subordination?

Bruce Ware, Wayne Grudem, and others insist that the Son of God eternally submits to the inherent authority of the Father, so that the authority-submission structure is a major factor in establishing the eternal distinctions between the persons. For these theologians, the submission of the Son to the Father in the economic state of incarnation is a reflection of the submission of the Son to the Father in the eternal preincarnate state. One often overlooked feature of such a proposal is that this understanding of the eternal relationship between Father and Son seems to entail a commitment to three distinct wills in the immanent Trinity. In order for the Son to submit *willingly* to the *will* of the Father, the two must possess distinct wills. This way of understanding the immanent Trinity does run counter to the pro-Nicene tradition, as well as the medieval, Reformation, and post-Reformation Reformed traditions that grew from it. According to traditional Trinitarian theology, the will is predicated of the one undivided divine essence so that there is only one divine will in the immanent Trinity.

By arguing for eternal authority and submission in the Godhead, Ware, Grudem, and others are not abandoning all traditional Trinitarian categories. Rather, drawing on the distinction between the one divine essence and the three divine persons (a distinction that is basic to Trinitarian orthodoxy from its earliest mature expressions), they are making a conscious and informed choice to conceive of will as a property of person rather than essence. This model of a three-willed Trinity then provides the basis for the conviction that structures of authority and submission actually serve as one of the means of differentiating the divine persons.[52]

Some may wonder why such a fine distinction is of any great consequence. However, one's conception of the will(s) of God as Trinity has inevitable christological consequences. According to the standard of christological orthodoxy, the Definition of Chalcedon, Jesus Christ is one person with two natures. The early medieval debates about the will/wills of Christ centered on this very issue. If will is associated with person, then Christ cannot possess a human will, but only a divine will because he is one divine person. However, if he did not possess a human will, then there is something fundamental to being human that Christ did not assume. For this reason among others, monothelitism (the view that the incarnate Son has only one will) was rejected by the sixth ecumenical council of the church in AD 681 in favor of a dyothelite (two wills) model, which was deemed to be consistent with Chalcedon and necessary to maintaining that Christ was made "like his brethren in all things" (Heb. 2:17).

This brief discussion of the property of will with respect to the triune being of God raises at least one important question related to the thesis of this essay. By affirming real correspondence between the economic and immanent Trinity with respect to the issue of Christ's submission to the Father, am I committing myself to a three-will understanding of the Trinity? Or, can the thesis of this essay be maintained within the framework of pro-Nicene categories, especially the conviction that the locus of the divine mind and will (along with all the other divine attributes) is the one essence/nature of the triune God?

According to the pro-Nicene Trinitarian grammar that dominated Western reflection on the doctrine of the Trinity for centuries, the three persons of the Godhead are eternally differentiated from one another in terms of relationships of origin. The unbegotten Father eternally generates the Son, and the Father and the Son eternally spirate the Holy Spirit. The begetting and spirating occur within the being of God so that each of the differentiated Trinitarian persons fully possesses the eternal being of God. A feature of this pro-Nicene model that is clearly

---

[52] Wayne Grudem indicates that the eternal functional subordination in role is the only means by which Father, Son, and Spirit are distinguished eternally. See his *Systematic Theology*, 251.

articulated by Augustine is of great significance to this discussion. The eternal relationships of origin, which differentiate the three persons in the immanent being of God, entail a fixed and irreversible order in the one eternal and indivisible divine essence. The order (Latin: *taxis*) of the divine being is always the same: Father, Son, Holy Spirit. This eternal and irreversible *taxis*, for Augustine, manifests itself particularly in the economic missions of the Son and the Spirit, as was shown above. Keith Johnson recognizes this feature of Augustine's theology:

> Augustine's mature account of Trinitarian agency involves two elements. On the one hand, the working of the Father, Son, and Holy Spirit is inseparably the work of the three *ad extra*. On the other hand, in this single act, the divine persons work according to their relative properties *ad intra*. The Father acts with the other divine persons according to his mode of being "from no one" (unbegotten). The Son acts with the other divine persons according to his mode of being "from the Father" (generation). The Spirit acts with the other divine persons according to his mode of being "from the Father and the Son" (procession). Combining these two elements we might say that the divine persons act inseparably through the intra-trinitarian taxis: from the Father, through the Son, in the Holy Spirit.[53]

In applying Augustine's theology to the question of submission and authority in the immanent Trinity, Johnson says, correctly, "There is no evidence that Augustine believed that the hypostatic distinction between the Father and the Son is constituted by eternal 'authority' (on the part of the Father) or eternal 'submission' (on the part of the Son)." However, while Augustine would almost certainly chafe at the terminology of "authority" and "submission" in the immanent Trinity, his understanding of the immanent Trinitarian *taxis* provides a tool for thinking about how the authority and submission between Father and Son in the incarnate state might find analogical correspondence in the immanent Trinity. Johnson observes that "Augustine does not explore the speculative question of whether any analogy might exist between the Son's filial mode of being eternally from the Father and his obedience to the Father

---

[53] Johnson, "Trinitarian Agency," 16.

in the state of humiliation."[54] It is just this "speculative question" which will be explored in the remainder of this essay. It is my contention that such an analogy does exist and can be articulated in a way that affirms Augustine's pro-Nicene account of Trinitarian agency.

Given Augustine's insistence on the eternal Trinitarian *taxis* of the one divine essence, let us now consider what implications this *taxis* has in terms of the one divine will. According to the doctrine of divine simplicity, the essence of God is infinitely coterminous with each of the attributes/properties of that essence, so that God does not merely *manifest* his mind, will, love, holiness, and so on. Rather, God just is his mind, will, love, holiness, and so on. Therefore, a fixed and irreversible *taxis* of the one divine essence entails a fixed and irreversible *taxis* of the one divine will. So, if the one essence of the Godhead subsists eternally as Father, Son, and Holy Spirit, then the one divine will subsists eternally as Father, Son, and Holy Spirit as well.[55]

In the incarnate state, the Son submitted his created human will to the eternal divine will of the Father. However, what does the eternal Trinitarian *taxis* of the one divine will look like *prior to* the incarnation of the Son of God? To say that the Son submits eternally to the will of the Father is, I propose, too strong precisely because it implies two distinct wills in relation to one another. It is preferable to say that, in the immanent Trinity, *the one eternal will of God is so ordered that it finds analogical expression in a created relationship of authority and submission: the incarnate Son submits to the will of his Father.*

Consider the incarnation as a test case. By the one united will of the triune God, the Son becomes incarnate in order to accomplish redemption for the people of God. On this point, the one will of the Trinity is exercised by the Trinitarian persons, each one willing according to his place in the intratrinitarian order of subsistence. The Father exercises the will of God for the incarnation according to his place as *first* in the order of subsistence. So, the Father wills the incarnation *as the one sending the Son*. The Son exercises the will of God for the incarnation

---

[54] Ibid., 24–25. Johnson footnotes this statement by referring to the theology of Hans Urs von Balthasar, who apparently does attempt to draw out such an analogy. How the analogy offered here compares with the one offered by Balthasar would have to be the subject of further research.
[55] The same could be said for all of the divine attributes. Each is predicated of the one divine essence and exists according to the eternal Trinitarian *taxis* that is basic to the divine essence: Father, Son, Holy Spirit.

according to his place as *second* in the order of subsistence. So, the Son wills the incarnation *as the one sent by the Father* to assume a human nature. The Spirit exercises the will of God for the incarnation according to his place as *third* in the order of subsistence. So, the Spirit wills the incarnation *as the one sent by the Father and the Son* to empower the human nature of Christ in the completion of his mission and to apply the merits of his work to the people of God.

This same model could be applied to any of the works of God in which his will has been revealed to man. Indeed, I propose that this manner of thinking about the one divine will according to an eternal Trinitarian *taxis* is necessitated by the pro-Nicene categories of Trinitarian theology. This immanent Trinitarian *taxis* of the one divine will finds analogical expression in terms of a relationship of authority and submission when it is applied to the Son in the incarnate state, living life as a man, submitting to the will of the Father.

In relation to the thesis of this essay, then, what is the main point of this final discussion? Although many gender complementarians have opted for a view of the Trinity that entails three distinct wills, thus making the authority and submission of gender complementarity a *direct* reflection of the immanent Trinity, this social model of the Trinity is not necessary to make the connection. Because the gender complementarity in 1 Corinthians 11:3 is said to be grounded *indirectly* in the immanent Trinity, the argument of this essay can be maintained within the boundaries of the Trinitarian grammar of the pro-Nicene tradition.

Conclusion

This essay has sought to answer an important theological question with respect to the hotly debated Pauline passage 1 Corinthians 11:2–16: Does 1 Corinthians 11:3 ground gender complementarity in the immanent Trinity? The importance of this question is apparent when one considers the extensive spate of literature on the correspondence between the immanent Trinity and social relationships, gender relationships being at the forefront of the debates. In this essay, I have argued that gender complementarity is grounded in the immanent Trinity indirectly. Thus, the basic contention of most gender complementarians that gender relationships reflect something about the very being of God is correct. However, this essay has argued that the correspondence must be seen as indirect and is best understood according to pro-Nicene Trinitarian categories rather than by the terminology of eternal immanent submission of the will of the Son to the Father.

In summary, this essay has argued as follows: 1 Corinthians 11:2–16 is best understood according to a gender complementarian reading; the submission of woman to man ("man is the head of woman") is grounded, in part, in the submission of the Son to the will of the Father ("God is the head of Christ"); the statement "God is the head of Christ" pertains *directly* to Christ in his incarnate state, in which his human will is submitted to the divine will of the Father; nevertheless, the submission of Christ to the Father, per his human will, is the analogical expression of the immanent Trinitarian *taxis* of the one eternal divine will. Therefore, one can legitimately conclude that 1 Corinthians 11:3 does indeed ground gender complementarity in the immanent Trinity, albeit *indirectly*.

4

"That God May Be All in All"

The Trinity in 1 Corinthians 15

JAMES M. HAMILTON JR.

Egalitarians do not like what complementarians say about ontological equality and functional subordination. What complementarians believe is that in what man and woman *essentially are* as human beings, they are ontologically equal, while in the *roles given to them by God*, there is functional subordination. In defense of this idea that ontologically equal beings can be functionally subordinate to one another, complementarians appeal to the relationship between God the Father and God the Son, observing that in what they *essentially are* they are ontologically equal, while in *what they do* there is clearly functional subordination. In a review of Philip B. Payne's *Man and Woman, One in Christ*, Craig Blomberg writes, "Like Rebecca Groothuis, Payne finds the concept of functional subordination within ontological equality virtually non-sensical, so he doesn't really consider it as an intermediate option."[1] This means that some egalitarians refuse to deal with the complementarian position.[2]

---

[1] Craig L. Blomberg, "Review of *Man and Woman, One in Christ: An Exegetical and Theological Study of Paul's Letters*," *Denver Journal*, February 5, 2010, http://www.denverseminary.edu/article/man-and-woman-one-in-christ-an-exegetical-and-theological-study-of-pauls-letters/.
[2] James M. Hamilton, "Payne's Refusal to Deal with the Complementarian Position," *For His Renown*, April 26, 2011, http://jimhamilton.info/2011/04/26/paynes-refusal-to-deal-with-the-complementarian-position/.

Kevin Giles and Millard Erickson, however, have addressed what complementarians have said about these matters, and my task in this essay is to consider how 1 Corinthians 15:20–28 contributes to this discussion. Neither Giles nor Erickson discusses this passage in the context of the argument Paul makes in 1 Corinthians 15. To be fair to them, that is not their purpose. Their discussions are systematic and wide-ranging. They discuss 1 Corinthians 15:24–28 in the context of the egalitarian-complementarian debate.

My purpose in this essay is first and foremost to understand what Paul is saying in 1 Corinthians 15:24–28 in light of what he is saying in the whole of 1 Corinthians 15. Once we have explored Paul's statements in light of the argument he is making, we will consider the claims Giles and Erickson make about Paul's words.

1 Corinthians 15:24–28 in Paul's Argument

Paul has dealt with schisms in the church in Corinth (1 Corinthians 1–4), sexual immorality and marriage issues (1 Corinthians 5–7), idolatry and worship (1 Corinthians 8–10), and what the church does when gathered (1 Corinthians 11–14).[3] In 1 Corinthians 15 he takes up the issue of the resurrection, and the burden of what he says in this chapter has to do with the resurrection of the dead as a necessary component of the gospel.

Paul begins in 1 Corinthians 15:1–4 by rehearsing the gospel he received and delivered to the Corinthians (v. 3). He states his intention to remind the Corinthians of the gospel he preached to them and in which they stand (v. 1), telling them of the gospel's power to save them if they hold fast to the Word he preached (v. 2). If they don't hold fast, their faith will be in vain and not result in salvation (v. 2). Paul then rehearses the gospel for them in verses 3b–4, "that Christ died for our sins in accordance with the Scriptures, that he was buried, that he was raised on the third day in accordance with the Scriptures." Because of Paul's focus in the rest of the chapter, we can be sure that he rehearses these aspects of the gospel because "some of [the Corinthians] say that there is no resurrection of the dead" (v. 12). Because of this, Paul em-

---

[3] On 1 Corinthians in Pauline and biblical theology, see further James M. Hamilton, *God's Glory in Salvation through Judgment: A Biblical Theology* (Wheaton, IL: Crossway, 2010), 457–61.

phasizes that the gospel he preached was that Christ died for our sins, was buried, and was raised on the third day. It is the resurrection that is in question, and Paul asserts at the outset that the resurrection of Jesus is a necessary component of the gospel he preached.

In 1 Corinthians 15:5–11 Paul explains that the resurrection of Jesus has been attested by the apostles and more than five hundred brothers at one time. Paul makes several interesting statements in these verses. We can note that Peter (Cephas) takes a prominent place and is listed first (v. 5), that Paul indicates that there were more than five hundred eyewitnesses, most of whom are alive and can be consulted (v. 6), and that James the brother of the Lord Jesus seems to be included among the apostles (v. 7); and then there are Paul's fascinating words about his own apostleship (vv. 8–10). He returns to his main point, however, in verse 11: "Whether then it was I or they, so we preach and so you believed." In other words, Paul and all the other apostles, along with the many eyewitnesses, all attest to the resurrection of Jesus from the dead as a necessary component of the gospel.

Paul connects the resurrection of Jesus from the dead to the situation in Corinth in 1 Corinthians 15:12–13: "Now if Christ is proclaimed as raised from the dead, how can some of you say that there is no resurrection of the dead? But if there is no resurrection of the dead, then not even Christ has been raised." Paul's point is simple: the Corinthians are saying there is no resurrection, but that means not even Jesus was raised, which in turn means that both Paul's preaching and the Corinthians' faith are emptied of content (15:14), with Paul and the apostles bearing false witness about God by claiming he did something he did not do: raise Christ from the dead (15:15). If Christ has not been raised, the faith of the Corinthians is futile and their sins have not been atoned for by Christ's death and resurrection (15:17). If Christ has not been raised (15:16), dead believers have perished (15:18) and Christians "are of all people most to be pitied" (15:19).

Paul's purpose in 1 Corinthians 15:12–19 has been to trace out the implications of the assertion that there is no resurrection from the dead: no resurrection means not even Christ has been raised. His purpose in 15:20–28 is to assert the contrary: Christ has been raised and he is the firstfruits of the general resurrection.

Paul counters the idea that apparently has some traction in Corinth, that there is no resurrection, by teaching in 1 Corinthians 15:20–28 that Christ is the firstfruits of the resurrection and will conquer all his enemies. Calling Christ "the firstfruits of those who have fallen asleep" invokes the Old Testament concept of the firstfruits (e.g., Lev. 23:9–14), where the firstfruits are dedicated to the Lord. The statement made by this act of worship seems to be that because the Israelites believe that the Lord will ensure the rest of the harvest, they gladly dedicate the firstfruits to him. In this way, the firstfruits are a kind of guarantee of the rest of the harvest. So here in 1 Corinthians 15:20–28, the resurrection of Jesus is a guarantee of the rest of the harvest. As Jay Smith writes, "Just as surely as the full harvest followed the firstfruits, so also all believers who have died in Christ will follow him in resurrection."[4]

From the assertion of Christ as firstfruits, Paul moves to Adam-Christ typology in 1 Corinthians 15:21–22, and he will return to it in 15:45. In 15:21–22 Paul states that death came by Adam, resurrection comes by Jesus, and as all die in Adam, so all shall be made alive in Christ. All shall be made alive. Everyone will be raised from the dead. Here, on the basis of the resurrection of Jesus, Paul means to overturn the Corinthian idea that there is no resurrection and establish that the connection between the first and last Adam (cf. 15:45) means that *everyone* will be raised from the dead.

Having established the resurrection, against what some in Corinth say (15:12), Paul now moves to the order of events in 1 Corinthians 15:23–25. At issue in these verses is the order of resurrections and the restoration of the kingdom to the Father when Christ has conquered all his enemies. Paul is clearly concerned with *when* these things will happen in relation to each other: "But each in his own order: Christ the firstfruits, then at his coming those who belong to Christ" (v. 23). Paul is saying that Christ has been raised from the dead, and when he comes "those who belong to Christ" will be raised. Incidentally, this fits very well with the depiction of two resurrections in Revelation 20:4–6, where believers are raised at Christ's coming, they reign with him for

---

[4] Jay E. Smith, "1 Corinthians," in *The Bible Knowledge Word Study: Acts—Ephesians*, ed. Darrell L. Bock (Colorado Springs: Victor, 2006), 312.

a thousand years, and then the rest of the dead are raised at the end of the thousand years.[5]

Synthesizing what Paul says in 1 Corinthians 15:20–28 with other New Testament teaching is one of the challenges of interpreting the passage. For this reason, and to explore what Paul is saying about the end and the resurrections that will take place, I will align Paul's comments with what John says about resurrections in Revelation 20.

Having described what John calls "the first resurrection" (Rev. 20:5–6), that of believers, in 1 Corinthians 15:23, Paul moves to what happens after that in 15:24–25: "Then comes the end, when he delivers the kingdom to God the Father after destroying every rule and every authority and power. For he must reign until he has put all his enemies under his feet." Again there is great harmony between what Paul says here and what John writes in Revelation 19–20. Paul says in 1 Corinthians 15:25 that Christ "must reign until he has put all his enemies under his feet," and this would match Christ's coming in conquest in Revelation 19 and setting up his thousand-year kingdom in Revelation 20:1–6, at the end of which he puts down Satan's final rebellion by defeating Gog and Magog in 20:7–10. "Then comes the end," Paul writes in 1 Corinthians 15:24, "when he delivers the kingdom to God the Father after destroying every rule and every authority and power."

What happens after Christ has reigned until all his enemies are under his feet (1 Cor. 15:25)? Paul seems to indicate that the resurrection of all those not raised at the coming of Christ—all those who do not belong to Christ (cf. 15:23)—comes next. This would appear to be the upshot of 1 Corinthians 15:26, "The last enemy to be destroyed is death." This matches John's depiction in Revelation 20:11–15, where "Death and Hades gave up the dead who were in them" (Rev. 20:13), and then "Death and Hades were thrown into the lake of fire" (20:14). To this point in 1 Corinthians 15:23–26 Paul has clearly been concerned with the events of the end, and his depiction of those events lines up very well with what John depicts in Revelation 20:1–15. This is the wider context in which 1 Corinthians 15:27–28 must be understood.

---

[5] On Revelation 20, see further James M. Hamilton, *Revelation: The Spirit Speaks to the Churches*, Preaching the Word (Wheaton, IL: Crossway, 2012), 365–79.

Paul does not appear to be discussing the difference between the human Jesus and the divine Jesus, nor is he making a statement about how all three members of the Trinity are involved in everything one member does. He is discussing the order of the events of the end and the way that Christ "must reign until he has put all his enemies under his feet" (1 Cor. 15:25). Paul will return to the events of the end—not an arcane topic when one is discussing the resurrection—in 15:50–57. What Paul says next in 15:27–28 guards against a possible misunderstanding of the idea that everything will be put in subjection to Christ.

It is interesting to observe that Paul's statement in 1 Corinthians 15:25, "For he must reign until he has put all his enemies under his feet," rephrases Psalm 110:1,

The LORD says to my Lord:
  "Sit at my right hand,
until I make your enemies your footstool."

Indeed, Paul's statement in 1 Corinthians 15:25 is based on this verse. He moves in 1 Corinthians 15:27 to Psalm 8:6, and the author of Hebrews is also concerned with the relationship between Psalm 8:6 and Psalm 110:1 (cf. Heb. 1:13; 2:5–9). Paul's concern in 1 Corinthians 15:27 is to establish that when Psalm 8:6 is realized and "all things are put in subjection," no one should think that the Father too will be made subject to Christ: "It is plain that he is excepted who put all things in subjection under him" (1 Cor. 15:27). So Paul is simply saying that when all things are subjected to Christ, that does not include the Father. Moreover, Paul is still concerned with the events of the end, as verse 28 will show.

Paul has established that Jesus is the firstfruits of the resurrection (1 Cor. 15:20). As Adam brought death to all, Jesus will give life to all (15:21–22). Paul then sets out the order of the events of the end: Christ is raised first, followed by all those who belong to him being raised at his coming (15:23). Christ will then reign until all his enemies are under his feet, at which point he, having defeated them all, will give the kingdom to the Father (15:24–25). Then death too will be defeated (15:26), and this seems to indicate, in keeping with Revelation 20, that the unbelieving dead will be raised.[6] Everything but the Father will be put in subjection to Jesus (1 Cor. 15:27).

What happens next? Paul tells us in 1 Corinthians 15:28: "When all things are subjected to him, then the Son himself will also be subjected to him who put all things in subjection under him, that God may be all in all." Once Christ has completed his work, apparently after his return and the resurrection of believers (15:23), after his thousand year reign, after his conquest of all his enemies (15:25), after the final defeat of death (15:26) and the resurrection of all unbelievers, and after everything is "subjected to him" (15:28), which could refer to the great white throne judgment (Rev. 20:11–15), then "the Son himself will also be subjected to" the Father. The reference to "God" being all in all in 1 Corinthians 15:28 most likely refers to the Father, because the Father is referred to in the phrase "him who put all things in subjection under him" (Christ) in the immediately preceding phrase of verse 28. Along these lines, too, is the fact that in 15:24 Paul has said, "Then comes the end, when he delivers the kingdom to God the Father." This reference to Christ's delivering the kingdom to God the Father is probably the same thing that Paul describes in verse 28 when he says that "the Son himself will also be subjected to him who put all things in subjection under him."

This seems to mean that at the end of history, after the millennium, after the great white throne judgment, Christ will "be subjected" to the Father (1 Cor. 15:28). This statement in 1 Corinthians 15:28 is in direct contrast with the statement in 15:27 that the Father will not be subjected to Christ.

Before considering what Erickson and Giles say about this passage, let's sketch in the rest of Paul's argument. Paul has asserted that the resurrection is a necessary component of the gospel (1 Cor. 15:1–4); he has grounded it in apostolic and eyewitness testimony (15:5–11); he has teased out implications of the "no resurrection" position some advocate in Corinth (15:12–19); and he has established that Christ is the firstfruits of the resurrection and set out the order of the resurrections and events of the end in 15:20–28.

---

[6] Cf. N. T. Wright, *The Resurrection of the Son of God*, vol. 3 of *Christian Origins and the Question of God* (Minneapolis: Fortress, 2003), 337n73.

Paul explains in 1 Corinthians 15:29–34 that if the dead are not raised, what the church does and what he suffers are alike pointless. If the dead are not raised, why baptize for the dead (v. 29)?[7] If the dead are not raised, why should Paul endure sufferings (vv. 30–32b)? Why not enjoy life while it lasts, live it up (v. 32c)? When he tells the Corinthians not to be deceived, that bad company corrupts good character, that they should awaken and cease sinning, and that he speaks to their shame (vv. 33–34), he makes plain that these rhetorical questions are meant to pursue the logical implications of the idea that there is no resurrection so that the Corinthians will reject that idea.

The question Paul begins to address in 1 Corinthians 15:35 apparently offends Paul, as can be seen by his harsh answer in verse 36, literally, "Fool!" This indicates that he considers the question of verse 35 an *argumentum ad absurdum*: "How are the dead raised? With what kind of body do they come?" Paul fleshes out the resurrection body by comparing death and resurrection to what happens to seed that is sown and then bears fruit (15:36–38). From there he contrasts different kinds of flesh—that of humans, animals, birds, and fish (15:39)—before moving to a discussion of the differing glories of the heavenly bodies: sun, moon, and stars (15:40–41). Paul then connects what he has said about seeds and fleshes and bodies to the resurrection of the dead in 15:42–49, before asserting in 15:50 that the resurrection must happen because "flesh and blood cannot inherit the kingdom of God." He summarizes the "mystery" of the events of the end in 15:51–57, a brief summary of what he has explained in 15:20–28, before calling the Corinthians to "be steadfast, immovable, always abounding in the work of the Lord, knowing that in the Lord your labor is not in vain" (15:58). It would appear that he wants them to be steadfast and immovable on the point of the resurrection, and that it is the resurrection that means that their labor now is meaningful and not "in vain" (cf. 15:58 and 15:2, 14).

To summarize, the whole argument of the chapter is that the resurrection of Jesus is a necessary component of the gospel, and to deny the general resurrection, as some Corinthians do, undermines the gospel. As with 1 Corinthians 11:17–34, where Paul answered the Corinthian

---

[7] Smith, "1 Corinthians," 315, writes, "The most plausible interpretation seems to be that some in Corinth were getting baptized vicariously for the dead, presumably believers who died before they were baptized."

error on the Lord's Supper with a gospel-focused explanation, so in 1 Corinthians 15, the Corinthian error on the resurrection is answered with a gospel-focused explanation of the events of the end. Table 1 seeks to bring together various statements by Paul and John on the order of the resurrections.

Paul has asserted that the resurrection of Jesus is a necessary component of the gospel (1 Cor. 15:1–4), grounded it in apostolic and eyewitness testimony (15:5–11), shown the implications of the Corinthian "no resurrection" position (15:12–19), shown Christ to be the firstfruits and explained the events of the end (15:20–28), argued that the "no resurrection" position would render the church's practice and Paul's sufferings pointless (15:29–34), answered the *argumentum ad absurdum* about resurrection bodies with comparisons to seed, fleshes, heavenly bodies, and Adam-Christ typology (15:35–49), shown that the resurrection is a requirement for the kingdom (15:50–57), and connected the resurrection to Christian living (15:58). With Paul's argument in 1 Corinthians 15 before us, we are now in position to consider what Erickson and Giles say about verses 24–28.

Erickson and Giles on 1 Corinthians 15:24–28

In their discussions of 1 Corinthians 15:24–28, both Erickson and Giles appeal to Calvin and other theologians, and appeal to the challenge of synthesizing what Paul says here with other statements in Scripture, but neither makes a direct appeal to the flow of Paul's argument. Having discussed Calvin and several others, and relying on a suggestion from Wolfhart Pannenberg, Giles writes:

> If this is the case, what Paul is teaching is that at the resurrection God the Father freely makes God the Son ruler over all, and at the end, God the Son freely gives back this rule to God the Father [footnoting Pannenberg]. Rather than speaking of fixed roles, or of an eschatological subordination of the Son, or of the demise of the Trinity, this text indicates a changing of roles in different epochs by two omnipotent divine persons.[8]

---
[8] Kevin Giles, *Jesus and the Father: Modern Evangelicals Reinvent the Doctrine of the Trinity* (Grand Rapids: Zondervan, 2006), 115; cf. 113–15.

Table 1. The sequence of resurrections according to Paul and John

	1 Cor. 15:20–28	1 Cor. 15:50–57	1 Thess. 3:13; 4:13–18	Revelation
Resurrection of Believers	15:23b: ". . . then at his coming those who belong to Christ."	15:51–52: "We shall not all sleep, but we shall all be changed. . . . The trumpet will sound, and the dead will be raised . . . and we shall be changed."	3:13: ". . . at the coming of our Lord Jesus with all his saints." 4:16–17: ". . . the sound of the trumpet of God. And the dead in Christ will rise first. Then we who are alive, who are left, will be caught up together with them in the clouds to meet the Lord in the air" (cf. Dan. 7:13; Acts 1:9–11).	11:11: resurrection of the two witnesses; followed by 11:15: trumpet, "The kingdom of the world has become the kingdom of our Lord and of his Christ." 20:4–5: ". . . those who had been beheaded for the testimony of Jesus and for the word of God. . . . came to life. . . . This is the first resurrection."
Millennial Reign of Christ	15:25: "He must reign until he has put all his enemies under his feet."			5:10: "They shall reign on the earth." 20:4: "They came to life and reigned with Christ for a thousand years."
Final Satanic Rebellion	15:24: ". . . he delivers the kingdom to God the Father after destroying every rule and every authority and power."			20:7–10: "Satan will be released . . . to deceive the nations . . . Gog and Magog. . . . The devil who had deceived them was thrown into the lake of fire . . . where the beast and the false prophet were" (cf. 19:20).
Resurrection of the Unbelieving Dead and Death Defeated	15:26: "The last enemy to be destroyed is death."	15:54: "Death is swallowed up in victory."		20:12–14: ". . . the dead, great and small. . . . Death and Hades were thrown into the lake of fire."
New Heaven and New Earth, Christ Subjected to the Father	15:28: "The Son himself will also be subjected to him . . . that God may be all in all."	15:57: "Thanks be to God, who gives us the victory through our Lord Jesus Christ."		chaps. 21–22; cf. esp. 21:3, 5, 23; 22:3–5

The problem with this statement is that in addition to 1 Corinthians 15:24, where Paul says that the Son will hand the kingdom over to the Father, Paul says in 15:28 that "the Son himself will also be subjected" to the Father. Giles observes that "the Greek verb translated 'subjected' in v. 28 can be read in the middle voice, 'Christ subjects himself,' or in the passive voice, 'Christ is subjected to the Father,'" but either way Paul is "speaking of fixed roles" and he is teaching the "eschatological subordination of the Son."[9] Whether the verb is passive or middle, Paul is dealing with what will take place at "the end" (v. 24), "when all things are subjected to" Christ (v. 28), and at that point the subjection of Christ clearly has to do with his role in relationship to the Father, not with ontology or the essence of his being.[10]

Giles also considers the "imaginative and evocative" proposal of Pannenberg, which, he says, "radically breaks with the tradition" and therefore "must be considered exploratory." As Giles explains it, Pannenberg's view would be "that the Father and the Son are mutually subordinate to one another."[11] But this seems to be exactly what Paul is guarding against in 1 Corinthians 15:27: "But when it says 'all things are put in subjection,' it is plain that he is excepted who put all things in subjection under him." Thus, contra Pannenberg and Giles, it is not Paul's point that when "the Father gives all rule to the Son" we can describe "the Father subjecting himself to the Son."[12] Just the opposite—the fact that all things are subject to the Son does not include the Father being subject to him (v. 27).

In a "theological postscript" to his discussion, Giles raises what he calls "two insurmountable theological problems" for "those who want to argue that the Son of God is eternally set under the Father's authority." First, he asserts that "in orthodoxy the divine three are thought of as indivisible in power and authority because they are indivisibly God. To suggest that the Son is eternally less in power and authority than the

---

[9] Ibid., 115. When Giles discusses Augustine, 190–94, he reports the way that Augustine dealt with this text, but it is not clear that Giles himself endorses Augustine's position. Giles (esp. on 198) also discusses Calvin's comments on the passage, calling his exegesis "significant." Calvin is synthesizing several lines of New Testament evidence, which will come up again when we consider Erickson.
[10] Leon Morris, *The First Epistle of Paul to the Corinthians* (Grand Rapids: Eerdmans, 1985), 213: "Paul is not speaking of the essential nature of either the Son or the Father. He is speaking of the work that Christ has accomplished and will accomplish."
[11] Giles, *Jesus and the Father*, 202.
[12] Ibid.

Father is to suggest that the Son is less fully God than the Father—what all the Arians taught."[13] The three are indivisibly God, but in 1 Corinthians 15:20–28 Paul is clearly distinguishing between the Father and the Son, and he seems to be indicating that at the end of all things the Son will be subject to the Father. There is a way of talking about these realities that both upholds orthodoxy and accounts for everything the text says, but it is a way of talking that Giles is not willing to grant: in what they are, Christ and the Father are ontologically equal; in what they do, Christ is functionally subordinate to the Father. The Arians would not have affirmed ontological equality.

The second concern Giles raises has to do with whether in eternity past and in eternity future "the language of commanding and obeying" can be applied to Father, Son, and Spirit. Giles writes, "Orthodoxy absolutely rejects the possibility that the divine three each have their own will."[14] We are up against the mystery of the Trinity here, but the passage considered in this chapter speaks of Christ being subjected to the Father at the end of all things, apparently for eternity future. Simon Gathercole has argued that the "sending" language in the Synoptic Gospels argues for Christ's preexistence, which would indicate that Christ was "sent" by the Father not just during the incarnation.[15] We must allow the Bible to shape our theology, rather than constraining the Bible with the cords of what we deem admissible.

Millard Erickson grants that Wayne Grudem's explanation of 1 Corinthians 15:24–28, holding to ontological equality and functional subordination, is "the plainest and most obvious interpretation."[16] But like Giles, Erickson appeals to Calvin, suggesting that passages such as Daniel 7:13 and 17, Luke 1:33, and 2 Peter 1:11, all of which point to Christ's everlasting kingdom, disallow the idea that Christ will be eternally subordinate to the Father. Calvin's answer, quoted by Erickson, is that what Paul means in 1 Corinthians 15:24 and 28 is that "we shall openly behold God reigning in his majesty."[17] I do not think Calvin's

---

[13] Ibid.
[14] Ibid., 203.
[15] Simon Gathercole, *The Preexistent Son: Recovering the Christologies of Matthew, Mark, and Luke* (Grand Rapids: Eerdmans, 2006).
[16] Millard J. Erickson, *Who's Tampering with the Trinity? An Assessment of the Subordination Debate* (Grand Rapids: Kregel, 2009), 115.
[17] Ibid., 136.

answer is difficult to harmonize with the idea that Christ is functionally subordinate to the Father even as he reigns with him. I have offered a reading of 1 Corinthians 15 that fits with John's depiction of the millennium in Revelation 20, and I think that what we are dealing with in 1 Corinthians 15:24 and 28 can easily be read in harmony with the kinds of statements we find in Revelation 21 and 22.

Consider, for instance, Revelation 22:3: "No longer will there be anything accursed, but the throne of God and of the Lamb will be in it, and his servants will worship him." Here the reference to God is clearly a reference to the Father, and the reference to the Lamb is likewise a reference to Jesus. This would indicate that the *role* of Christ as the Redeemer remains relevant in eternity future. Further, whereas in the millennial depiction of Revelation 20, Christ reigns (20:4) and there is no mention of the Father reigning on a throne on earth in that passage, undoubtedly the one who sat on the throne in Revelation 4 was the Father, and he surely continues to reign from his heavenly throne through the millennium. Still, Christ reigns before his people on earth in Revelation 20:4, and then it is God the Father and the Lamb who reign from the throne in Revelation 22:3. Both are God, as 22:3 speaks in the singular of *his* servants worshiping *him*, referring back to both God and the Lamb. And yet the hierarchy and roles seen from Revelation 4–5, where the Lamb approached the one on the throne, remain in that depiction of the new heaven and new earth. So it would seem natural to conclude that by continuing to depict Jesus as the Lamb in Revelation 22:3, John is saying in a different way what Paul said in 1 Corinthians 15:24 and 28—that Christ has rendered the kingdom to the Father and been subjected to him. Thus, Christ's kingdom is everlasting, but he reigns in the kingdom he has delivered to the Father, in which he is subject to the Father.

Erickson also cites Charles Hodge, noting that Hodge held to the eternal subordination of the Son to the Father but did not believe it was taught by 1 Corinthians 15:24–28. In his exposition, Hodge distinguishes between "the eternal Logos, the second person of the Trinity," and "the Logos as incarnate," suggesting that "the subordination, however, here spoken of, is not that of the human nature of Christ separately considered, as when he is said to suffer, or to die, or to be ignorant; but it is the official subordination of the incarnate Son to God as God."[18] A distinction such as this may help us understand a passage like Mark 13:32, where Jesus says that not even the Son knows the day but only the Father does; but I see no indication that Paul means to distinguish between the Son as incarnate man and the Son as divine Logos. I do not think the cited switch from "Christ" in 1 Corinthians 15:23 to "Son" in 15:28 does this, because it is Christ in verse 23 who delivers the kingdom to the Father in verse 24. I would suggest that Hodge means to synthesize what Paul says here with other passages, and that because there is no exegetical warrant for this distinction, it does not help Erickson's case.

Conclusion

No analogy is perfect, and with any analogy aspects of the things being compared will not align perfectly. The comparison between the ontological equality and functional subordination in the members of the Trinity, on the one hand, and the equality and diverse roles of men and women, on the other, is *simply* an analogy. The relationships between the one help us understand the relationships between the other; and from what Paul says about headship in 1 Corinthians 11:3 and marriage in Ephesians 5, we have scriptural warrant for comparing divine and human relationships. First Corinthians 15:24 and 28 indicate that Christ will hand the kingdom over to the Father, that Christ will be subject to the Father, and that God will be all in all. God's glory will cover the dry lands as the waters cover the seas, and the best way to talk about Jesus the Son being subjected to God the Father is to affirm that they are ontologically equal as God while the Son takes up a functionally subordinate role.

---

[18] Ibid., 136–37.

5

Eternal Generation in the Church Fathers

ROBERT LETHAM

We believe in one God the Father Almighty, maker of heaven and earth and of all things visible and invisible; And in one Lord Jesus Christ the Son of God, the Only-begotten, begotten by his Father before all ages, Light from Light, true God from true God, begotten not made.

Niceno-Constantinopolitan creed, AD 381

If anyone shall not confess that the Word of God has two nativities, the one from all eternity of the Father, without time and without body; the other in these last days, coming down from heaven and being made flesh of the holy and glorious Mary, Mother of God and always a virgin, and born of her: let him be anathema.

Capitulum 2, The Second Council of Constantinople, AD 553

Critical Reservations

Despite these clear statements on the eternal generation of the Son by two ecumenical councils, confessed down the centuries by the church—East and West; Orthodox, Catholic, and Protestant—many evangelicals, such as John S. Feinberg,[1] Millard Erickson[2] and Bruce Ware,[3] have voiced reservations or openly opposed them. Robert L. Reymond asked for definite exegetical evidence before the church is asked to accept the doctrine.[4] Many of these criticisms proceed on the assumption that theology is to be an assemblage of biblical texts strung together, explicit statements required for each and every affirmation. Consequently, the absence of explicit statements to justify a matter renders it speculative. In contrast, Patristic and medieval exegesis was constantly checked against the deposit of faith.[5] The Westminster Confession of Faith considers the whole counsel of God to include good and necessary deductions from Scripture.[6]

Precipitating Cause

From the second century, the Greek apologists were faced with threats from Gnosticism and Neoplatonism, which if applied to the Son would subordinate him to, or view him as an emanation from, the One. Either of these ideas would have destroyed the gospel, for a Christ who is less than the Father could not reveal God or save his people. The doctrine of generation protected against this danger. The orthodox fathers, to a man, held that the generation of the Son by the Father in eternity repulsed heresy by asserting that the Son belonged on the side of God. Eventually it provided the cement that bound together the church's doctrine of the Trinity.[7]

Development of the Doctrine

Justin

Possibly the earliest reference to the generation of the Son is from Justin, in his *Dialogue with Trypho the Jew*. Since the apostles confess Christ

---
[1] John S. Feinberg, *No One Like Him: The Doctrine of God* (Wheaton, IL: Crossway, 2001), 488–92.
[2] Millard J. Erickson, *God in Three Persons: A Contemporary Interpretation of the Trinity* (Grand Rapids: Baker, 1995), 305–10.
[3] Bruce A. Ware, *Father, Son, and Holy Spirit: Relationships, Roles, and Relevance* (Wheaton, IL: Crossway, 2005), 162.
[4] Robert L. Reymond, *A New Systematic Theology of the Christian Faith* (New York: Nelson, 1998), 324–38.
[5] Paul Hartog, "The 'Rule of Faith' and Patristic Biblical Exegesis," *TrinJ* 28 (2007): 65–86; Manlio Simonetti, *Biblical Interpretation in the Early Church: An Historical Introduction to Patristic Exegesis* (Edinburgh: T&T Clark, 1994), 121–37; Christopher A. Hall, *Reading Scripture with the Church Fathers* (Downers Grove, IL: InterVarsity, 1998), 177–200; Bertrand de Margerie, SJ, *An Introduction to the History of Exegesis*, vol. 1, *The Greek Fathers* (Petersham, MA: Saint Bede's, 1993), 119f.
[6] Westminster Confession of Faith, 1.6. See Benjamin Breckinridge Warfield, *The Westminster Assembly and Its Work* (New York: Oxford University Press, 1934), 226–27.
[7] See Basil Studer, "Trinity," in *Encyclopedia of the Early Church*, ed. Angelo Di Berardino, 2 vols. (New York: Oxford University Press, 1992), 851–52.

as the Son, he says, "we have understood that he proceeded before all creatures from the Father."[8] The Logos was begotten in a unique way by the Father and afterward became man by the virgin.[9]

Irenaeus

In contrast to the heretics' use of the Logos doctrine to subordinate the Son, Irenaeus refers frequently to Isaiah 53:8—"who shall declare his generation?" (KJV)—pointing to his ineffable and indescribable relation to the Father, surpassing human generation. Since it concerns the relations between the Father and the Son, it is eternal, asserting that the Son is with the Father from eternity.[10]

Tertullian

Opposing the modalist Praxeas, Tertullian holds that the Father, the Son, and the Holy Spirit are distinct but inseparable.[11] Wisdom—effectively the Son—was generated.[12] The Father is the whole substance of God, while the Son is the derivation of the whole.[13] In his contest with Praxeas, Tertullian moved close to subordinationism, stressing the distinctions between the persons. Generation refers to the relations between the Father and the Son.[14]

Origen

Origen held that the Son was born of the Father before creation, without a beginning, and before any creatures came into existence.[15] The Father always generates his Wisdom.[16] Generation is incomprehensible and inexpressible.[17] It cannot be compared to human generation; it is incom-

---

[8] Justin, *Dialogue with Trypho the Jew* 100; *The Ante-Nicene Fathers* (hereafter *ANF*), ed. Alexander Roberts and James Donaldson, 10 vols. (1885–1887; repr., Edinburgh: T&T Clark, 1993), 1:249. See also Justin, *Dialogue with Trypho the Jew* 102; *ANF* 1:250.
[9] Justin, *Dialogue with Trypho the Jew* 105.1; *ANF* 1:251.
[10] Irenaeus, *Against Heresies* 2.28.5–9; *ANF* 1:400–406.
[11] Tertullian, *Against Praxeas* 9; *Patrologia Latina* (hereafter *PL*), ed. J. P. Migne et al. (Paris, 1878–1890), 2:164; *ANF* 3:603.
[12] Tertullian, *Praxeas* 6; *PL* 2:161; *ANF* 3:601.
[13] Tertullian, *Praxeas* 9; *PL* 2:164; *ANF* 3:603–4.
[14] Ibid.
[15] Origen, *On First Principles*, preface, 4; *Patrologia Graeca* (hereafter *PG*), ed. J. P. Migne et al. (Paris, 1857–1866), 11:117; *ANF* 4:240.
[16] Origen, *On First Principles* 1.2; *ANF* 4:246.
[17] Origen, *On First Principles* 1.4; *ANF* 4:247.

parable.[18] This flows from its being eternal.[19] It is by nature, not by an external act.[20] The Son is one in nature and subsistence with the Father.[21]

Athanasius

With Athanasius the doctrine of eternal generation comes into its own. The main issue for him in the Trinitarian crisis is not so much the Son's being *homoousios* (of the same being) with the Father but the distinction between created and uncreated.[22] He remarks that in the New Testament the verb γεννάω ("beget") is used of the Son but not of creatures, while ποιέω ("make") is never connected with the Son.[23] Correspondingly, the Word is Creator and not a creature.[24] He has no beginning, since he is alone with the Father and begotten, having his beginning with the Father, who is without beginning, so that he himself is without beginning (ὁ δὲ Λόγος τὸ εἶναι οὐκ ἐν ἄλλῃ ἀρχῇ ἔχει, ἀλλ' ἐν τῷ Πατρὶ, τῷ καὶ κατ' ἐκείνους ἀνάρχῳ, ἵνα καὶ αὐτὸς ἀνάρχως ὑπάρχῃ ἐν τῷ Πατρὶ, γέννημα καὶ οὐ κτίσμα τυγχάνων αὐτοῦ).[25] This relation transcends human fatherhood and sonship. Since the Son is of the Father's essence (οὐσία), he is eternal and the generation is eternal. It does not happen in time, nor is it a sequence. The Son is of the Father's *ousia* from eternity,[26] the proper offspring of the Father's *ousia*.[27] As the offspring of the Father, he is like him.[28] As Thomas Weinandy indicates, for Athanasius, the nature of God "the Father begetting the Son is eternally, and so immutably and unalterably, constitutive of what the one God is."[29]

---

[18] Ibid.
[19] Ibid.
[20] Ibid.
[21] Origen, *On First Principles* 1.6; ANF 4:248.
[22] Panayiotis Christou, "Uncreated and Created, Unbegotten and Begotten in the Theology of Athanasius of Alexandria," *Augustinianum* 13, no. 3 (1973): 399–409; Georges Florovsky, "St. Athanasius' Concept of Creation," in *The Collected Works of Georges Florovsky*, vol. 4, *Aspects of Church History*, ed. Richard S. Haugh (Vaduz, Liech.: Büchervertriebsanstalt, 1987), 39–62; Paul Gavrilyuk, "Creation in Early Christian Polemical Literature: Irenaeus against the Gnostics and Athanasius against the Arians," *Modern Theology* 29, no. 2 (2013): 22–32.
[23] Athanasius, *Orations against the Arians* 2.57; PG 26:268; *Nicene and Post-Nicene Fathers of the Christian Church* (hereafter NPNF[1] or NPNF[2] [First or Second Series]), ed. Philip Schaff and Henry Wace, Second Series (Edinburgh: T&T Clark, 1886–1900), 4:378–79.
[24] Athanasius, *Orations against the Arians* 2.57–58; PG 26:269; NPNF[2] 4:378–80.
[25] Athanasius, *Orations against the Arians* 2.57; PG 26:269; NPNF[2] 4:378.
[26] Athanasius, *Orations against the Arians* 1.16; PG 26:45; NPNF[2] 4:315–16.
[27] Athanasius, *Orations against the Arians* 2.2; PG 26:149; NPNF[2] 4:349. See also, 2.22–23; PG 26:192–93; NPNF[2] 4:359–60.
[28] Athanasius, *On the Decrees of the Synod of Nicea* 17; PG 25:452; NPNF[2] 4:160–61.
[29] Thomas G. Weinandy, *Athanasius: A Theological Introduction* (Aldershot: Ashgate, 2007), 63; see 60–65, 136–37.

Generation for Athanasius is virtually synonymous with participation. The Son participates in all that the Father is, and the Father participates in all the Son is, and so to be generated by the Father is to participate in God (τό γὰρ ὅλως μετέχεσθαι τὸν θεὸν, ἴσον ἐστὶ λέγειν, ὅτι καὶ γεννᾷ· τὸ δὲ γεννᾶν τί σημαίνει ἢ Ὑιόν),[30] for the Son and the Father are one (αὐτὸς καὶ ὁ Πατὴρ ἕν εἰσι).[31] Indeed, generation is the foundation of creation. As Anatolios remarks with reference to Athanasius's comment that the Son is the offspring of the Father's being,[32] "[God] has the power to create as internal to his being . . . as something that is fulfilled precisely in the generation of the Son. The priority of theology over economy, in Athanasian terms, is thus the priority of divine generation over creation."[33] In other words, God's free decision to create is an exercise of that same nature in the context of which the Father generates the Son.[34] This is why Bavinck makes the point that creation would be impossible apart from the generation of the Son.[35]

Consequently, human and divine creating differ. Humans are composed of parts and lose substance in begetting, whereas God is indivisible and simple, with no partitions. Human fathers exist before their sons; God always is.[36] Thus, in his *Letters to Serapion on the Holy Spirit*, Athanasius can say that the Son is "whole of whole" and "whole God."[37] Since the Son is the proper offspring of the Father's being, the Son is all that the Father is, except for being the Father. The Son is the whole image and radiance of the whole. He is the perfect expression of the Father. He is not part of God or less than the whole God.[38] He and the Father mutually indwell one another.[39] The Father is never without the Son, nor vice-versa.[40]

---

[30] Athanasius, *Orations against the Arians* 1.16; PG 26:44–45. See Khaled Anatolios, *Athanasius: The Coherence of His Thought* (London: Routledge, 1998), 107.
[31] Athanasius, *Orations against the Arians* 1.16; PG 26:44–45; NPNF[2] 4:315–16.
[32] Athanasius, *Orations against the Arians* 2.2; PG 26:149; NPNF[2] 4:349.
[33] Anatolios, *Athanasius*, 122.
[34] Ibid., 122–25.
[35] Herman Bavinck, *Reformed Dogmatics*, ed. John Bolt, trans. John Vriend, vol. 2, *God and Creation* (Grand Rapids: Baker Academic, 2004), 420.
[36] *On the Decrees* 11–12; PG 25:441–45; NPNF[2] 4:157–58; Athanasius, *Orations against the Arians* 1.27–28; PG 26:68–69; NPNF[2] 4:322–23.
[37] Athanasius, *Letters to Serapion on the Holy Spirit* 1.16; PG 26:568–69; *Works on the Spirit: Athanasius and Didymus*, trans. Mark DelCogliano, Andrew Radde-Gallwitz, and Lewis Ayres (New York: St Vladimir's Seminary Press, 2011), 78.
[38] Athanasius, *Orations against the Arians* 1.20–21; PG 26:53–57; NPNF[2] 4:318–19.
[39] Athanasius, *Orations against the Arians* 3.3–4; PG 26:328–29; NPNF[2] 4:395.
[40] Athanasius, *Orations against the Arians* 1.25; PG 26:64; NPNF[2] 4:321.

Panayiotis Christou concludes that "by his teaching, Athanasius himself changed the direction of theology from the genesis of the Son (as, of course, also of the Spirit) to the begetting; from γένεσις to γέννησις."[41] Again, Athanasius "did not accept identity of the Divine Persons, but identity of the essence of the Persons."[42] As uncreated, each possesses the entirety of the divine nature and is God. As for internal relations, Athanasius preserves the divided state within the Trinity. The οὐσία is identical; the persons act distinctly.[43]

Basil

Basil opposes any numeration in God, in terms of first, second, and third, that would imply difference of rank. Instead, we confess the distinction of persons but hold to the monarchy of the Father. The one Godhead is seen in the Father and the Son. "For the Son is in the Father, and the Father in the Son (Υἱὸς γὰρ ἐν τῷ Πατρὶ καὶ Πατὴρ ἐν τῷ Υἱῷ); such is the former, such is the latter, and such is the latter, such is the former; and in this is the One."[44] Thus, referring to John 1:1, he stresses that the Son is ever with the Father.[45]

Since the Son transcends time, his generation is eternal and beyond human comprehension and, for that reason, cannot be compared to human generation, which occurs in time.[46] Thus, we need to abandon all material comparisons and consider generation in a manner worthy of God, for the generation of the Son is without passion or divisions and is timeless. Moreover, since this occurs eternally within the Trinity, it cannot entail subordination. The whole nature of the Father is impressed on the Son like a seal (ὥσπερ ἐν σφραγίδί τινι τῆς ὅλης φύσεως τοῦ Πατρὸς ἐναποσημανθείσης τῷ Υἱῷ).[47] Basil, in *Epistola* 9, refers to the phrase "light from light" in the Creed of Nicea and understands it to refer to and support the *homoousial* relation of the Son to the Father. "Being of this mind, the fathers at Nicaea spoke of the Only-begotten as 'Light of Light,' 'Very God of Very God,' and so on, and then con-

---
[41] Christou, "Uncreated and Created," 406.
[42] Ibid., 408.
[43] Ibid.
[44] Basil of Caesarea, *On the Holy Spirit* 45; *PG* 32:149b; *NPNF*² 8:28.
[45] Basil of Caesarea, *On the Holy Spirit* 14; *PG* 32:89; *NPNF*² 8:8–9.
[46] Basil of Caesarea, *On the Holy Spirit* 14; *PG* 32:88–89; *NPNF*² 8:8–9.
[47] Basil of Caesarea, *Against Eunomius* 2.16; *PG* 29:604–5.

sistently added the homoousion.... It is impossible to understand the being of the Only-begotten in relation to the Father in any other way"[48]

Hildebrand argues that John 14:9 is crucial for Basil, for it "expresses what it means for the Son to be divinely begotten, and what it means for him to be the Image and Resemblance: 'divine generation' (stripped of all corporeal and material connotations) means that the Son perfectly makes known the Father."[49] Generation refers to the relations between the persons and has nothing to do with οὐσία. That it also denotes *an order* between the persons is clear from Basil's arguments against Eunomius over τάξις, which the Arians took as a difference of rank, but Basil—and the orthodox followed this—understood in terms of order or appropriate disposition.[50]

Gregory of Nyssa

Gregory agrees with his brother that generation is according to hypostasis, not essence. There is an order between the three; the Son is from the Father, the Son and the Holy Spirit are inseparable, and both are from the Father. Thus, the Father is the cause according to the personal relations (κατὰ τὴν ὑπόστασιν).[51] Generation entails identity of nature, since the begotten resembles the begetter, and so it is impossible for us to describe it.[52] However, since the nature of the Son is the same as the Father, there is no subordination of the former to the latter.[53] Since the Son is said to be "only-begotten," it is impossible for there to be rivals.[54] His generation "surpasses all power of speech or thought," so Scripture borrows language while rejecting everything else in earthly generation. Consequently, "community of nature alone is left, and for this reason by the title 'Son' is declared ... the close affinity and genuineness of

---

[48] Basil of Caesarea, *Letters* 9.3; *PG* 32:272; *NPNF*[2] 8:123. See also Basil of Caesarea, *On the Holy Spirit* 15; *PG* 32:89, 92; *NPNF*[2] 8:9–10, where he emphasizes that the expression "at the right hand of God" cannot signify any inferiority to the Father but rather expresses a relation of equality.
[49] Stephen M. Hildebrand, *The Trinitarian Theology of Basil of Caesarea* (Washington, DC: Catholic University of America, 2007), 190; see also 168–70.
[50] Milton V. Anastos, "Basil's Κατὰ Εὐνομίου: A Critical Analysis," in *Basil of Caesarea: Christian, Humanist, Ascetic: A Sixteen-Hundredth Anniversary Symposium*, ed. Paul Jonathan Fedwick (Toronto: Pontifical Institute of Medieval Studies, 1981), 88, 93; G. W. H. Lampe, *A Patristic Greek Lexicon* (Oxford: Clarendon, 1961), 1372–73.
[51] Basil of Caesarea, *Letters* 38.4; *PG* 32:329; *NPNF*[2] 8:137–41. This is considered to have been composed by Gregory of Nyssa, although some scholars think it was written by Gregory of Nazianzus.
[52] Gregory of Nyssa, *Against Eunomius* 1.33–34; *NPNF*[2] 5:77–81.
[53] Gregory of Nyssa, *On the Holy Trinity, and of the Godhead of the Holy Spirit*, in *NPNF*[2] 5:327.
[54] Gregory of Nyssa, *Against Eunomius* 2.8; *NPNF*[2] 5:112–13.

relationship which mark his manifestation from the Father." His is "an existence at once derived from and existing with the Father," "no interval intervening."[55]

Gregory of Nazianzus

With Nazianzen there is an apparent tension between his claim that the Father is the ἀρχή (source) in relation to cause, not to nature, and other passages where he appears to teach that the monarchy belongs to the whole Trinity. The Father as αἴτιος (cause) is greater than the Son (ὅτι τῷ αἰτίῳ μείζων ὁ Πατὴρ τοῦ Υἱοῦ).[56] Gregory's opponents make the Father greater in nature; Gregory denies this, saying that the Father is greater in terms of cause. He is cause of the hypostatic (personal) relations, but the being of God is one and invisible, the Son equal with the Father,[57] for "we do not divide the power, for there is neither greater nor less."[58] All three persons are equal, so Gregory is afraid that using ἀρχή might indicate he viewed the Son to be inferior.[59] Indeed, "we hold that, to subordinate any of the Three, is to destroy the whole. For we worship and acknowledge them as Three in their properties but One in their Godhead."[60]

Thomas Noble considers this an inherent ambiguity in Gregory's thought.[61] Gregory wants the monarchy to be the whole Trinity but, within the Trinity, in terms of *hypostasis*, also wants to preserve the ἀρχή of the Father.[62] This agrees with Gregory's famous statement that, considering the one οὐσία, he saw the three as equal in essence, glory, and power, but when considering the three, he observed an order (τάξις) in which the Father is greater as ἀρχή and αἴτιος of the Son and the Spirit. Both these perspectives must be held together.[63]

---

[55] Gregory of Nyssa, *Against Eunomius* 2.9; NPNF² 5:114–15.
[56] Gregory Nazianzen, *Oration 29: On the Son* 15; PG 36:93; NPNF² 7:306; *St. Gregory of Nazianzus: On God and Christ*, trans. Frederick Williams and Lionel R. Wickham (Crestwood, NY: St Vladimir's Seminary Press, 2002), 83.
[57] Gregory Nazianzen, *Oration 40: On Holy Baptism* 43; PG 36:420; NPNF² 7:375–76.
[58] Gregory Nazianzen, *Oration 31: On the Holy Spirit* 14; PG 36:149; NPNF² 7:322; *St. Gregory of Nazianzus: On God and Christ*, 127–28.
[59] Gregory Nazianzen, *Oration 40* 43; PG 36:420; NPNF² 7:375–76.
[60] Gregory Nazianzen, *Oration 43: The Panegyric on St. Basil* 30; NPNF² 7:405.
[61] Thomas A. Noble, "Paradox in Gregory Nazianzen's Doctrine of the Trinity," in *Studia Patristica* 27 (Louvain: Peeters, 1993), 94–99.
[62] Ibid., 97.
[63] Gregory Nazianzen, *Oration 40* 41; PG 36:417; NPNF² 7:375; Noble, "Gregory Nazianzen," 97–99.

Gregory repeats in his brilliant way the common teaching we have already seen in Athanasius and his fellow Cappadocians. The generation of the Son is incomprehensible: "You explain the ingeneracy of the Father and I will give you a biological account of the Son's begetting and the Spirit's proceeding—and let us go mad the pair of us for prying into God's secrets."[64] It is best honored in silence.[65] Again, it points to identity of nature. Indeed, as Christopher Beeley observes, for Gregory "the unity and oneness of the Trinity . . . is constituted by the Father's begetting of the Son and sending forth of the Spirit."[66]

Augustine

In the West, Augustine is seminal. Central to his Trinitarianism are the union of the three in the one divine being and the indivisibility of the Trinitarian works. He fully accepted the Trinitarian settlement at Constantinople I.[67] The Father and Son are one being.[68] Given this, for Augustine the Son is born from the Father, who is the beginning (*principium*) of the whole divinity.[69] The Father alone is he from whom the Son is born and the Holy Spirit principally proceeds.[70] As such the Son has two births: one in eternity, the other from the virgin.[71] His generation is eternal, since there is no point at which the Father and the Son are not.[72]

John of Damascus

The Damascene's great work *The Orthodox Faith* represented the distillation and consolidation of Patristic orthodoxy. In it, he confesses that we are unable to understand heavenly things; we must believe God's

---

[64] Gregory Nazianzen, *Oration* 31 8; *PG* 36:141; *NPNF*² 7:320. The translation here is from *St. Gregory of Nazianzus: On God and Christ*, 122.
[65] Gregory Nazianzen, *Oration* 29 8; *PG* 36:84; *NPNF*² 7:303; *St. Gregory of Nazianzus: On God and Christ*, 75–76.
[66] Gregory Nazianzen, *Oration* 29 10, 16; *PG* 36:88, 96; *NPNF*² 7:304–7; *St. Gregory of Nazianzus: On God and Christ*, 78, 83–84; Christopher A. Beeley, *Gregory of Nazianzus on the Trinity and the Knowledge of God: In Your Light Shall We See Light* (Oxford: Oxford University Press, 2008), 200.
[67] See Robert Letham, *The Holy Trinity: In Scripture, History, Theology, and Worship* (Phillipsburg, NJ: P&R, 2004), 184–200; Lewis Ayres, *Nicaea and Its Legacy: An Approach to Fourth-Century Trinitarian Theology* (Oxford: Oxford University Press, 2004).
[68] Augustine, *De Trinitate* 4.20.29; *The Works of Saint Augustine: The Trinity*, trans. Edmund Hill (Hyde Park, NY: New City, 1991), 174.
[69] Augustine, *De Trinitate* 15.17.29; *The Trinity*, 419.
[70] Augustine, *De Trinitate* 15.26.45–48; *The Trinity*, 430–33.
[71] Augustine, *On the Creed* 8; *NPNF*¹ 3:371–72; Augustine, *On the Gospel of John* 48.6; *NPNF*¹ 7:267–68; *John* 54.7; *NPNF*¹ 7:298.
[72] Augustine, *On the Creed* 8: *NPNF*¹ 3:371.

118 Robert Letham

Word.[73] He distinguishes generation from creation. Whereas in creation the Maker produces something externally of an absolutely different nature, generation entails the begetter producing out of his essence offspring similar in essence. Generation is out of nature; creation is an act of will.[74] Generation involves unity of essence and differentiation of person.[75] In short, "the Father, the Son, and the Holy Spirit are one in all respects, save those of not being begotten, of birth, and of procession."[76] John has a lengthy and developed discussion of the perichoresis (mutual indwelling) of the three persons in the context of his consideration of generation and procession.[77]

Calvin

Moving beyond the Fathers, Calvin's adherence to eternal generation has recently been called into question. Robert L. Reymond claimed that Calvin rejected "the ancient doctrine of the Father's eternal generation of the Son."[78] That this is untenable is clear from Calvin's writings. In the *Institutes of the Christian Religion*, he is emphatic that Christ is the only begotten Son of God (*unigenitus Dei Filius*), the Word begotten of the Father (*sermo ante secula ex Patre genitus*), for by virtue of eternal generation he always possessed sonship (*ab aeterna genitura semper hoc habuit ut Filius esset*). The only begotten Son of God was brought into the world (*in mundum productus est unigenitus Dei Filius*). Repeatedly Calvin refers to Christ as the begotten by the Father.[79] While we are called "sons," God calls Christ alone the Only Begotten (*unigenitus*).[80]

In his commentary on Acts 13:33, where Luke cites Psalm 2:7—"You are my Son; / today I have begotten you"—referring to Christ's resurrection, Calvin agrees that God begot Christ when he was openly acknowledged as the only begotten of God at his resurrection. However, "that does not prevent Christ being the Word begotten by the eternal

---

[73] John of Damascus, *On the Orthodox Faith* 1.1–4; NPNF² 9:1–4.
[74] John of Damascus, *On the Orthodox Faith* 1.8; NPNF² 9:6–11. This is one of the most important passages in the literature.
[75] John of Damascus, *On the Orthodox Faith* 1.6; PG 9:4–5.
[76] John of Damascus, *On the Orthodox Faith* 1.8; PG 9:10.
[77] John of Damascus, *On the Orthodox Faith* 1.8; NPNF² 9:6–11.
[78] Reymond, *A New Systematic Theology*, 327–30.
[79] John Calvin, *Institutes*, 2.14.5.
[80] Ibid., 2.14.6.

Father before time. But that is the secret generation. But David now declares that it was revealed to men." (*Neque tamen hoc obstat, quominus Christus sapientia sit, ab aeterno Patre ante tempus genita, sed illa arcana est generatio. Nunc autem praedicat David manifestatum fuisse hominibus.*) The begetting in the resurrection reveals the secret eternal generation by the eternal Father before time. It is a temporal manifestation of the eternal reality.[81]

Again, Calvin considers that in Colossians 1:15 the Son is called firstborn "because he was begotten by the Father, that [creatures] might be created through him" (*sed quia in hoc a Patre sit genitus*). His generation by the Father is the ground of creation.[82]

Basic Entailments

As Herman Bavinck states, "God's fecundity is a beautiful theme." He argues that the doctrine of the generation of the Son displays God as "no abstract, fixed, monadic, solitary substance, but a plenitude of life. It is his nature to be generative and fruitful."[83] Creation would be impossible if the Son were not generated from eternity. "Without generation, creation would not be possible. If, in an absolute sense, God could not communicate himself to the Son, he would be even less able, in a relative sense, to communicate himself to his creature."[84] In this, Bavinck reflects the classic Trinitarian doctrine that the persons are oriented to the other. The Father is the Father of the Son, the Son is the Son of the Father. The three are inherently relational. This relationality underlies God's free determination to create—an act of his will, exercised in harmony with his nature.

Generation Is Ineffable

Generation reflects the incomprehensibility of God and is a transcendent mystery, beyond the grasp of our minds to master. We can say very

---

[81] John Calvin, *Calvin's Commentaries: The Acts of the Apostles 1–13*, trans. John W. Fraser and W. J. G. McDonald (Grand Rapids: Eerdmans, 1965), 378–79; Calvin, *Commentariorum in Acta Apostolarum liber primus*, Ioannis Calvini Opera Exegetica (Geneva: Librairie Droz, 2001), 389–90.
[82] John Calvin, *Calvin's Commentaries: The Epistles of Paul to the Galatians, Ephesians, Philippians, and Colossians*, trans. T. H. L. Parker (Grand Rapids: Eerdmans, 1965), 308–9; Calvin, *Commentarii in Pauli Epistolas*, Ioannis Calvini Opera Exegetica (Genève: Librairie Droz, 1992), 398.
[83] Bavinck, *Reformed Dogmatics*, 2:308.
[84] Ibid., 2:420.

little about it; it is a matter of faith. This should pose no insuperable problem, or else faith would be based on our own capacities and limited exclusively to what we know. This was uniformly recognized by the Fathers; for them it was a great mystery. The idea that they were given to speculative attempts to explain it is not borne out by the sources.

Generation Is Not to Be Compared to Human Generation: It Denotes Unity of Nature

The Arians made deductions from the generation of human sons, who come into existence and in turn become fathers when they beget sons. From this the Arians concluded that the Son of God had a beginning, that God became Father at that point. The premise generated the heresy. The one correspondence between the two forms of generation is that the generated is of the same nature as the generator. This was the central point made by Athanasius and the Fathers. This alerts us to the danger of reading back into the Trinity patterns intelligible in the created order; if anything, the latter reflects the former.

Generation Is Contrasted to Creation: "Begotten, Not Made"

That generation is not creation was the basic issue in the Trinitarian crisis, the one foremost for Athanasius. The doctrine of eternal generation obviates any notion of the Son as a creature. In the creed the positive "begotten" and the negative "not made" are equally vital. The confession of his begetting denies creation, underlining again his identity of nature with the Father.

Generation Indicates Personal Distinction between the Father and the Son

Simultaneously the dogma asserts identity of nature and distinction of the persons—the heart of the doctrine of the Trinity. The three are one indivisible being, while irreducibly distinct. The Son is not the Father, the Father is not the Son, and the Holy Spirit is neither the Father nor the Son. Yet the three are one.

Generation Highlights an Irreversible Hypostatic Order

The New Testament authors refer to the three persons in differing orders (Matt. 28:19–20; 1 Cor. 12:4–6; 2 Cor. 13:14; Eph. 4:4–6; Rev. 1:4–5). However, there is a general pattern evident throughout the economy of creation, providence, and grace: from the Father through the Son by the Holy Spirit (Matt. 28:19). In turn, our response to God's grace is enabled by the Spirit, is offered through the Son, and rests on the Father (Eph. 2:18). God's revelation in human history reflects eternal antecedent realities, for he is faithful to himself. He acts in conformity with who he is.

Thus, the Father sends the Son, the Spirit proceeds from the Father, and the Spirit is sent by the Son—never the reverse. While each of the three is exhaustively God and is of the one indivisible being, there is a relation between them that is eternally true.

The relations of sending and being sent reflect the order of begetting and being begotten. Both the Western and Eastern churches have understood these as missions and processions. According to the processions, the Son and the Spirit are begotten and proceed eternally from the Father. The missions concern the sendings of both in history. There is a distinction but an inseparable connection.

The Dogma of Eternal Generation Is the Cement Holding Together the Doctrine of the Trinity

The generation is eternal since the Father and the Son are eternal. As Bavinck puts it, "Rejection of the eternal generation of the Son involves not only a failure to do justice to the deity of the Son, but also to that of the Father," for "it is not something that was completed and finished at some point in eternity, but an eternal unchanging act of God, at once always complete and eternally ongoing. . . . The Father is not and never was ungenerative; he begets everlastingly."[85] Since God is eternal and transcends time—which he created—the Trinitarian relations are eternal. There is not a punctiliar moment when the Father begat the Son, for that would place generation within the parameters of space-time and be contrary to its place within the eternal life of the indivisible Trinity.

---
[85] Ibid., 2:310.

Illegitimate Conclusions

Arguing from Human Realities to God: The Arian Method

The Arian argument that human sons are subordinate to their fathers led to their contention that the Son is subordinate to the Father. The church rejected the conclusion as heretical and opposed the premise as mistaken. Rather, the Son is equal with the Father in status, power, and glory. He is identical in being from eternity. In short, to take the created reality as definitive of the life of God is a serious error, leading to dire results.

Subordination

John V. Dahms, in defending eternal generation, argues that it supports the eternal subordination of the Son.[86] He considers that "eternal generation provides the ontological basis for eternal subordination and eternal subordination lends significance to eternal generation."[87] While Dahms qualifies this conclusion by affirming the essential equality of the Father and the Son, he claims that without the Son being eternally subordinate to the Father, the doctrine of eternal generation is superfluous, merely pointing to undefined distinctions.[88] Dahms's preoccupation throughout appears to be an insistence on subordination.

However, the language of subordination entails that the one subordinated has no choice but is subjected by his superior. The subject of active forms of the verb "to subordinate" subordinates another. This could hardly be the case in the Trinity. It was typical of the Arian heresy.

Instead, the idea of *submission* is compatible with an order among the Trinitarian persons and with their equality of status and identity of being. The subject of active forms of the verb "to submit" is a free agent. Submission is a free act among humans. The New Testament sees it as the epitome of godliness; Kevin Giles agrees.[89] We are called to submit to one another (Eph. 5:21), to look to the interests of others

---

[86] John V. Dahms, "The Johannine Use of *Monogenēs* Reconsidered," *New Testament Studies* 29 (1983): 222–32; Dahms, "The Generation of the Son," *JETS* 32 (1989): 493–501; Dahms, "The Subordination of the Son," *JETS* 37 (1994): 351–64.
[87] Dahms, "The Subordination of the Son," 363.
[88] Ibid.
[89] Kevin Giles, *The Trinity and Subordinationism: The Doctrine of God and the Contemporary Gender Debate* (Downers Grove, IL: InterVarsity, 2002), 18, 31, 116–17.

(Phil. 2:1–5), for this is the attitude of Christ. From that it is reasonable to conclude that Christ's life of service is revelatory of who the Son eternally is, and so of the way the three relate to one another in the unity of the indivisible Godhead. This is what God is like. Given that, there is an order—from the Father through the Son by the Holy Spirit—but not one of superior and inferior. Rather, it is an order of equals, in the identity of the indivisible Trinity, including both initiation and submission in loving exocentric union.

Failure to Recognize Personal Distinctions
While all three persons work inseparably in all God's works, each work is attributable peculiarly to one Trinitarian person: only the Son died on the cross, although he offered himself by the Spirit to the Father (Heb. 9:14). This inseparable action should keep us from conceiving of only one person being at work in this or that; talk of "roles" that each of the persons undertakes is potentially misleading. Notwithstanding, the appropriation of a particular work to a particular person should prevent us from confusing the persons, as if the Father died on the cross or the whole Trinity came at Pentecost. This confusion is evident in some attempts by egalitarians in their discussions of the Trinity.

Are Implications for Human Living Possible?
The relation between the Father and the Son is unique. It is more than difficult to draw clear-cut applications to human life. However, humanity was made in the image of God and the Son took human nature into personal union; so while the Creator-creature distinction is paramount, there is also a compatibility between the Son and humans. From this we have some justification for tentative proposals.

Unity and Indivisibility of Being and Equality of the Persons Are Not Undermined by an Order of Personal Subsistence or Economic Mission
It is clear that in terms of deity the Father and the Son are of one being, equal in power and glory, possessing all God's attributes. However, in

terms of personal relations there is a distinction. The Father begets the Son, and the Son is begotten—never the reverse. The Son receives from the Father—never the reverse. The incarnate Son obeys the Father; he is never said to obey the Holy Spirit, although it is clear that the Spirit upheld him throughout his life and ministry. As Calvin said, "To the Father is attributed the beginning of activity, and the fountain and wellspring of all things; to the Son, wisdom, counsel, and the ordered disposition of all things; but to the Spirit is assigned the power and efficacy of that activity."[90] And again, "For in each hypostasis the whole divine nature is understood, with this qualification—that to each belongs his own peculiar quality."[91] So "when we speak simply of the Son without regard to the Father, we well and properly declare him to be of himself; and for this reason we call him the sole beginning. But when we mark the relation that he has with the Father, we rightly make the Father the beginning of the Son."[92] And

> because the peculiar qualities in the persons carry an order with them, e.g., in the Father is the beginning and the source, so often as mention is made of the Father and the Son together, or the Spirit, the name of *God* is peculiarly applied to the Father. In this way, unity of essence is retained, and a reasoned order is kept, which yet takes nothing away from the deity of the Son and the Spirit.[93]

An Order in Human Relationships Does Not in Itself Entail a Breakdown in Ontological Unity and Equality

It follows from this that identity of nature and equality of status are compatible with an order. If this is so in the eternal God, it cannot be illegitimate in humanity, his creature. However, here as well there are grave dangers lurking on both sides. Abuse of one person over another, wherever it occurs, is an offense against the unity of the race, made in the image of God. This can occur in any context: in ethnic contexts, in religious contexts, or in relationships between men and women.

---

[90] John Calvin, *Institutes of the Christian Religion*, ed. John T. McNeill, trans. Ford Lewis Battles (Philadelphia: Westminster Press, 1960), 1.13.18.
[91] Ibid., 1.13.19.
[92] Ibid.
[93] Ibid., 1.13.20.

We could—very loosely—characterize it as a subordinationist or even tritheist error.

On the other hand, blurring of the distinctions in humanity between male and female is akin to a modalist error. Unity trumps diversity; order is set aside and distinctions are flattened. If God's revelation of himself in human history as the Father, the Son, and the Spirit did not reflect who he is but was merely a set of roles akin to those performed by an actor, singularities not indicative of who he is, we would have no true knowledge of God. Furthermore, if there were no differentiations between the Trinitarian persons in God's works, the result would be confusion akin to patripassianism, in which the Father is said to have died on the cross.

6

True Sonship—Where Dignity and Submission Meet

A Fourth-Century Discussion

MICHAEL J. OVEY

> Therefore, if God existed, only in one way could he serve human liberty—by ceasing to exist.
>
> Mikhail Bakunin, *God and the State*, 1871

"Arians" are the people in black hats.[1] Arian positions were anathematized by the church from AD 325 onward, and Arianism is rightly seen as fatal for Christian belief. Peter Adam notes that by applying the term to opponents now, one implies "they are not Christians at all."[2] The battle against Arianism has epic status in the church's history,[3] and later generations have sometimes used it as a framework to interpret

---
[1] Arian theology developed over the fourth century, and had significant variations, but a central principle is that the Son is a creature, albeit an exalted one and with a unique mode of creation, but still, ultimately, a creature. Hence the immense significance of the Nicene Creed's asserting that the Son is "begotten not made." Athanasius of Alexandria catches the Nicene thought aptly: "If He is a Son, He is not a creature; but if a creature, then not a Son" (*De synodis* 36). The flagship Arian text is the Septuagint of Prov. 8:22, κύριος ἔκτισέν με, which was construed as "the Lord created me."
[2] Peter Adam, "Honouring Jesus Christ," *Churchman* 119, no. 1 (2005): 35.
[3] Note the title of Maurice Wiles's *Archetypal Heresy: Arianism through the Centuries* (Oxford: Clarendon, 1996).

their own struggles and thus to work out who really are the people in black hats in their own time.[4]

This means there is enormous freight in laying the charge of Arianism against Trinitarian positions which hold that the Son is subject to the Father.[5] The charge necessarily implies that those holding to an ordinal relationship in which the Son is subject are heretics.[6] Of course, serious recent scholars on Arianism note the dangers in theologians' today using this particular ancient term to discredit current opponents.[7] However, this does not mean the charge is never rightly made.[8] Is the charge rightly made here? If so, the ordinal submission of the Son *must* be rejected.

Before answering, we must be clear what the charge precisely is. Reference has been made to the ordinal or relational superordination of the Father and correlative submission of the Son. It is, though, common ground in this debate that the Bible does indeed speak of the obedience of the Lord Jesus Christ (e.g., John 14:31; Phil. 2:8). However, Kevin Giles and others interpret this obedience as restricted to the incarnate human Jesus.[9] Obedience is only in the humanity.[10] This means that the precise question runs, Is it necessarily Arian to assert that the eternal relationship of the Father and Son is one of superordination and submission respectively?

The answer is no.

---

[4] For example, John Henry Newman's use of the Arian struggle to interpret the debates of his own day.
[5] Particularly vociferous along these lines in recent years have been Kevin Giles (e.g., Giles, "Father and Son: Divided or Undivided in Power and Authority?" [paper presented at the annual meeting of the Evangelical Theological Society, Washington, DC, November 16, 2006]) and the former archbishop of Perth, Peter Carnley (e.g., Carnley, *Reflections in Glass* [Sydney: HarperCollins, 2004]). Peter Adam, in "Honouring Jesus Christ," feels that Carnley's charge is playing ecclesiastical politics, but even so the charge must be considered and answered.
[6] This essay employs terms in the range of *subject*, *obey*, and *submission* to describe the relationships under discussion. Obviously, these can be emotive terms. They are adopted here not to provoke but because they best represent the original terms in the Patristic material we shall examine, namely, the ὑποτάσσω word group in Athanasius of Alexandria's account and the *subicio* and *obsequor* word groups in Hilary of Poitiers's accounts. They are also the translations used in the well-known *NPNF* series.
[7] Thus Rowan Williams, *Arius, Heresy and Tradition* (London: Dartman, Longman and Todd, 1987), is critical of Newman's appropriation of the Arian controversy.
[8] Thus many see the Jehovah's Witness movement precisely as contemporary Arianism.
[9] Adam, "Honouring Jesus Christ," 38, summarizes Giles's position thus: "Giles' basic claim is clear. It is that no 'subordination' of any kind will be found in the operations of the Triune God, except that in the Incarnation the human Jesus is subordinate to the Father."
[10] It is beyond the scope of this chapter to consider whether this formulation so separates the divine from the human that it undermines the hypostatic union and is to that extent "Nestorianizing." Clearly, the fourth-century pro-Nicene theologians do distinguish between things done by the Son through his human nature (eating, dying, etc.) and things done through his divine nature; the question is whether this is rightly applied to the matter of whether the person, the Son, can be said to obey.

This chapter contributes to that answer by examining some Patristic evidence. Part of the evidence comes from significant creedal and confessional material in the period 340–365, and part from three anti-Arian theologians of that period: Athanasius of Alexandria, Hilary of Poitiers, and Basil of Ancyra.[11]

This period is central. If one wants to know what counts as Arianism, then an obvious place to look is this period, when the historical controversy took place and the arguments were being crystallized. This period is of particular import because the creed known as the Sirmium *Blasphemia* (357) falls within it. This creed, or "manifesto,"[12] significantly focused the real issues between the plethora of theological positions that had existed since 325. R. P. C. Hanson puts it thus: "It enabled everybody to see where they stood. At last the confusion which caused Westerners to regard Easterners as Arians can be cleared up. This is an Arian creed. Those who support it are Arians. Those who are repelled by it are not."[13] This means that reactions to the subordinationism that the *Blasphemia* contains will have sharper focus.[14]

Now, the Sirmium *Blasphemia* unquestionably sees the Son as subject to the Father.[15] Further, anti-Arian theologians unquestionably see the *Blasphemia* as Arian. But is this submission section in the *Blasphemia* part of what made the *Blasphemia* obnoxious to the anti-Arians? Or did the *Blasphemia*'s critics themselves have a submission understanding? And if so, why did they think that was not *necessarily* Arian? To answer these questions we must examine creedal and confessional material from the period other than the *Blasphemia*,[16] as well as the writings of key anti-Arian theologians who react to it.

Four further introductory comments are necessary. First, as a cau-

---

[11] Of these, Athanasius and Hilary are strongly Nicene, while Basil of Ancyra is often seen as semi-Arian, but definitely opposed to full Arianism.
[12] Both Lewis Ayres, *Nicaea and Its Legacy: An Approach to Fourth-Century Trinitarian Theology* (Oxford: Oxford University Press, 2004), 137, and R. P. C. Hanson, *The Search for the Christian Doctrine of God: The Arian Controversy 318–381* (Edinburgh: T&T Clark, 1988), 347, use the term "manifesto" to describe the Sirmium Creed of 357.
[13] Hanson, *The Search*, 347. For similar evaluations of the Sirmium *Blasphemia*, see Ayres, *Nicaea and Its Legacy*, 137ff., and Carl L. Beckwith, *Hilary of Poitiers on the Trinity: From* De Fide *to* De Trinitate (Oxford: Oxford University Press, 2008), 56. Key evidence for this view occurs in Hilary of Poitiers, who notes that Eastern and Western bishops were united in their condemnation of the *Blasphemia* (*De synodis* 2–3).
[14] Arianism was to develop further after 357 into still more obvious forms, but the *Blasphemia* remains a watershed.
[15] The relevant section is quoted below.
[16] Creedal material is significant because it represents something formulated with some kind of consent. Valuable as, for example, Athanasius's writings are, they are first and foremost his, not a conciliar product.

tion, we must remember that the debate from the late 350s increasingly focused on whether *ousia* language could properly be used in relation to God. The superordination of the Father was not the immediate issue. Care should be taken over imposing anachronistic questions onto the fourth-century debate, especially when presuppositions about the legitimacy or otherwise of power and authority can be so very different in our own era.[17] Second, as a related point, Arianism was not the only erroneous Trinitarian theology that the orthodox needed to combat in this period. Varieties of Sabellianism remained real threats.[18] Third, restraint must be exercised over constructing arguments merely from fourth-century silence. Fourth, Giles and others rightly see much at stake here, especially concerning our understanding of the relationship between love and authority: those arguing for the superordination of the Father envisage not merely that true love and legitimate authority can coexist, but that they are in fact inseparable in the Father's relation to his Son.[19] Thus, just as Giles and Carnley fear Arianism, so those arguing for the superordination of the Father have their own theological fear, that the non-superordination case distorts and disfigures the eternal love between Father and Son. These are high stakes.

Creedal and Confessional Material

The creedal and confessional material we will examine shows that, overall, Arian, Nicene, and non-Nicene sources alike commonly held to the submission of the Son outside the incarnation.[20] However the material also shows that the Son's submission may be grounded differ-

---

[17] What one might call cynicism about power has a long history. Thus the Sophists of the fifth century BC did pose the question of whether justice was simply the interest of the stronger (see the character Thrasymachus in Plato's *Republic*, bk. 1). However, the postmodern turn of our own period, especially under the influence of Friedrich Nietzsche and Michel Foucault, gives a wide and strong antiauthoritarian flavor to the current cultural West.

[18] The name Sabellius was associated with the Trinitarian heresy of modalism, the idea that there is only one person in the godhead, who appears in three different guises or characters. During the mid-fourth century, Marcellus was held by many Easterners to have a Sabellian account of the relations between Father and Son, as was Photinus, against whom at least one creed was aimed.

[19] Obvious areas of impact include the Open Theism theology associated with Clark Pinnock (who does tend to see true love and authority as mutually opposed), as well as the nature of the Son's lordship and relations between humans in family, state, and church. Jürgen Moltmann rightly stresses that there are implications from Trinitarian theology for these sets of relationships between humans, but does so from an egalitarian standpoint.

[20] The idea of "non-Nicene" as a theological position that is not opposed to but is independent of the Nicene formula is helpfully used by Ayres (e.g., *Nicaea and Its Legacy*, 139). While independent of the Nicene formula, a non-Nicene position is not necessarily Arian. It might, of course, be seen as that or as insensitive to the Arian question.

ently, with Arian versions of submission being associated with the Son as creature, while others stress that the Son's submission arises from his sonship and not from being a creature.

The material we will look at comprises the Dedication Creed (341), the Encyclical of Serdica (343), the Macrostich (345), the First Creed of Sirmium (351), and the Second Sirmium Creed, the *Blasphemia* of 357. This covers Eastern and Western perspectives, as well as pro-Nicene, Arian, and non-Nicene material.

The Second Antioch Creed (the "Dedication" Creed), 341

In 341 a new church was dedicated in Antioch, built under the auspices of the emperor, Constantius. This offered the Eastern bishops gathered there the opportunity to restate their own theological position.[21] There was some need for this since the Westerner Pope Julius had recently vindicated two bishops from the East who had been deposed, Athanasius of Alexandria and Marcellus of Ancyra.[22] A number of creedal documents were produced, notably the Second or Dedication Creed.[23] It has several interesting features.

First, it does not exactly reproduce the language of Nicaea 325, which insisted that the Son is born of the Father's essence.[24] Nor does it employ *homoousios* terminology. Essence language is used, but, differing slightly from Nicaea, the Son is "unable to change or alter, the unvarying image of the *essence* and might and glory of the Godhead."[25]

Second, there is material that could suggest the superordination of the Father.[26] The creed describes the Son as "the Mediator between

---

[21] Athanasius, who was understandably incensed by his treatment by his Eastern fellow bishops, speaks of their need to write something "since they were in general and lasting odium for their heresy" (*De synodis* 22). No doubt the presence of Constantius, his least favorite emperor, would not have thrilled him either.
[22] Ayres, *Nicaea and Its Legacy*, 117. It is easy to underestimate the difficulties created by the Western reception of Marcellus. Unlike Athanasius, Marcellus had been deposed for unorthodoxy. The unorthodoxy apparently related to positions over the divine unity that had Sabellian or monarchian overtones. Franz Dünzl, *A Brief History of the Doctrine of the Trinity in the Early Church* (London: T&T Clark, 2007), 65, remarks, "We can understand why the Nicene Creed was discredited for so many years, since Marcellus was one of its most ardent champions!" The outline of Marcellus's theology in ibid., 65–69, is succinct and helpful.
[23] Both Athanasius and Hilary refer to it in their respective works entitled *De synodis*, suggesting its importance, as Ayres rightly concludes (*Nicaea and Its Legacy*, 118).
[24] See Ayres, *Nicaea and Its Legacy*, 120.
[25] Hilary, *De synodis* 29 (emphasis added).
[26] The First Creed of Antioch, formulated on the same occasion but earlier than the Dedication Creed, also contains material that could suggest the subordination of the Son. It speaks of the Son who "fulfilled his Father's will" (quoted by Athanasius, *De synodis* 22). The Fourth Creed does not have material referring explicitly to the Father's will.

God and man" and then explains this: "For He said, *I came down from heaven, not to do Mine own will, but the will of Him that sent me* [John 6:38 KJV]."

Further material in an ordinal direction comes at the end of the creed,[27] where the baptismal formula of Matthew 28:19 is quoted:

> Our Lord Jesus Christ ordained His disciples, saying, *Go ye, and teach all nations, baptizing them in the name of the Father, and of the Son, and of the Holy Ghost*, manifestly, that is, of a Father who is truly Father, and clearly of a Son who is truly Son, and a Holy Ghost who is truly a Holy Ghost, these words not being set forth idly and without meaning, but carefully signifying the Person, and order [translating *ordo* in Hilary, *De synodis* 29 and τάξις in Athanasius, *De synodis* 23], and glory of each of those who are named, to teach us that they are three Persons, but in agreement one.

Now the reference to doing the Father's will, from John 6:38, could refer to obedience only during the incarnation. After all, John 6:38 is cited at a point where the Dedication Creed has the incarnation in view. Matthew 28:19, though, is explained in terms of the order and glory of each person. "Order" could suggest an eternal superordination of the Father more strongly, but the alternative of a purely incarnational superordination is not impossible.

Overall the creed's agenda is against Sabellianism, and probably, given the historical circumstances, the deposed Bishop Marcellus.[28] Hilary sees the creed in anti-Sabellian terms,[29] although Athanasius sees it rather as "Arian."[30] This may reflect later unhappy developments. The creed contains much a pro-Nicene could agree with, particularly the idea of Father, Son, and Spirit being truly Father, truly Son, and truly Spirit. This is critical, as will become apparent later. Equally, Arian sympathizers could endorse the creed. Thus the creed covers disparate theologies "that eventually followed separate paths."[31] The creed's vice,

---

[27] See Dünzl, *A Brief History*, 76.
[28] It is easy to forget how important Marcellus of Ancyra was and what disquiet he excited in the East. The West's reception of him was bound to make Easterners suspicious.
[29] *De synodis* 32; although he is acutely alive to the creed's potential inadequacies in speaking of the persons' "being in agreement one" (31). Such language has ready precedent in Origen, but obviously Arius would be quite happy with a unity between Father and Son that was *only* of agreement.
[30] Ayres, *Nicaea and Its Legacy*, 121.
[31] Ibid.

perhaps, for a pro-Nicene was precisely that it did not clearly enough exclude Arians. This, though, does not mean the creed was intended by all to be a stalking horse for Arians.[32] It is easy to forget how an Eastern bishop might retort that the Nicene Creed was defective because Marcellus could subscribe to it.[33]

This means that the Dedication Creed, while not clearly excluding all forms of Arianism, contains some material suggesting the superordination of the Father. As with other issues, though, the creed is not clear whether this is a purely incarnational superordination.

The Serdica Encyclical, 343

Obviously, a creed that did not clearly exclude Arians was unlikely to win over supporters of Athanasius and Marcellus. The encyclical issued at Serdica is therefore very important for our purposes because of who composed it. Its composers (largely anti-Arians) did have the Arian question at the front of their minds;[34] by this time they were (understandably) suspicious of Arian sophistry; they had a relatively free hand, given the withdrawal from the council of various bishops holding sees within Emperor Constantius's sphere of influence;[35] and they had before them the Dedication Creed with its seeming superordination language. Would these highly sensitive anti-Arians react to this?

The document is indeed strongly anti-Arian and understands Arianism very broadly. Ayres wryly remarks, "'Arianism' is also defined in such broad terms that almost any theology which was willing to insist on there being more than one *hypostasis* was in error."[36] In accordance with this program, the encyclical insists that the Son belongs on the Creator side of the Creator-creature divide. The Son is indeed begotten,

---

[32] So Dünzl, *A Brief History*, 77, whose judgment is supported by the way the First Creed of Antioch distances the bishops from being followers of Arius. The cynical might feel, though, that lack of clarity remains.
[33] Dünzl perceptively remarks, "The second Antiochene formula had nothing to do with the Nicene Creed; rather, it was to be a substitute for this creed which had been discredited by the teaching of Marcellus" (Ibid.).
[34] We recall Hilary's argument that the Dedication Creed was addressing those who "presumed to attribute the three names to the Father" (*De synodis* 32), i.e., Sabellians.
[35] These might have been expected to argue more strongly for a Dedication Creed approach. They refused to attend, given the presence of Marcellus and Athanasius, whom they regarded as duly deposed. See Dünzl, *A Brief History*, 80.
[36] Ayres, *Nicaea and Its Legacy*, 125, citing Thomas A. Kopecek, *A History of Neo-Arianism*, vol. 1 (Philadelphia: Philadelphia Patristic Foundation, 1979), 85: Serdica "issued an encyclical which defined Arianism so broadly that nearly every easterner who had ever heard of Origen was considered Arian."

but not begotten as a creature.[37] The encyclical is sensitive to charges of Sabellianism:

> We do not say that the Father is Son nor that the Son is Father. But the Father is Father and the Son is Son of the Father. We confess that the Son is the power of the Father. We confess the Logos of God the Father, alongside whom there is no other, and this Logos as true God, wisdom and power. We teach him as true Son.[38]

We should note the fruitful way the notion of true Son appears in this anti-Sabellian section. A true son cannot be his own father.[39] But "true Son" is exactly a category shared with the Dedication Creed.

However, the next question is whether the anti-Arian program of the Serdica Encyclical extends to objecting to superordination language. On the contrary, Serdica endorses superordination language: "None (of us) ever denies the statement: 'The Father is greater than I' [John 14:28]—but that does not apply to another hypostasis or any difference but (only) because the name of the Father is in itself greater than that of the Son."[40]

Three comments should be made. First, Ayres and Dünzl both suggest that the Father and Son are not adequately differentiated or individuated.[41] Such personal distinction or individuation as there is revolves around the idea of "name." Naturally, this must be taken with the earlier statement that the Son is a true son (and hence the Father a true father). The name conveys a reality.[42] Second, one cannot say that being "greater" here is restricted to the incarnation. It cannot be restricted to the incarnation because what is in view is the eternal relationship between the one who is eternally Father and the one who is eternally Son. The Son did not start to be Son at the incarnation. The Arian controversy primarily occurs with regard to that relationship. Third, an egalitarian explanation might stress that, at this stage, what

---

[37] The obvious comparison is with Nicaea's "begotten not made."
[38] Using the text and translation of Dünzl, *A Brief History*, 82. Dünzl is relying on the text and German translation of J. Ulrich, *Die Anfänge der abendländischen Rezeption des Nizänums* (Berlin: de Gruyter, 1994).
[39] As Tertullian had long ago observed in his anti-Sabellian work *Against Praxeas*.
[40] Dünzl, *A Brief History*, 83.
[41] Ayres, *Nicaea and Its Legacy*, 125; and Dünzl, *A Brief History*, 83.
[42] This is a standard position for Nicene theologians, but it is developed with great force by Hilary. Note his statement in *De Trinitate* 1.27: "It is the easiest of tasks, after demonstrating His right to the Name of Son, to shew [sic] that the Name truly describes His relation to the Father."

it is to be "greater" is not explicitly spelled out in terms of submission and obedience.

That said, the Serdica material shows that a strongly anti-Arian council, with a very broad understanding of what amounted to Arianism, did not balk at such sentiments as the Dedication Creed apparently holds. Rather it accepted some species of superordination of the Father precisely in the eternal relationship. It is not clear, of course, what that superordination might comprise.

The Macrostich ("Long-Lined" Creed), 345

It is unsurprising that, in the circumstances, the Serdica Encyclical was not universally accepted. Not only was Marcellus present, but the Serdica material bears traces of his theology.[43] Anti-Arians might protest that the Dedication Creed was not sufficiently exclusive, but anti-Marcellans might feel the same about Serdica.

Nevertheless, the need for rapprochement was increasingly apparent, and Eastern bishops proposed the Macrostich.[44] It is important to remember that the Macrostich was intended to reassure Westerners that Eastern bishops were orthodox.[45] Plausibly, then, the Macrostich would try to allay rather than inflame concerns about Arianism. With that in mind, two sections speak very strikingly of the Son's subordination. These sections occur in the commentaries on two of the creed's anathemas.

Thus the fourth anathema condemns those who say "that Christ is not God." The commentary on it states, "For we acknowledge, that *though He be subordinate to His Father and God*,[46] yet, being before ages begotten of God, He is God perfect according to nature and true, and not first man and then God, but first God and then becoming man for us, and never having been deprived of being."

The intention here is to support the anathema condemning those who deny that Christ is God. The phrase "perfect according to nature

---

[43] Dünzl, *A Brief History*, 84: "All in all, one cannot disguise the overwhelming influence of Marcellus of Ancyra on the creed of Serdica." In the circumstances, this is not a compliment.
[44] Preserved in Athanasius, *De synodis* 26.
[45] The creed concludes, "Thus much, in addition to the faith before published in epitome, we have been compelled to draw forth at length, not in any officious display, but to clear away all unjust suspicion concerning our opinions . . ." The language of "Eastern" and "Western" is in the original. Ayres, *Nicaea and Its Legacy*, 129, speaks of a "conciliatory tone."
[46] In Athanasius, *De synodis* 26, the phrase is ὑποτέτακται τῷ πατρί καὶ θεῷ (emphasis added).

and true" supports the Son's deity, and the phrase "never having been deprived of being" means the Son cannot be a creature. Yet the Macrostich's framers do not see the Son's subjection as inconsistent with their high account of his divinity. We must note, though, the context of that subjection. It is "to his Father and God." This opens the door to understanding the subjection within the context of the eternal Father-Son relationship. The subjection is emphatically not that of creature to Creator, for the Son is not a creature.

The second relevant section occurs in the commentary on the seventh anathema, which condemns those who say "that the Son is Ingenerate; or that the Father begat the Son, not by choice or will." The original concern here is twofold. First, the Son must not be seen as a "Twin" of the Father, which would be the inference from stating that both Father and Son were ingenerate. They would not then be distinguishable.[47] Second, there is a fear that if one says that the Father did not beget by will, then he was under an external constraint.

The commentary reads:

> Believing then in the All-perfect Triad, the most Holy, that is, in the Father, and the Son, and the Holy Ghost, and calling the Father God, and the Son God, yet we confess in them, not two Gods, but one dignity of Godhead, and one exact harmony of dominion, *the Father alone being Head over the whole universe wholly, and over the Son Himself, and the Son subordinated to the Father*[48] but, excepting Him, ruling over all things after Him which through Himself have come to be, and granting the grace of the Holy Ghost unsparingly to the saints at the Father's will. For that such is the account of the Divine Monarchy towards Christ, the sacred oracles have delivered to us.

We should note how central divine cosmic monarchy is. For Athanasius there is no real God without divine cosmic monarchy.[49] Likewise, Tertullian had earlier stressed divine monarchy as the Father's monarchy in which the Son shared as Son.[50] The significance of asserting di-

---

[47] Their characteristics would be identical, so that, while individual, each person would not be unique. One would be interchangeable with another.
[48] The phrase "and the Son subordinated to the Father" translates τοῦ δὲ υἱοῦ ὑποτεταγμένου τῷ πατρί (Athanasius, *De synodis* 26 [emphasis added]).
[49] Notably *Contra Gentes* 6.
[50] Tertullian stresses that there is one divine and undivided rule, and the Son has no independent dominion (no *alia dominatio*), because he is given authority by his Father (*Against Praxeas* 4).

vine monarchy is in the context of asserting that there is only one God. The Son is therefore explicitly subject to the Father, although—in a key anti-Arian stance—the Son belongs on the Creator side of the Creator-creature divide, for he rules over all he has made.

This material, in a document attempting to lay to rest fears about Arianism, clearly does see the eternal Father-Son relationship in super-/subordination terms, and does so in relation to the stock idea of divine monarchy. If anything, the Macrostich develops and intensifies the subjection themes of the Dedication and Serdica Creeds. There are, though, two kinds of subjection at stake here. One is the subjection of the Son to the Father, who is his head.[51] The other subjection is that of creatures to their Creator. It is far from easy to reconcile the Macrostich statements with the idea that the Son's subjection is purely for the incarnation, or that it is without authoritative content.

The First Creed of Sirmium, 351

Unfortunately, the opportunity provided by the Macrostich was not grasped,[52] though this was not because of misgivings about the two sections reproduced above. We turn next to the First Creed of Sirmium,[53] not to be confused with the *Blasphemia* of 357. The First Sirmium Creed was aimed not primarily at the Arian question, but rather at the theology of Photinus of Sirmium.[54]

We need here to examine the seventeenth anathema of the Sirmium Creed, which reads:[55]

> If any man says that the Lord and the Lord, the Father and the Son are two Gods, because of the aforesaid words: let him be anathema. *For we do not make the Son the equal or peer of the Father, but*

---

[51] It is not possible to explore here possible implications this may have for exegeting the use of "head" in 1 Cor. 11:3. Suffice it to say that "head" here occurs in the context of dominion, and the Father is not the "source" of the cosmos in the same way that he is the "source" of the Son. The Arian controversy turns precisely on the point that origination by creation is not the same as origination by begetting.
[52] For detail, see Ayres, *Nicaea and Its Legacy*, 129.
[53] Recorded by Athanasius in his *De synodis* 27 and by Hilary in his *De synodis* 38.
[54] Photinus is associated with the theology of Marcellus of Ancyra; see Ayres, *Nicaea and Its Legacy*, 134. That Photinus was not the originator of his heresy is suggested by Hilary's comment (*De synodis* 39) that the Sirmium proceedings were necessary "because the heresy which Photinus *was reviving* was sapping our Catholic home by many secret mines" (emphasis added).
[55] This follows Hilary's enumeration of the first Sirmium anathemas. The anathema quoted is numbered 18 in Athanasius, *De synodis* 38.

understand the Son to be subject.[56] For He did not come down to Sodom without the Father's will, nor rain from Himself but *from the Lord*, to wit by the Father's authority; nor does He sit at the Father's right hand by His own authority, but He hears the Father saying, *Sit thou on My right hand*.

Again, the Son's subjection is explicit, and, as with the Macrostich seventh anathema, the context is the denial that there are two Gods. The Son acts on the Father's authority, and his reign is established by his Father's command (thus the quotation of Ps. 110:1). The subjection of the Son cannot be restricted to the incarnation, because the example cited is the destruction of Sodom and Gomorrah in Genesis 19:24. The biblical text reads: "Then the LORD rained on Sodom and Gomorrah sulfur and fire from the LORD out of heaven" (NRSV).

The obvious difficulty here is how to understand the double reference to "the LORD," a difficulty underlined by the use of the covenant name in both instances. The First Sirmium Creed takes the first occurrence as referring to the Son, and the second occurrence as referring to the Father.[57]

To state the obvious, Sodom and Gomorrah were destroyed before the incarnation. So, if the Son is obedient to the Father in Genesis 19:24, his obedience cannot purely be in his human nature.

It would be tempting to retort that the First Sirmium Creed is simply exegetically wrong on Genesis 19:24. This, though, misses the point. Even if the creed's framers wrongly exegeted this verse,[58] they clearly thought that the Son's subjection to his Father did not deny the Son's divinity.[59] This suggests that the framers of the First Sirmium Creed did not think it was a contradiction to have a fully divine Son subjected to his Father. It also means that explaining obedience purely through the humanity assumed in the incarnation would not meet their understanding of the biblical material. Further, this subjection in Genesis 19:24 is

---

[56] The clause "*For we do not make the Son the equal or peer of the Father, but understand the Son to be subject*" (emphasis added), translates Athanasius, *De synodis* 27, οὐ γὰρ συντάσσομεν υἱὸν τῷ πατρί, ἀλλ' ὑποτεταγμένον τῷ πατρί, and Hilary, *De synodis* 38, "Non enim exaequamus vel comparamus Filium Patri, sed subjectum intelligimus."
[57] Anathema 16 (17 in Athanasius, *De synodis* 38) of the First Creed reads, "If any man does not understand *The Lord rained from the Lord* to be spoken of the Father and the Son, but that the Father rained from Himself: let him be anathema. For the Lord the Son rained from the Lord the Father."
[58] In fact, this is a quite usual Patristic exegesis of Gen. 19:24.
[59] Anathemas 1 and 3 place the Son on the Creator side of the Creator-created divide.

understood, put simply, as the Son's obeying the Father's will. Obviously one might retort that the First Sirmium Creed is in fact "Arianizing" (possibly unintentionally). This means that we must examine responses to it, but first we must revisit the Sirmium *Blasphemia*.

The Second Sirmium Creed (the Blasphemia*), 357*

We have already outlined the "landmark" significance of the *Blasphemia*. It is important to remember, though, that while the *Blasphemia* indeed opposed the Nicene formula,[60] it also stood against the Dedication Creed.[61] Hence it clarified who was and who was not an Arian. Both pro-Nicenes and "non-Nicenes"[62] were treated as defective by the *Blasphemia*. The relevant section reads:

> There is no question that the Father is greater. No one can doubt that the Father is greater than the Son in honour, dignity, splendour, majesty, and in the very name of Father, the Son Himself testifying, *He that sent Me is greater than I. And no one is ignorant that it is Catholic doctrine that there are two Persons of Father and Son; and that the Father is greater, and that the Son is subordinated to the Father, together with all things which the Father has subordinated to Him.*[63]

We can now see that the *Blasphemia* was not at all unusual in containing material relating to the Son's subordination; earlier Eastern and Western documents have this theme. Nor is it unusual to place this subjection material in the context of denying that there are two Gods. Divine monarchy is an important theological value across the spectrum, Nicene, non-Nicene, Arian, and, indeed, Sabellian.

What is unusual compared with earlier material is to bracket the subjection of the Son along with subjection of all things to the Father. Such phrasing repays attention.[64] It suggests that the Son is subject *in*

---

[60] Evidenced starkly in its outlawing of discussion using *ousia* terminology.
[61] Hanson, *The Search*, 347, says that the creed "attacks [the Nicene formula], no longer covertly, but directly and openly, as it also attacks the Dedication Creed of 341."
[62] I'm using again Ayres's helpful term for a position that is independent of the Nicene formula, but does not repudiate it (Ayres, *Nicaea and Its Legacy*).
[63] As quoted by Hilary, *De synodis* 11 (emphasis added). Athanasius's account is found in his *De synodis* 28 and differs little at this point. The phrase "the Son is subordinated to the Father" translates *filium subiectum* (Hilary, *De synodis* 11) and τὸν δὲ υἱὸν ὑποτεταγμένον τῷ πατρί (Athanasius, *De synodis* 28).
[64] See the very percipient footnote 5389 of the *NPNF*² translation of Athanasius, *De synodis*.

the same kind of way as created things. This implies that in the Creator-creature divide, the Son stands on the side of the creatures: the classic Arian position.[65]

Here, then, we probably do have a subordinationist statement that is genuinely Arian. This matters because it shows that the fears expressed by Giles, Carnley, and others are not *always* groundless: some types of subordination are Arian in this crucial sense: that they treat the Son as a creature. The next question is whether after the crystallization the *Blasphemia* created, those opposing it would see *all* species of subordination as treating the Son as a creature.

Responses to the "Arianizing" Thought of the *Blasphemia*

In fact, the anti-Arian theologians we shall examine show that subordination, if based on the Father-Son relationship, is orthodox, even though those theologians have to react to the *Blasphemia*, among other things. For all three the idea of true Son is central.[66] This is not a theological speculation but something they construe the biblical revelation as emphasizing. In fact, this idea is critical to the anti-Arian project. Its source lies in the biblical material, notably the Gospel of John, in which Jesus's sonship is a vital issue that precipitates opposition to Jesus, and does so on the grounds of blasphemy.[67] This insistence on true sonship earlier grounded the Nicene formula that to be begotten is not the same as being made. Arianism is deficient because it fails to see the Son as true Son since it treats him as a creature.

Basil of Ancyra

The critical move that Basil makes in his reaction to the *Blasphemia* is the distinction between a Father-Son relationship and a Creator-creature relationship. Basil writes: "We have therefore believed in a Father, a Son and a Holy Spirit not in a creator and a creature. For 'creator and

---

[65] This is reinforced by the way the attributes of being without beginning, invisibility, immortality, and impassibility are predicated of the Father, but there is a pointed silence over whether the Son enjoys these.
[66] We have already seen that the non-Arian creedal material relies on "true Son" ideas.
[67] In particular, see John 5:18; 10:30–39; 19:7. Indeed, on the Arian account that the Son claims only to be a creature, it is hard to see how the charge of blasphemy would arise, especially in the form given in John 10:33.

creature' are one thing but 'father and son' are another, since these two concepts differ in meaning."[68] Basil develops this distinction between the two kinds of relationship with some sophistication. He needs to do this since on any view notions of physicality need to be abstracted from the two kinds of relationship if one is to compare them fittingly with respect to God. Even if the second person is a Son, his sonship is not exactly on all fours with human sonship.

Thus with regard to the Creator-creature relationship, Basil comments that "a creature is made by an impassible creator and is perfect, stable and as its creator intended."[69] Whereas for the Father-Son relationship, once physical passion has been abstracted, "only the generation of a living being of like essence will be left—for every 'father' is understood to be the father of an essence like his."[70] Basil uses this distinction between the two types of relationship vigorously, precisely in order to stop the Son from being reduced to a creature, even if a unique creature.

However, after this analysis, Basil turns his thoughts to authority in the Father-Son relationship. He writes,

> And if anyone says that the Father is the Father of the only begotten Son by authority only, and not the Father of the only-begotten Son by authority and essence alike—thus accepting only the authority, equating the Son with any creature, and denying that he is actually the true Son of the Father—let him be anathema.[71]

This repays close attention. Basil's point is that there is authority in the Father-Son relation, but also a fatherhood based on essence, in which the Son is like in essence to his Father. To assert authority *only*, without the likeness of essence, would be to reduce the Son to a creature. That, then, would be an account of the Father's authority that was Arian precisely because it amounted to "equating the Son with any creature." Basil does recognize that some accounts of the Father's authority can

---

[68] Reproduced in Epiphanius of Salamis, *Panarion* 73.3.4. Epiphanius views Basil as defective since he is a "semi-Arian."
[69] Ibid., 73.3.8. Basil stresses the impassibility of the Creator, but the contingency of the creature as something that exists purely according to its Creator's will. Compare Rev. 4:11 for the contingency of creatures as dependent on God's will.
[70] Ibid., 73.4.2. Later, Hilary will argue in *De synodis* that "like essence" can only be understood in an innocent sense if it is taken as "of the same essence," i.e., as *homoousios*. See also Athanasius's argument in his *De synodis*.
[71] Epiphanius, *Panarion* 73.11.9.

become Arian, but not that all are. The implication is that there is a proper place for authority in the relationship between Father and Son.

Athanasius of Alexandria

True sonship forms an important part of Athanasius's response to Arianism.[72] In particular he uses true sonship to show that the Son is not a creature. For Athanasius the two relations are mutually exclusive.[73] However, Athanasius obviously envisages differences between human sonship and divine sonship. For instance, divine sonship is incorporeal and without passion.[74]

Clearly, the next question is whether Athanasius thinks that a relation of superordination-submission between the Father and the Son is an area where human and divine fatherhood differ. Athanasius has two very instructive lines of thought that bear on this and indicate that he does not think human and divine fatherhood differ on this point.[75]

THE LANGUAGE OF "SERVANT" APPLIED TO SONS

First, Athanasius observes that the Bible applies "servant" language to both human sons and the eternal Son. He knows and accepts that sons can be called servants by their fathers. Thus in *Contra Arianos* 2.3, while discussing the distinction between "begotten" and "made," he recounts that fathers do call their sons servants. He explains that this comes "from their authority as being fathers."[76] It does not imply a difference of nature. Therefore Athanasius sees that a natural human father has authority over his son. This authority arises from the paternal relationship. Paternity, therefore, has two applications in Athanasius's argument: first, it allows him to assert identity of nature (humans beget humans); second, it also allows him to explain "servant" language as a consequence of this same relationship.

---

[72] Although his use of the idea is not restricted to directly anti-Arian polemic. It is present in both *Contra Gentes* 46 and *De incarnatione* 32.
[73] See, e.g., *Contra Arianos* 2.3, picking up the "begotten not made" distinction of the Nicene Creed.
[74] "Passion" in the sense of a bodily desire that masters one. Divine impassibility does not, for Athanasius, mean God does not love.
[75] The material is taken from the *Contra Arianos* discourses, composed over the period 356–360. Conceivably some of this material may predate the *Blasphemia*, but Athanasius's arguments after the *Blasphemia* remain similar, although in later years he works hard at establishing common ground with those holding to "of like essence."
[76] *Contra Arianos* 2.3. The word translated "authority" is ἐξουσία.

Athanasius's appeal to paternal authority may sound politically incorrect in the modern cultural West. It is, though, utterly unsurprising in the social conditions of the Roman Empire of the fourth century. Christian and Jewish ethical codes greatly emphasized filial obedience, since the fourth commandment of the Decalogue stipulates this. This is also true of Greek and Roman pagan culture. One considers, for instance, the way the idealized Roman hero Aeneas is presented as *pious*, encapsulated by his care and reverence for his father Anchises.[77] It would be more surprising if Athanasius did not share this view of filial piety toward a father.

Athanasius then meets the major point that, like human sons, the Son too is called a servant.[78] The Arian argument Athanasius faces runs along the lines that if the Son is a servant, then he is a servant like other servants, and hence created, just like them. It is therefore critical for him both to acknowledge the biblical description of the Son as servant (for this is a given of the scriptural material); and also to preserve the nature of the Son as identical with the Father.

He argues that Solomon is rightly called both son by nature and servant of his father, David, because of a father's authority. He notes that Arians find this interpretation perfectly acceptable concerning Solomon and David. If it is acceptable in that context of human fatherhood, there is no reason why it is not equally acceptable in the case of the divine Father-Son relationship. Thus, Athanasius's argument turns precisely on the parallel between human and divine father-son relations on this point of paternal authority. It is vital to grasp this.

Thus, Athanasius accepts that relationships of authority between persons do not automatically imply inferiority of nature. He does not accept the presupposition that identity of nature must always rule out a relationship of submission/superordination. For Athanasius does not explain the "servant" terminology by suggesting that the "servant" title is a mere courtesy without content. He accepts that a human father has genuine authority, and presupposes that human sons are not of a different, inferior nature from their fathers.

---

[77] See, in particular, Vergil's presentation of Aeneas's care and reverence for his father Anchises during the fall of Troy, in *Aeneid*, bk. 2. The Son's *pietas* is highly significant in Hilary's discussion of the Son's relation with the Father.
[78] *Contra Arianos* 2.4.

Further, for Athanasius to refute Arianism, he must deal with the relation of the Father and the Son *outside* the incarnation. He cannot use the strategy suggested by Giles and others, namely, that obedience language is restricted to the incarnation. Athanasius is, of course, perfectly well aware of such arguments, for he ascribes other problematic texts to the humanity of the incarnate Son. However, he conspicuously does not use this argument to deal with servant language applied to the Son. The reason is not far to seek: the Arian case focuses on servant language applied to the Son *outside* the incarnation. Giles's answer deals with servant issues within the incarnation and thus simply leaves the Arian case intact. Sadly, Giles's strategy leaves orthodoxy exposed to exactly the Arian challenge that so exercises him.

It might be said that Athanasius is mistaken in applying servant language to the Son in his eternal relation with the Father. This, though, misses the point: even were Athanasius wrong on this, he nevertheless does think paternal authority on the part of the Father is orthodox, not necessarily Arian.

Bad Sons and Revolt

The second line of thought comes from Athanasius's observations about two sons of David, Absalom and Adonijah, in *Contra Arianos* 3.7. The context is the refutation of the Arian charge that an uncreated Son would be inconsistent with monotheism. Athanasius comments on what David heard about Absalom[79] and Adonijah.[80] Both cases involve revolt from David by disloyal sons attempting to overthrow their father's kingdom. Yet, says Athanasius, the Son is not like Absalom and Adonijah. The difference is that there is no "rivalry,"[81] nor has the Son called himself God and fomented revolt from the Father.[82]

Of course, it might be said that an egalitarian relationship without submission/superordination would ensure just such non-rivalry as well as would a submission/superordination between Father and Son. However, this is not the reason Athanasius supplies for the absence of rivalry between Father and Son. Appealing to John 6:38, Athanasius explains

---
[79] 2 Sam. 15:13.
[80] 1 Kings 1:11.
[81] *Contra Arianos* 3.7; the word is ἄμιλλα, which can have the sense of contest for superiority, e.g., in a race.
[82] Ibid.

that there is no rivalry because the Son has glorified the Father and done his will.[83] So, for Athanasius, what denies the possibility of the Son's being a rival for his Father's throne, as Absalom was for David's, is that the Son does his Father's will. This is a very different rationale from saying there is no rivalry because "the Son adheres to the mutually and equally agreed plans of Father and Son together" or something similar. The note of obedience is unmistakable.

Again, it is insufficient for Athanasius's purpose if John 6:38, with its note of obedience, refers only to Jesus's human nature. Athanasius needs to repel Arian charges precisely about the relation of Father and Son outside the incarnation.

However, Athanasius's remarks about bad sons show that rivalry with their fathers is assumed to be unacceptable. This coheres with Athanasius's earlier remarks about "servant" language being applied to sons. Further, his appeal to John 6:38 and the obedience motif that it contains fits neatly with what he has also said about paternal authority.

Athanasius, then, recognizes that natural sons sometimes infringe their fathers' sovereignty, "unnatural" though that is. Such rivalry against a father is ethically condemned. By contrast, the Son is a good son precisely because he does his Father's will—again, as one would expect. Athanasius does not directly address the question of whether a son conforming to an egalitarian father-son relationship on the model of the twenty-first-century cultural West would be a good son.[84]

Hence we must conclude that Athanasius did not see paternal authority belonging to the Father as necessarily making the Son a creature. Rather he uses paternal authority to explain the biblical data, how a true son can be called servant and is not a rival to his father.

Hilary of Poitiers

Like Athanasius and Basil of Ancyra, Hilary emphasizes the Son as a true son of the Father. It would be fanciful to see Hilary as an Arian fellow-traveler. He wrote extensively against Arianism and was exiled

---
[83] Ibid., quoting John 6:38.
[84] The obvious difficulty is whether this actually counts as fulfilling the fourth commandment, as expounded by Paul in Eph. 6:1–3 and Col. 3:20. See also 1 Tim. 3:4 for obedience in the children of presbyters, and Rom. 1:30 for the association of rebelliousness toward parents with the disintegrative effects of sin. Jesus likewise upholds the fourth commandment in the dispute over corban (Mark 7:9ff. and parallels).

146 *Michael J. Ovey*

for opposing the "Arianizing" bishop Saturninus of Arles. By the time he wrote his two great anti-Arian works, *De synodis* and *De Trinitate*, he had become familiar with the positions of Eastern theologians[85] and had before him the *Blasphemia*.

Hilary's Reaction to Sirmium, 351

We have seen that the First Creed of Sirmium (351) asserts submission/superordination between the Father and Son, and that this cannot be explained by restricting the Son's obedience to the incarnation. The first question is how Hilary reacts to the subordinationist material that creed set out in its seventeenth anathema. In fact, Hilary's commentary on the seventeenth anathema shows his support for the First Sirmium Creed:

> God is One on account of the true character of His natural essence and because from the Unborn God the Father, who is the one God, the Only-begotten God the Son is born, and draws His divine Being only from God; and since the essence of Him who is begotten is exactly similar to the essence of Him who begot Him, there must be one name for the exactly similar nature. *That the Son is not on a level with the Father and is not equal to Him is chiefly shewn* [sic] *in the fact that He was subjected to Him to render obedience [dum subditus per obedientiae obsequelam est], in that the Lord rained from the Lord and that the Father did not, as Photinus and Sabellius say, rain from Himself, as the Lord from the Lord*; in that He then sat down at the right hand of God when it was told Him to seat Himself; in that He is sent, in that He receives, *in that He submits* [obsequitur] *in all things to the will of Him who sent Him. But the subordination of filial love* [pietatis subjectio] *is not a diminution of essence, nor does pious duty cause a degeneration of nature, since in spite of the fact that both the Unborn Father is God and the Only-begotten Son of God is God, God is nevertheless One, and the subjection and dignity* [subjectio . . . et dignitas] *of the Son are both taught in that by being called Son He is made subject* [subjicitur] *to that name which because it implies that God is His Father is yet a name which denotes His nature. Having a*

---
[85] He had been exiled to present-day Turkey.

name which belongs to Him whose Son He is, He is subject to the Father both in service [obsequie subjectus] and name; yet in such a way that the subordination of His name [subjectio nominis] bears witness to the true character of His natural and exactly similar essence.[86]

Several points emerge from this. First, the language of subjection and obedience is extensive and not incidental.

Second, the Son's subjection is theologically significant since it is used in the context of upholding the oneness of God. This implies that without the Son's subjection, divine unity is undermined.

Third, Hilary describes the Son's submission as the "subordination of filial love" (*pietatis subjectio*). Obviously this echoes John 14:31, where Jesus links his obedience to his Father with his love for his Father. Jesus does not appear to consider his obedience demeaning or inconsistent with love. However, this is a unique love. For Jesus is the unique Son of the Father, and thus a subordination arising from this relationship will be unique too, and to that extent different from the love shown by a creature. A creature, after all, is by definition not a natural Son.

Fourth, Hilary heavily stresses names. For Hilary, like other pro-Nicenes, the names are not mere titles but convey a reality. The name of "Son" for Hilary indicates two things about the Son. First, as Son he is fully divine, but, second, he has a relation of subjection to his Father. This means that subjection is not an alternative to the Son's dignity. As Son, the Son has *both* dignity *and* subjection. In this way the category of "names" used by the Serdica Encyclical does have fruitful content for delineating relations between the first and second persons of the Trinity. It opens up the possibility also that if one denies the subjection of the Son arising from his character as Son, one also undermines the grounds on which one says the Son is of the same nature as the Father.

However, are these statements of Hilary explicable merely as comments on someone else's defective confession? We must now turn to later material in *De synodis* for Hilary's own opinion.

---

[86] *De synodis* 51 (emphasis added).

Hilary's Own Confession in *De Synodis* 64

After outlining creedal material from others, Hilary articulates his own position:

> Kept always from guile by the gift of the Holy Spirit, we confess and write of our own will that there are not two Gods but one God; nor do we therefore deny that the Son of God is also God; for He is God of God. We deny that there are two incapable of birth, because God is one through the prerogative of being incapable of birth; nor does it follow that the Unbegotten is not God, for His source is the Unborn substance. There is not one subsistent Person, but a similar substance in both Persons. There is not one name of God applied to dissimilar natures, but a wholly similar essence belonging to one name and nature. *One is not superior to the other on account of the kind of His substance, but one is subject [subjectum] to the other because born of the other. The Father is greater because He is Father, the Son is not the less because He is Son. The difference is one of the meaning of a name and not of a nature.* We confess that the Father is not affected by time, but do not deny that the Son is equally eternal. We assert that the Father is in the Son because the Son has nothing in Himself unlike the Father: we confess that the Son is in the Father because the existence of the Son is not from any other source. We recognize that their nature is mutual and similar because equal: we do not think them to be one Person because they are one: we declare that they are through the similarity of an identical nature one, in such a way that they nevertheless are not one Person.[87]

By now, the position Hilary outlines is very familiar because of similar statements from Antioch, Serdica, the Macrostich, and the First Creed of Sirmium. There is but one God, and both Father and Son are rightly called God. They are two persons, as they have two names. The Father's superiority is explicitly not based on his being of a different substance.[88] Rather it arises from the reality of the relationship, in which the Father begets the Son.[89] The anti-Arian Hilary therefore does himself hold that the Father-Son relationship is one of superordination/submission.

---

[87] Ibid., 64 (emphasis added).
[88] "One is not superior to the other on account of the kind of His substance . . ."
[89] ". . . but one is subject to the other because born of the other."

The Importance of the Subordination of the Son for Hilary

However, the argument might run that this position is fundamentally peripheral for Hilary, a throwaway remark. But to say that would misunderstand Hilary's overall argument in *De synodis*.

He notes that one can use *homoousios* terminology wrongly.[90] Such wrong uses can nurture "Sabellianizing" positions. Given Eastern fears about the Western reception of Marcellus of Ancyra, this point needs to be made. Hilary then moves on to outline how *homoousios* is rightly used.[91] Because the term could be misunderstood, Hilary stipulates, "Let no one think that the word ought to be used by itself and unexplained."[92] He moves on to what the proper explanation of *homoousios* involves:

> Let us bring forward no isolated point of the divine mysteries to rouse the suspicions of our hearers and give an occasion to the blasphemers. *We must first preach the birth and subordination of the Son [subjectio] and the likeness of His nature*, and then we may preach in godly fashion that the Father and the Son are of one substance.[93]

Hence for Hilary *homoousios* can be properly taught *only* in the context of the Son's filial subjection. For Hilary, filial subordination is not the fast track to Arianism, but actually *necessary* for Nicene orthodoxy. On this view it would be tragically mistaken to try to defend Nicene orthodoxy by eliminating filial subjection. Eliminating filial subjection would imply that the second person is not "true Son."

The Coherence of Hilary's Position

But is Hilary's position simply incoherent? He may mean to defend orthodoxy against Arianism, but he actually lets it in unawares through the back door by defending the Son's subjection. A key question, then, is whether the subjection the *Blasphemia* sets out and the subjection Hilary espouses can really be distinguished.

Hilary knows perfectly well that his position involves stating that both the Son and all other things are subject to the Father. His point

---

[90] *De synodis* 67.
[91] Ibid., 69.
[92] Ibid., 70.
[93] Ibid. (emphasis added).

is that the subjection arises from different relationships: "A distinction [namely, between the Son's subjection and that of all other things] does exist, *for the subjection of the Son is filial reverence, the subjection of all other things is the weakness of things created.*"[94] Hilary's argument here turns on the Son as Son. Nicene theology, of course, draws very heavily on the thought that the Son is begotten, not made. As begotten, the Son is not a creature. However, just as begottenness entails the Son's full deity, so it also entails subjection. Hilary has earlier emphatically linked begotten-ness with subjection.[95]

This means that for Hilary, the subjection of the Son is orthodox because it does not arise from a Creator-creature relationship. This is very intelligible, because Arianism understands the Son ultimately in just that Creator-creature relationship. Further, the *Blasphemia* sets out an authentically Arian subjection in that the Son's obedience is bracketed with that of the creatures.

Concluding Theological Reflections

The question posed at the beginning of this chapter was this: Is it necessarily Arian to assert that the eternal relationship of the Father and Son is one of superordination and submission respectively? The material we have examined shows that the key Arian text, the *Blasphemia*, does indeed envisage the Son's submission. However, Nicene and non-Nicene texts before the *Blasphemia* also commonly envisage the Son's submission, and not only in the incarnation. Anti-Arian texts after the *Blasphemia* continue to assert the Son's submission. There is a telling absence of objection to the mere notion of the Son's submission.

There is a perfectly coherent basis for this. The difference between an Arian account of the Son's submission and a non-Arian, orthodox, account of the Son's submission lies in the rationale on which that submission is asserted. In the Arian account, the Son submits because he is a creature—a unique creature, but still a creature. In the orthodox account, the Son submits because he is truly a son. Sons submit to their fathers because this is what good sons do. The eternal Son is not

---
[94] Ibid., 79; the emphasized phrase translates "cum subjectio Filii naturae pietas sit, subjectio autem caeterorum creationis infirmitas sit."
[95] Ibid., 64, 67.

different in this respect, obeying his Father in the key Old Testament epiphany of Genesis 19. All this means a *no* to the question we have posed, because, while Arianism sees the Son ultimately as created, the orthodox account refuses to see the Son as a creature, but insists that he is a true son, including having a son's submission to his father.

The terms used to express this in the material we have examined revolve around the ὑποτάσσω word group in Athanasius's account and the *subicio* and *obsequor* word groups in Hilary's accounts. In the New Testament, the ὑποτάσσω word group is used to describe Jesus's submission to his earthly parents (Luke 2:51), demonic submission to the name of Jesus (Luke 10:17), and submission to earthly political authorities (Rom. 13:1). These usages resonate with the way the non-Arian material stresses submission in the context of divine monarchy and the authority that goes with it.[96] This vocabulary is shared by the *Blasphemia* and the orthodox alike. The point of difference, as noted above, is not whether submission is asserted outside the incarnation, but whether that submission is rooted in the Creator-created relationship or the father-son relationship.

The stress both Nicenes and non-Nicenes lay on the Son as true Son derives finally from their reading of the biblical revelation. Yet the ramifications of true sonship are profound. Nicene orthodoxy came to assert *homoousios* precisely because this is what true sonship will entail in the divine begetting. For, if he is the true Son, then the Son will be of the same nature as his Father, since fathers beget sons in their own nature, not in a different nature. What the Father is, that the Son is also, except Father.[97] There is, then, an asymmetry between Father and Son. The asymmetry does not lie in one being truly divine and the other not, but rather at the level of relationship. The Trinitarian persons are not simply distinguishable as individuals; they are unique individuals who

---

[96] Of course, the ὑποτάσσω word group is also employed in the context of husband-wife relationships (Eph. 5:24; Col. 3:18). Thus the question of the eternal Father-Son relationship has possible implications for husband-wife relations. The point is sometimes made that Paul uses ὑποτάσσω in relation to husbands and wives but ὑπακούω in relation to children and parents, and that there is clear semantic blue water between the two word groups in that the former does not have connotations of obedience while the latter does. Space precludes full semantic discussion. Suffice it to say both that ὑποτάσσω is used of Jesus in relation to his parents in Luke 2:51—and the perfect Jesus can hardly be a model of disobeying the fourth commandment—and that the two word groups seem to have semantic overlap in 1 Pet. 3:1, 6.

[97] A motto especially associated with Athanasius, but the thought is common among Nicenes. Its biblical support comes especially from John 5:26, where Jesus states that the Father and Son each has "life in himself."

differ from each other relationally and are not interchangeable. Hence the insistence that the Trinitarian persons are not "three brothers," or "three friends."[98] Such symmetrical relationships in which there is individuality but not uniqueness falls short of the biblical revelation, which, the Nicenes insist, is of Father, Son, and Spirit, not three friends or brothers. As has often been noted, this Nicene position has profound implications for human society in the way it grounds both fellowship and diversity.[99]

Further ramifications of true sonship can be used to safeguard orthodox belief in a number of ways. Hilary expresses this very clearly in the developed thought of his *De Trinitate*. True sonship refutes both Arianism and Sabellianism. It refutes Arianism because true fathers beget sons in their own substance, and this means the Arian proposition that the Son is a creature cannot be correct, because a creature is not of the same substance as its Creator. It refutes Sabellianism because a true father is genuinely distinguishable from his son and is not his own son; a true father-son relationship is not ultimately a reflexive relationship in which a father is his own son.[100] For Hilary, further, the Son's true sonship underpins the Father's identity as true Father.[101] This means that losing the notion of true Son undermines the repudiation of Sabellianism, Arianism, and the eternal character of the Father as Father.

The Son's submission contributes to this theology of true sonship. Thus, for Athanasius a true son is a good son, over whom a father has a legitimate authority because of the paternal relationship. A true son fulfills norms of obedience and is rightly called his father's servant. This implies that a son who cannot rightly be described as servant is not a perfect son, and his true sonship would be in doubt.[102] For Hilary,

---

[98] For Athanasius, this simply departs from the biblical revelation of sonship: see *Contra Arianos* 1.14; compare also *De synodis* 51.
[99] Particularly illuminating in this regard is the work of Colin Gunton. See notably Gunton, *The One, the Three and the Many* (Cambridge: Cambridge University Press, 1993).
[100] Tertullian's work *Against Praxeas* majors on just this point; note *Against Praxeas* 23.
[101] Hilary comments, "They deny the Father by robbing the Son of His true Sonship" (*De Trinitate* 2.4). One of the casualties created by Sabellianism was that it left a hidden God at the heart of Christian belief, because there was an identity "behind" the masks of Father and Son. Patristic theologians since Origen were acutely aware that arguments about who the Son was had corollaries for who the Father was (especially helpful is Peter Widdicombe, *The Fatherhood of God from Origen to Athanasius* [Oxford: Oxford University Press, 2000]).
[102] This could be developed in terms of the Son's righteousness as the one who keeps God's law and is the last Adam. Conversely, if the Son is not a "good son," the question arises as to whether he can be a perfect law keeper. This in turn could affect how the Son is counted as he who keeps the law for us, and whose righteousness is imputed to us.

true sonship necessitates *both* identity of nature *and* filial submission. Hence, removing filial submission undermines identity of nature, since filial submission is a consequence of true sonship. In the confessional material, the Son's submission is regularly used to repudiate charges of ditheism and to uphold the unity of God. On that thinking, rejecting the Son's submission undermines the monotheism of orthodox Trinitarian thought.[103] In the light of these considerations, it is not surprising that Hilary argues that *homoousios* can *only* be properly taught along with filial submission.

In short, then, the Patristic theology we have examined runs along these lines: If one loses filial submission, one imperils true sonship, for filial submission is a natural consequence of true sonship. And if one loses true sonship, one loses Nicene Trinitarian theology, particularly in its repudiation of Arianism, which is obviously not the intention of Giles, Carnley, and others.

Naturally, in terms of broader debate, this raises the key question of where submission fits in a Christian theology that operates in the postmodern cultural West. A full hermeneutics of suspicion may argue that power is normally exploitative and self-interested, or that it can only be amoral and it is a mistake in categories to evaluate it in ethical terms.

It is, though, just here that the Nicene true-Son theology we have examined searches us most closely. Given that the relations between the persons are eternal and perfect, if true sonship includes filial submission, then the Father-Son relationship features a relation of superordination and submission that is by definition perfect and good. It is not only possible but necessary to speak of perfect relationships that involve submission.[104] Jesus, after all, speaks of showing his love for his Father by doing his Father's will (John 14:31; see also 15:10). One might well ask how Jesus reveals his love for his Father without this obedience. In the Gospel of John, Jesus also speaks emphatically of his Father's love for him, but sees no contradiction between the fatherly love that will give him all authority (see, e.g., John 3:35; 17:2) and the tasks—even including the cross—that the Father has set him to obey.

---

[103] It is worth noting that one prominent current exponent of non-submission in the Trinity, Jürgen Moltmann, has been criticized precisely for a tritheistic account of the Trinity.
[104] Although this does not entail that all relationships must feature superordination and submission.

Perhaps if Jesus sees no necessary contradiction between authority and love, there is none.

Here, though, we touch not merely on the question of submission and authority, but also on what the nature of love is. Augustine, of course, recognizes that love in its authentic form is other-person centered, and in its sinful and perverted form has become disastrously curved in on itself. The consequences of which kind of love is in operation when one either wields authority or is called on to submit to authority are drastic. Augustine famously compares the outcomes as he talks about two contrasting "cities" or ways of life:

> We see then that the two cities were created by two kinds of love: the earthly city was created by self-love reaching the point of contempt for God, the Heavenly City by the love of God carried as far as contempt of self. In fact, the earthly city glories in itself, the Heavenly City glories in the Lord. The former looks for glory from men, the latter finds its highest glory in God, the witness of a good conscience. The earthly lifts up its head in its own glory, the Heavenly City says to its God: "My glory; you lift up my head." In the former, the lust for domination lords it over its princes as over the nations it subjugates; in the other both those put in authority and those subject to them serve one another in love, the rulers by their counsel, the subjects by obedience. The one city loves its own strength shown in its powerful leaders; the other says to its God, "I will love you, my Lord, my strength."[105]

The late Patristic theologian Augustine challenges us that one can exercise authority and one can submit to it in genuine other-person-centered love. The implication of the Nicene and non-Nicene material we have examined is that the eternal Trinitarian Father-Son relationship reveals both other-person-loving authority and other-person-loving submission, because the Son is a true son, and the Father a true father.

---

[105] Augustine, *City of God*, trans. Henry Bettenson (New York: Penguin Putnam, 1972), 14.28.

7

Augustine and His Interpreters

JOHN STARKE

> A trinity is what we are looking for, and not for any kind of trinity either but the one that God is.
>
> Augustine, *De Trinitate*

Augustine of Hippo serves as a pivot point in the history of Christian theology. He is like an elbow to an arm: he sets a direction by which all subsequent theology can be measured for alignment or lack thereof.

It is not at all surprising, then, that when two parties disagree on a particular theological issue or interpretation, Augustine is usually sought after for support. The problem occurs when *both sides* claim Augustine for support, as is the case for our current debate on whether there is an order of authority and submission among the persons of the Trinity. The challenge seems to come at us in two ways: (1) Augustine wrote a great deal on the Trinity, so it's easy to find a quote or two to support one side of the argument, even while finding a number of quotes for the other. (2) Augustine did not write with our modern-day debates in mind, so those who appeal to him for support can often misinterpret his original intentions, since the opponents he was writing against often looked very different from our own today.

Nevertheless, that does not mean that Augustine is of no use for our current debate or that he did not have anything to say. He did and this essay intends to show that. But it might be useful to concede at the beginning that to mine Augustine's works for quotes that support either side of this debate would be a bad way to begin. However, it is just as dangerous to believe we can come to any text unbiased, as if we don't bring our own questions. Therefore, the most prudent thing to do, it seems, is to admit our biases and pray for wisdom. That is the spirit in which, Lord willing, this essay is written.

Summary of Opposing Arguments

At the heart of the disagreement is the egalitarians' cry of *foul!* when complementarians[1] appeal to Augustine's explanation of how the sending of the Son by the Father reveals an eternal order of authority and submission. Many egalitarians claim that Augustine's understanding of eternal generation and inseparable operations among the persons of the Trinity makes the complementarian appeal to Augustine illegitimate.

The purpose of this essay is to show that the egalitarian argument proves too much. A more faithful alternative is to see that Augustine's doctrines of eternal generation and inseparable operation undergird and support an order of authority and submission, and to deny an order of authority and submission would be inconsistent with Augustine's most basic orthodox assumptions and out of step with Augustine's most prominent interpreters.

Consider the following quote from Augustine:[2]

> If however the reason why the Son is said to have been sent by the Father is simply that *the one is the Father and the other the Son* then there is nothing at all to stop us believing that the Son is equal to the Father and consubstantial and co-eternal, and yet that *the Son is sent by the Father*. Not because one is greater and the other less, but

---

[1] I do not see Millard Erickson's plea to employ "gradational" and "equivalent" in the place of "complementarian" and "egalitarian" in this debate as a good alternative (see Millard J. Erickson, *Who's Tampering with the Trinity: An Assessment of the Subordination Debate* [Grand Rapids: Kregel, 2009], 17–21). For one, "gradational" seems to carry with it the same baggage "subordination" carries. Second, "gradational" has absolutely no sense of equality, which complementarians would want to strongly affirm in the Trinity, as it relates to essence. Therefore, despite the baggage of gender debates, "complementarian" seems to be the only good available option in order to affirm in the Godhead both an equality in essence and an order of authority and submission among the persons.

[2] All citations of *De Trinitate* are taken from Augustine, *The Trinity*, trans. Edmund Hill (Brooklyn: New City, 1991).

because one is the Father and the other the Son; one is the begetter, the other begotten; the first is the one from whom the sent one is; the other is the one who is from the sender. For *the Son is from the Father, not the Father from the Son*. In the light of this we can now perceive that the Son is not just said to have been sent because the Word became flesh, but that he was sent *in order for the Word to become flesh*. (*De Trinitate* 4.27 [172], emphasis mine)

Wayne Grudem depends upon this quote to show that Augustine, along with other figures in church history, from the early church to the modern era, affirms an order of authority and submission in the persons of the Trinity.[3]

Robert Letham, in disputing with Kevin Giles over the use of this quote, argues:

> His [the Son's] sending preceded the incarnation, and so his incarnate life and ministry can (as appropriate) reveal something of his eternal relations. If this were not so, we would be left with agnosticism, in flat contradiction of Jesus' own words that he who has seen him (in his lowliness) has seen the Father (John 14:9 et al.).[4]

Bruce Ware concludes from the quote above that, "as Augustine affirmed, the distinction of Persons is constituted precisely by the differing relations among them, in part manifested by the inherent authority of the Father and inherent submission of the Son."[5] Ware goes on to argue that

> Augustine denies the egalitarian claim that all subordination of the Son to the Father rests fully in the Son's incarnate state. To the contrary, Augustine affirms that "the Son is not just said to have been sent because the Word became flesh, but that he was sent in order for the Word to become flesh." In other words, the sending of the Son occurred in eternity past in order that the eternal Word, sent

---
[3] Wayne Grudem, *Evangelical Feminism and Biblical Truth: An Analysis of More than 100 Disputed Questions* (Colorado Springs: Multnomah, 2004; repr., Wheaton, IL: Crossway, 2012), 418.
[4] Robert Letham, *The Holy Trinity: In Scripture, History, Theology, and Worship* (Phillipsburg, NJ: P&R, 2004), 494.
[5] Bruce A. Ware, *Father, Son, and Holy Spirit: Roles, Relationships, and Relevance* (Wheaton, IL: Crossway, 2005), 79–80. See also Ware, "Tampering with the Trinity," in *Biblical Foundations for Manhood and Womanhood*, ed. Wayne Grudem (Wheaton, IL: Crossway, 2002), 246.

from on high from the Father, might take on human flesh and then continue his role of carrying out the will of his Father.[6]

Millard Erickson, however, contends that in other places, Augustine's doctrine of inseparable operations rejects the type of arguments complementarians have made when appealing to Augustine. He quotes Augustine saying, "Wherefore, since the Father sent Him by a word, His being sent was the work of both the Father and His Word; therefore the same Son was sent by the Father *and the Son*, because the Son Himself is the Word of the Father that wisdom must needs appear in the flesh" (*De Trinitate* 2.9 [103], emphasis mine). Erickson thus argues that Augustine's understanding of inseparable operations undercuts the complementarian position of an order of submission and authority.[7] "Consequently," he argues, "while it is said that the Father sent the Son because they are referred to respectively as the Father and the Son, *it can as well be said that the Son also sent himself.*"[8]

Kevin Giles provides only a spattering of quotes from Augustine that do little to further the debate, since he only employs quotes that argue against the Arian error that the one sending is greater than the one sent in nature, which is why Giles consistently accuses complementarians of tending toward Arian and semi-Arian heresies.[9] Complementarians, of course, want to do nothing of the sort. Like Erickson, Giles suggests that Augustine's inseparable operation doesn't allow for an order of submission and authority in the Godhead.[10]

However, Keith E. Johnson offers a more diligent argument for why Augustine's understanding of eternal generation and inseparable operation does not allow for an order of authority and submission. Much more space will be devoted to his arguments throughout this

---

[6] Ware, *Father, Son, and Holy Spirit*, 81.
[7] Erickson, *Who's Tampering with the Trinity?*, 158.
[8] Ibid., 159 (emphasis added).
[9] Kevin Giles, *Jesus and the Father: Modern Evangelicals Reinvent the Doctrine of the Trinity* (Grand Rapids: Zondervan, 2006), 190–94. Giles provides the following short quotes on p. 191: "He [Augustine] says, 'in error' they presume, 'the one who sends is greater than the one sent'" (*De Trinitate* 2.7). "Texts that speak of the Son's sending by the Father do not teach that 'the Son is less than the Father, but that he is from the Father. This does not imply any dearth of equality, but only his birth from eternity'" (*De Trinitate* 2.3). "Such texts 'mark him neither as less nor equal, but only intimate that he is from the Father'" (*De Trinitate* 2.3). Giles makes similar arguments in "The Subordination of Christ, the Subordination of Women," in *Discovering Bible Equality: Complementarity without Hierarchy*, ed. Ronald W. Pierce and Rebecca Merrill Groothuis (Downers Grove, IL: InterVarsity, 2004), 341–42.
[10] See Giles, *Jesus and the Father*, 194, and "The Subordination of Christ," 341–42.

essay.[11] Augustine maintains, according to Johnson, "that 'being sent' does not imply inferiority on the part of the Son. It simply reveals that the Son is eternally *from* by [sic] the Father."[12]

Despite the language of a "sender" and "one sent," Augustine argues that the Father, Son, and Spirit act inseparably. Johnson shows that Augustine sees the basis of inseparable operation as (1) that the Son is *from* the Father and (2) that the Father *abides in* the Son as he works.[13]

How, then, does Augustine's understanding of eternal generation and inseparable operation, according to Johnson, come to bear upon complementarians who appeal to Augustine as holding to an order of authority and submission? Johnson claims that complementarians misinterpret Augustine as affirming an order of authority and submission in the "sent" language of Scripture. According to Johnson, "Augustine insists that the Father and Son—who "have but one will and are indivisible in their working (*De trin.* II.9)—were both involved in sending the Son."[14] He quotes Augustine at length:

> What we are saying may perhaps be easier to sort out if we put the question this way, crude though it is: In what manner did God send his Son? Did he tell him to come, giving him an order he complied with by coming, or did he ask him to, or did he merely suggest it? Well, whichever way it was done, it was certainly done by word. But God's Word is his Son. *So when the Father sent him by word, what happened was that he was sent by the Father and his Word. Hence it is by the Father and the Son that the Son was sent, because the Son is the Father's Word* (*De trin.* II.9, emphasis Johnson's).

This has consequences for complementarians, according to Johnson. He argues:

> Inseparable action, therefore intrinsically qualifies all the working of the Father and Son, including the "sending" of the Son by the Father. EFS [Eternal Functional Subordination] proponents, therefore,

---

[11] Keith E. Johnson, "Trinitarian Agency and the Eternal Subordination of the Son: An Augustine Perspective, *Themelios* 36, no. 1 (2011): 7–25.
[12] Ibid., 13.
[13] See Johnson's larger argument, ibid., 13–16. Johnson adequately shows that Augustine did indeed base the Father and Son's inseparable operation in eternal generation and their intratrinitarian ontological unity (*Tractates on the Gospel of John 11–27*, vol. 79 of *The Fathers of the Church*, trans. John W. Rettig (Washington, DC: Catholic University of America Press, 1988).
[14] Johnson, "Trinitarian Agency," 20.

misread Augustine when they sever his comments about the Father's "sending" the Son from Augustine's unequivocal affirmation that the divine persons act inseparably.[15]

What is the cause of this misreading by complementarians? Johnson suggests that since *some* complementarians, such as Ware and Grudem, reject eternal generation, which marks a substantive difference between them and Augustine, these differences "fuel misreadings of Augustine."[16] Johnson argues later on that "in Ware's theology, 'submission' effectively replaces 'eternal generation' as the distinguishing property of the Son. Augustine is then read through the lens of this alternative understanding of personal properties."[17] Therefore, Johnson concludes, complementarians misrepresent Augustine when appealing to him for support of an order of authority and submission.

To summarize: Although Giles, Erickson, and Johnson are not completely alike in their critiques of complementarians, two common themes can be observed: (1) Complementarians read too much into Augustine's doctrine of eternal generation in saying that Augustine is also affirming an order of authority and submission. (2) Augustine's inseparable operation does not allow for an order of authority and submission. To affirm an order of this kind must surrender inseparable operation, tearing asunder the one will of God and leading to a forfeiture of unity of nature.

Response

Before engaging in the substance of the arguments, I should say something on the use of language in the debate. The descriptive and emotive language often employed to summarize or refute the arguments of complementarians skews the debate, at best, and, at worst, misrepresents complementarians horribly.

For example, the following unfortunate language is commonly used in representing the complementarian position: "difference of rank" among the persons; the "superiority of the Father" and "inferiority"

---
[15] Ibid.
[16] Ibid., 19.
[17] Ibid., 22.

of the Son; the Father's will is "unilaterally imposed"; a "superiority-submission structure"; "hierarchy"; "command structures"; "subordination*ism*." Language of this sort only clouds the matter and implies that its users either misunderstand the complementarian position or misrepresent it intentionally. This neither furthers the debate nor displays prudence and charity.

However, the substance of arguments against the complementarian position is another matter. The remainder of this essay will respond to the claims that (1) Augustine's doctrine of eternal generation does not imply an order of authority and submission, and (2) inseparable operation does not allow for it.

Eternal Generation

In order to show that the doctrine of eternal generation does indeed imply an order of authority and submission in Augustine, we'll attempt to answer the following three questions, which summarize the arguments against a complementarian reading of Augustine.

Does a Rejection of Eternal Generation Necessarily Impair a Correct Interpretation of Augustine?

Keith Johnson's initial tactic against a complementarian understanding of Augustine is peculiar. After laying out his argument, he begins with the charge that since complementarians like Ware and Grudem reject Augustine's doctrine of eternal generation, their differences "fuel misreadings of Augustine,"[18] and "Augustine is "read through the lens of an alternative understanding of personal properties."[19] In other words, their rejection of Augustine's eternal generation impedes their ability to interpret Augustine rightly.

However, while it is one thing to argue that Augustine's view of eternal generation *does not* incorporate a relationship of authority and submission (which Johnson does attempt to show), it does not follow that because *some* complementarians do not hold to Augustine's scheme *in toto*, then they are hindered from rightly interpreting him.

---
[18] Ibid., 19; but see his preceding arguments, 9–19.
[19] Ibid., 22.

Johnson contends that since in "Ware's theology, 'submission' effectively replaces 'eternal generation' as the distinguishing property of the Son,"[20] his interpretation is skewed from the beginning. While it seems unclear whether Ware *replaces* eternal generation with submission,[21] Johnson doesn't give any explanation as to why other complementarians, such as Letham[22] and Stephen Wellum,[23] who strongly hold to eternal generation, yet see it as grounds for an order of authority and submission in Augustine.

Ware's and Grudem's rejection of eternal generation does not give evidence to a misreading of Augustine, nor does it explain away other complementarians who do hold to it.

Does the Language of "Being Sent" Reveal an Order of Authority and Submission?

Both Johnson and Giles argue that eternal generation can have no further implication for how the persons relate to each other, since "being sent" only reveals one who is unbegotten, begotten, and in procession.[24] Therefore, Augustine does not distinguish the divine persons on the basis of their work or function.[25] Being "sent" merely "reveals that the Son is eternally *from* by [sic] the Father,"[26] and nothing more. It does not reveal an order of authority and submission from eternity.

These arguments by Johnson and Giles have further implications for the problem of inseparable operations, but the obvious question for now is this: Is that all Augustine wanted to affirm in eternal generation? The answer must be no.

For example, consider Augustine's comments on John 5:19, "So Jesus said to them, 'Truly, truly, I say to you, the Son can do nothing of his own accord, but only what he sees the Father doing. For whatever the Father does, that the Son does likewise." Johnson argues from Au-

---

[20] Ibid.
[21] See Ware's developed argument in *Father, Son, and Holy Spirit*, 71.
[22] See his arguments against Giles in Letham, *The Holy Trinity*, 494–95—not to mention countless other contemporary and historical Augustinian theologians whom Johnson himself references in his articles, such as John Owen and Herman Bavinck. See below how in Owen and Bavinck eternal generation is the ground for an order of authority and submission.
[23] Stephen J. Wellum, "Irenic and Unpersuasive: A Review of Millard J. Erickson, *Who's Tampering with the Trinity?*," *JBMW* 15, no. 2 (Fall 2010): 45–56. See especially, 55.
[24] See Johnson, "Trinitarian Agency," 13–16; Giles; *Jesus and the Father*, 191.
[25] Giles, "The Subordination of Christ," 342.
[26] Johnson, "Trinitarian Agency," 13,

gustine's exposition of this text that this passage merely points to the Son's being *from* the Father. (Johnson also argues that inseparable operation keeps it from going any further, which we will discuss below.)[27]

However, that conclusion only follows if Augustine attributes this saying to the Son in *forma servi*, not *forma Dei*. When Augustine argues from this text in *De Trinitate*, he makes it clear that "this is not spoken in the form of a servant, but in the form of God" (1.1 [100]).[28] What the Son does (function) depends upon what the Father does. The order is never reversed. It can never be said that the Father does only what he sees the Son doing (*Tractates* 20.4 [133]).[29] Therefore, any qualification that inseparable operation has on how Augustine interprets the text—and it does have qualifications—does not take away Augustine's stress on the *functional order* of the Father and Son. There is an initiation by one and a reception by the other. Equality cannot be reduced to a reversal of this order.

Equally important is that Augustine stresses that not only does the functional order flow *from* Father *to* the Son, but so does the power to carry it out. "Since, then the power of the Son is of the Father, therefore also the substance is of the Father; and since the substance of the Son is of the Father, therefore the power of the Son is of the Father" (*Tractates* 20.4 [133]). Is it the selfsame power? Most affirmatively. But Augustine continues, "[Jesus] said, 'The Son cannot of Himself do anything.' Because He is not Son from Himself, therefore He is not able from Himself" (*Tractates* 20.4 [133]).

One response could be that there is a reciprocal relationship to "power" and "substance" in Augustine: "Since the power of the Son is of the Father, therefore also the substance is of the Father; *and* since the substance of the Son is of the Father, therefore the power of the Son is of the Father" (*Tractates* 20.4 [133]). And since there is a reciprocal relationship, there is not a logical order, that is, *from* substance *to* power; or *from* substance *to* function. But that objection skirts the question.

---
[27] Ibid., 15. Johnson argues from Saint Augustine, *Tractates on the Gospel of John 11–27*.
[28] Johnson may argue that Augustine's homily is a more mature form of his Trinitarianism, since he makes note that he quotes Augustine's *Tractates* rather than *De Trinitate*. But it's not clear how Augustine's Trinitarianism has developed from his statements in *De Trinitate*, nor how his "maturity" would change the *forma Dei* and *forma servi* distinction.
[29] All citations from Augustine's *In Joannis Euangelium Tractatus CXXIV* are taken from Augustine, *Lectures or Tractates on the Gospel according to John*, vol. 7 of *Nicene and Post-Nicene Fathers*, First Series, ed. Philip Schaff (Peabody, MA: Hendrickson, 2004), 133.

The question is whether the Son's generation *from* the Father has any bearing on what he does. Augustine would most clearly say yes. It has bearing not only on *what* the Son does, but also on the power by which he does it. The order is a noncompetitive initiating authority and receptive obedience between the Father and Son.

John Calvin makes the same argument, depending much on Augustine, that the Father is the *beginning of deity*[30] and the *beginning of activity*.[31] "To the Father is attributed the beginning of activity and the fountain and wellspring of all things; to the Son, wisdom, counsel, and the ordered disposition of all things."[32] For Calvin, just as it is for Augustine, the Father is the beginning of the Son, and what the Son does comes from the Father as the wellspring and initiator of all things.

So too, John Owen agrees with Augustine that the "Son receives all from the Father, and the Father nothing from the Son. Whatever belongs unto the person of the Son, as the person of the Son, he receives it all from the Father by eternal generation."[33] Eternal generation, for Owen, is the ground for an order of authority and submission: "As unto *authoritative designation*, it was the act of the Father. Hence he is said to send 'his Son in the likeness of sinful flesh,' Rom. viii. 3; Gal. iv. 4";[34] and to the Son, "all the holy obedience which proceeded from [the human nature], was consequent in order of the nature unto this union."[35] In other words, for Owen, the human obedience is a consequence of its union with the obedient divine Son, submitting to the Father's authoritative designation.

It might be more helpful to quote Owen at length to see how he uses Augustine's categories of eternal generation *and* inseparable operation in order to provide a clear order of authority and submission:

---

[30] John Calvin, *Institutes of the Christian Religion*, ed. John T. McNeill, trans. Ford Lewis Battles (Louisville, KY: Westminster John Knox, 1960), 1.13.25–26.
[31] Ibid., 1.12.18.
[32] Ibid.
[33] John Owen, *The Glory of Christ*, trans. William H. Goold, vol. 1 of *The Works of John Owen* (Edinburgh: Banner of Truth, 2000), 71. In Owen's preface to vol. 1, he stresses his dependence upon Augustine's *De Trinitate*; see pp. 7, 10, 21, 23, 25, and 26. But his dependence is most clearly seen on 70–79 and 218–19, where Owen nearly quotes Augustine word for word from books 6 and 7 on how the Son is the image of the Father. Owen links Augustine's theme of the Son as the image of the Father directly to the order of operations. Therefore, for Owen, the order of being and operations is directly related to mankind's knowledge of and acceptance with God.
[34] Owen, *The Glory of Christ*, 225 (emphasis added).
[35] Ibid., 227.

> The sum of what we can comprehend in this great mystery ariseth from the consideration of the *order* of the holy persons of the blessed Trinity in their operations; *for their order herein doth follow that of their subsistence.* Unto this great work there are peculiarly required, authority, love, and power—all directed by infinite wisdom. These originally reside in the person of the Father, and the acting of them in this matter is constantly ascribed to him. He sent the Son as he gives the Spirit, *by an act of sovereign authority.* . . . The Son, who is the second person in the order of the subsistence, in order of operation puts the whole authority, love, and power of the Father in execution.[36]

But this order raises questions for Giles and Johnson as it relates to interpreting Augustine. For Giles, an order of authority and submission ultimately means a "lack of power" in the Son.[37] Even Johnson implies that if "being sent" means an order of submission and authority, then it necessitates an *inferior* Son.[38] Worse, for some it has serious implications for the omnipotence of the Son.[39]

Yet, Augustine's sermon on John 10:17-18 puts that concern to rest. Verses 17-18 read, "For this reason the Father loves me, because I lay down my life that I may take it up again. No one takes it from me, but I lay it down of my own accord. I have authority to lay it down, and I have authority to take it up again. This charge I have received from my Father."

The Son has complete and utter divine authority over his own body. The power is of the eternal Word (*Tractates* 47.13 [264]) to lay down the flesh and raise it up. This power over life and death is the selfsame power that is *from* the Father. This power is omnipotent and complete, yet *from* the Father.[40]

Therefore, when the text says that the power to lay down his flesh or raise it up is wielded by the charge or command of the Father, it is not in contrast to his omnipotence (*Tractates* 47.13 [264]). Drawing from Augustine's sermon, Michael Allen and Scott Swain argue:

---

[36] Ibid., 219 (emphasis added).
[37] Giles, *Jesus and the Father*, 191.
[38] Johnson, "Trinitarian Agency," 13.
[39] See Thomas Joseph White, "Intra-Trinitarian Obedience and the Nicene-Chalcedonian Christology," *Nova et Vetera* 6 (2008): 389, cited in Michael Allen and Scott Swain, "The Obedience of the Eternal Son," *International Journal of Systematic Theology* 15, no. 2 (2013): 116.
[40] See Augustine's extended argument on simplicity in books 6 and 7.

The charge and command of the Father does not negate the will and power of the Son—in Trinitarian fashion, they are both not only valid affirmations but necessary aspects of the gospel proclamation. Jesus wills to do this, and he exercises real authoritative power in so doing, and yet his action in this regard is according to his Father's charge.[41]

Is It Fitting for an Eternal Son to Be in Union with an Obedient Human Nature?

The claim that the eternal Son of God yields obedience to the Father only during the incarnation raises some serious christological concerns. The most obvious concern is the *kind* of separation between the eternal Word, for whom submission and obedience to the Father would be inappropriate, and the assumed humanity, which does submit to the Father. Letham raises the question, "Is there something about the Son that makes it compatible for him to unite to himself a human nature that lives in obedience to the Father? Is there something in the Son *as Son* that makes this union with an *obedient* human nature fitting?"[42]

Letham warns that if the answer to that question is no—that there is nothing about the Son *as Son* that makes personal union with an obedient human nature appropriate and fitting—then "we would be in peril of a Nestorian separation"[43] between the two natures: one for which submission and obedience to the Father would be inappropriate and another which does submit to the Father.

Certainly this conclusion would be out of step with Augustine's Catholic orthodoxy and, as Letham notes, out of step with orthodox Christianity going forward. For example, the Second Council of Constantinople set forth the dogmas of *anhypostasia*, that the human flesh of Christ has no independent existence apart from the union with the divine nature, effected by the Word, and *enhypostasia*, that the Word, the eternal Son provides the personal center of Christ. Therefore, argues Letham, "all actions of the incarnate Christ according to both natures are attributed to the person of the Son."[44] He concludes, "Thus, the

---
[41] Allen and Swain, "The Obedience of the Eternal Son," 130. I owe much of this argument on the problem of the Son's omnipotence and the Son's obedience to this article.
[42] Letham, *The Holy Trinity*, 394. Much of the following argument is from Dr. Letham.
[43] Ibid.
[44] Ibid., 395.

Word *incarnate* obeys the Father. At the same time, it is the *Word* incarnate who obeys the Father."[45]

Inseparable Operation

Most certainly, the weight of the egalitarian claim that it is illegitimate for complementarians to appeal to Augustine is in his doctrine of inseparable operation. For Johnson, it is inconsistent to hold to an order of authority and submission while holding to inseparable operation. It will be important to follow Johnson's argument all the way through. He charges that when complementarians interpret an order of submission and authority in the "sending" of the Son, they misinterpret Augustine, because "they sever his comments about the Father 'sending' the Son from Augustine's unequivocal affirmation that the divine persons act inseparably."[46]

Johnson quotes Augustine to show that both the Father *and* the Son were involved in sending the Son:

> What we are saying may perhaps be easier to sort out if we put the question this way, crude though it is: In what manner did God send his Son? Did he tell him to come, giving him an order he complied with by coming, or did he ask him to, or did he merely suggest it? Well, whichever way it was done, it was certainly done by word. But God's Word is his Son. *So when the Father sent him by word, what happened was that he was sent by the Father and his Word. Hence it is by the Father and the Son that the Son was sent, because the Son is the Father's Word* (De trin. II.9, emphasis Johnson's).

Johnson continues to quote Augustine: "So it is that the invisible Father, together with the jointly invisible Son, is said to have sent this Son by making him visible" (*De Trinitate* 2.9 [103]). Therefore, according to Johnson, when Bruce Ware quotes Augustine in saying not merely that the Son has been sent because he became incarnate "but that he was sent in order for the Word to become flesh" (*De Trinitate* 4.27 [172])[47] as proof that Augustine believed in an obedient Son,

---
[45] Ibid., 395 (emphasis original).
[46] Johnson, "Trinitarian Agency," 20.
[47] Ware, *Father, Son, and Holy Spirit*, 80–81.

Ware misreads Augustine. "As we have seen above," says Johnson, "the sending of the Son was not merely the work of the Father but the inseparable work of the Father and the Son," and to hold to an order of authority and submission would break the one will of the Father and Son into two.[48]

Therefore, "inseparable action intrinsically qualifies all the working of the Father and Son, including the 'sending' of the Son by the Father,"[49] and "the 'sending' language in Scripture does not reveal that the Son is somehow eternally subordinate to the Father . . . but simply reveals that the Son is eternally 'from the Father' (i.e., eternal generation)."[50] Here, then, are the main points Johnson argues, according to Augustine:

1. An order of authority and submission is incompatible with Augustine's inseparable operation, since the work of "sending" the Son was the inseparable work of the Father *and* Son.
2. An order of authority and submission not only is incompatible with inseparable operation, but would divide the one will of the Father and Son.
3. Incompatibility with Augustine's inseparable operation and division of the one will of the Father and Son would therefore lead to a position incompatible with *homoousian*.

Let us examine each one.

1. *An order of authority and submission is incompatible with Augustine's inseparable operation, since the work of "sending" the Son was the inseparable work of the Father and Son.*

This first point is difficult to maintain, since in arguing against an order of authority and submission by appealing to inseparable operation, Johnson ends up flattening the order completely—even the order Augustine wants to maintain in eternal generation. In other words, Johnson's argument proves too much.

Johnson is correct in emphasizing that Augustine was "unequivocal" in affirming that the divine persons act inseparably. However, the unity in which the persons operate is one of *harmony*, not *unison*, since

---
[48] Johnson, "Trinitarian Agency," 20.
[49] Ibid.
[50] Ibid., 21.

for Augustine each person is irreducibly distinct. Johnson seems to take away any harmony and leaves room only for a "unison of action." But as we have seen above, the Father initiates, and the Son obediently responds, since the Son does only what he sees his Father doing, and the power to do it comes from his Father (John 5:19).

Yet, as Johnson points out in Augustine, the Son is sent by the Father *by* word, and his Word is his Son. But Augustine is not interested in disposing of the Trinitarian order. Rather, the Son is not only the "one sent" but also the "means" by which he is sent. So then, we can affirm with Johnson that the sender is both the Father and the Son, but the Son is not the sender *in the same way* the Father is the sender. The Son does not initiate; the Father does. The Father initiates by way of his Word, and the Son obeys. Johnson seems to be overemphasizing the inseparability to the extent of undermining Augustine's eternal generation, threatening the integrity of the person.

If we take Johnson's explanation of inseparable operation to other places in the Scripture, what we find is troubling. In Luke 3, when Jesus is being baptized and the heavens opened, the Father said to Jesus, "You are my beloved Son; with you I am well pleased" (Luke 3:22). Now let's for a moment consider Augustine's inseparable operation. Clearly, the Father is speaking to the Son and speaking *by* his word. But if we used Johnson's understanding of inseparable operation, it would be nonsensical—worse, it would be modalism—to say it is *also* the Son who says, "You are my beloved Son."

Another example would be the prayer of Jesus in Gethsemane, "My Father, if it be possible, let this cup pass from me" (Matt. 26:39). According to Augustine, inseparable operation means not that the Father is the one also speaking, but that the Father is abiding in all the Son does (see *Tractates* 20.6 [134]; John 10:15).[51] Using Johnson's scheme, however, we are *en route* to patripassionism if the Father *also* says, "Let this cup pass from me." Indeed, Geerhardus Vos gave an appropriate warning: "To emphasize that unity [of the being of God] so strongly that the Persons can no longer enter into judicial terms with each other would lead to Sabellianism and would undermine the

---

[51] See Lewis Ayres on Augustine's understanding of inseparable operation, in Ayres, *Nicea and Its Legacy* (New York: Oxford, 2004), 371–72.

reality of the work of salvation with its relations between Person and Person."[52]

Again, these conclusions are clearly out of step with Augustine's Catholic orthodoxy. Rather, if the Father is the beginning of *substance* and *activity* (eternal generation) and there is unity in operation (one of harmony, not unison) among the persons, then a better alternative to Johnson's understanding of Augustine would be that the Father initiates the activity, and the Son faithfully accepts and joyfully carries out the Father's plan. As Letham writes, "This order is not to be understood in terms of human arrangements, such as rank or hierarchy, but in terms of an appropriate disposition."[53] This sort of order allows for both eternal generation *and* inseparable operation without one impeding on the other, or the whole scheme giving way to gross error.

2. *An order of authority and submission not only is incompatible with inseparable operation, but would divide the one will of the Father and Son.*

Johnson insists that if the Son is obedient to the Father, then the Father and Son must have different wills, therefore leaving no room for inseparable operation.[54] Giles agrees.[55] Is this the only option in Augustine or might there be an excluded middle?

Thomas Aquinas, attempting to work diligently within the parameters of Augustine's eternal generation and inseparable operations, asks and answers this question in his commentary on John 5:30:[56]

> But do not the Father and the Son have the same will? I answer that the Father and the Son do have the same will, but the Father does not have his will from another, whereas the Son does have his will from another, i.e., from the Father. Thus the Son accomplishes his own will as from another, i.e., as having it from another; but the Father accomplishes his will as his own; i.e., not having it from another. Thus he says: I am not seeking my own will, that is, such

---

[52] Geerhardus Vos, *Verbondsleer in de Gereformeerde Theologie*, 25. Quoted in G. C. Berkouwer, *Divine Election: Studies in Dogmatics* (Grand Rapids: Eerdmans, 1960), 164.
[53] Letham, *The Holy Trinity*, 383.
[54] Johnson, "Trinitarian Agency," 20.
[55] Giles, *Jesus and the Father*, 191.
[56] I'm indebted to Allen and Swain, "The Obedience of the Eternal Son," 127, for this insight.

as would be mine if it originated from myself, but my will, as being from another, that is from the Father.[57]

This suggests not a second will that the Son has *apart* from the Father, but a will that he shares *from* the Father.[58]

3. *Incompatibility with Augustine's inseparable operation and division of the one will of the Father and Son would therefore lead to incompatibility with* homoousian.

Johnson is correct to assume that if complementarians reject the inseparable operations of the Father and Son, that would lead to incompatibility with *homoousian*. In fact, all three—Giles, Erickson, and Johnson (Giles being the most egregious of the three)—tend to use Augustine to show that the Trinitarianism of complementarians is or tends to be less than *homoousian*.

However, the force of Augustine's argument is toward his Homoian opponents, who, as Johnson even confesses, "argued that the one who sends is 'greater than the one who is sent.'"[59] Clearly, complementarians make no such claim. Therefore, many of the quotes Johnson, Erickson, and Giles use against complementarians to show that Augustine opposed an "inferior-superior" or "greater than–less than" relation result in a *non sequitur*. Even more, as shown above, an order of authority and submission is a better alternative than the egalitarian one to uphold Augustine's doctrine of eternal generation and inseparable operation.

Conclusion

It is, therefore, not illegitimate for complementarians to appeal to Augustine's understanding of eternal generation as a ground for an order of authority and submission. For Augustine, eternal generation is the ground of an irreversible order of operations: a noncompetitive order of initiating authority and receptive submission between the Father and the Son.

---

[57] Thomas Aquinas, *Commentary on the Gospel of John, Chapters 1–5*, trans. Fabian Larcher and James A. Weisheipl (Washington, DC: Catholic University of America Press, 2010), 294–95.
[58] Allen and Swain, "The Obedience of the Eternal Son," 127. The authors note, "This is not to deny dyothelitism, but to suggest that the Son's obedient human will is determined by and expressive of his obedient divine will, i.e., the proper filial manner in which he executes the undivided divine will *ad extra*. See Thomas, *Summa Theologiae*, 3a.48.6."
[59] Johnson, "Trinitarian Agency," 21.

Nor does Augustine's inseparable operation qualify the "sent" language in Scripture to such an extent that an order of authority and submission would be incompatible with it. Rather, since Augustine emphasizes an inseparable operation of harmony, not unison, an order of authority and submission allows for both eternal generation *and* inseparable operation without one impeding on the other or the whole scheme giving way to gross error.

8

"To Devote Ourselves to the Blessed Trinity"

Eighteenth-Century Particular Baptists, Andrew Fuller, and the Defense of "Trinitarian Communities"

MICHAEL A. G. HAYKIN

It is a curious fact that although the concept of the encyclopedia has its origins within the ideological matrix of the eighteenth-century Enlightenment, when it comes to conservative expressions of theology, this era was not really conducive to encyclopedic or systematic summaries of the Christian Faith.[1] In this regard, a work like John Gill's (1697–1771) *Complete Body of Doctrinal and Practical Divinity* (1769–1770) was definitely out of sync with conservative theological trends. The other great Baptist theologian of this era, Andrew Fuller (1754–1815), was more typical. Though he was entirely capable of drawing up a systematic theology, he resisted doing so until it was too late. When he finally

---

[1] The title of this chapter comes from Andrew Fuller, "Strictures on Some of the Leading Sentiments of Mr. R. Robinson," in *The Complete Works of the Rev. Andrew Fuller* (hereafter *WAF*), ed. Joseph Belcher, 3 vols. (1845; repr., Harrisonburg, VA: Sprinkle, 1988), 3:601. For the term "Trinitarian communities," see Andrew Fuller, *Socinianism Indefensible on the Ground of Its Moral Tendency*, in *WAF* 2:258. Portions of my earlier paper "A Socinian and Calvinist Compared: Joseph Priestley and Andrew Fuller on the Propriety of Prayer to Christ," *Nederlands Archief voor Kerkgeschiedenis/Dutch Review of Church History* 73 (1993): 178–98, have been used in this essay with permission from E. J. Brill, the publisher of this journal.

began to write something in this vein, he had about sixteen months to live, and he never got beyond writing down his thoughts on the prolegomena of theology, the being of God, the necessity of revelation along with the inspiration of the Bible, and the doctrine of the Trinity.[2]

Fuller was well aware of his era's aversion to systematizing theology, for as he noted in a sermon he gave at the annual meeting of the Baptist churches of the Northamptonshire Association in 1796, "Systematic divinity . . . has been of late years much decried," and that because such a way of doing theology was regarded as "the mark of a contracted mind, and the grand obstruction to free inquiry."[3] In other words, the Enlightenment exaltation of rational inquiry unfettered by such external authorities as divine writ and holy church had made a significant imprint upon the world of Christian writing. Fuller went on to note, however, that only in the realm of religious thought was such an attitude acceptable. In other spheres of thought and action, such as philosophy, agriculture, or business, it would be regarded as folly to dispense with a foundational system of first principles.[4]

Fuller was convinced that there is a system of truth to be found in the Scriptures, even though that truth is not arranged systematically.[5] But the same was true of the world of nature, he argued. There one sees a "lovely variety but amidst all this variety, an observant eye will perceive unity, order, arrangement, and fullness of design."[6] Whatever difficulties might therefore attend the discovery of the systematic interlocking of biblical truths, it was vital to recognize that, from God's perspective, there was a unified body of truth. As Fuller noted in another context, to simply abandon the idea of theological truth because key aspects of it were disputed is, at best, absurd and, at worst, "infinitely . . . pernicious"; for "if all disputed subjects are to be reckoned matters of mere speculation, we shall have nothing of any real use left in religion."[7]

One of the most disputed theological *loci* in the eighteenth century

---

[2] See his *Letters on Systematic Divinity*, in WAF 1:684–711. Fuller was asked to draw up this "System of Divinity" at the request of his close friend John Ryland (1753–1825). He deals with the doctrine of the Trinity in the ninth and final letter (WAF 1:707–11). He would have written this final letter no earlier than October 1814.
[3] *The Nature and Importance of an Intimate Knowledge of Divine Truth* (1796), in WAF 1:164.
[4] Ibid., 1:165.
[5] "The Manner in which Divine Truth Is Communicated in the Holy Scriptures," in WAF 3:537.
[6] *Intimate Knowledge of Divine Truth*, in WAF 1:165.
[7] *A Defence of a Treatise Entitled The Gospel of Christ Worthy of All Acceptation Containing A Reply to Mr. Button's Remarks and The Observations of Philanthropos*, in WAF 2:511.

was also one that had been absolutely central to the Christian tradition, namely, the doctrine of the Trinity. The Trinitarianism of the ancient church had remained basically unchallenged until the seventeenth and eighteenth centuries. Even during the Reformation, a most tumultuous theological era, this vital area of Christian belief did not come into general dispute, though there were a few, like Michael Servetus (1511–1553) and the Italians Lelio Francesco Sozzini (1525–1562) and his nephew Fausto Sozzini (1539–1604),[8] who rejected Trinitarianism for a Unitarian perspective on the Godhead. However, as Sarah Mortimer has argued in her ground-breaking study of seventeenth-century English Socinianism, in the century after the Reformation the Socinian understanding of human beings as "inquiring, reasoning and active individuals who must take responsibility for their own spiritual lives" did come to play a critical role in undermining the way that "Trinitarian communities" in England had established theological boundaries for themselves.[9] This was part of a growing tide of rationalism in the seventeenth century, and the one following that led to a "fading of the trinitarian imagination" and to the doctrine coming under heavy attack.[10] Informed by the Enlightenment's confidence in the "omnicompetence" of human reason, increasingly the intellectual *mentalité* of this era either dismissed the doctrine of the Trinity as a philosophical and unbiblical construct of the post-apostolic church and turned to classical Arianism as an alternate, though admittedly odd, perspective, or simply ridiculed it as utterly illogical and argued for deism or Socinianism.[11] Of course, this retooling of theological perspectives did not happen without significant conflict. Contrary to the impression given by various historical overviews of the doctrine of the Trinity, the late seventeenth and eighteenth centuries were actually replete with critical battles over Trinitarianism. And some of these involved the Trinitarian community of which Andrew Fuller was a member, the Particular Baptists.

---

[8] His surname is sometimes rendered Socinus, hence Socinianism.
[9] *Reason and Religion in the English Revolution: The Challenge of Socinianism* (Cambridge: Cambridge University Press, 2010), 240–41.
[10] See especially William C. Placher, *The Domestication of Transcendence: How Modern Thinking about God Went Wrong* (Louisville, KY: Westminster John Knox, 1996), 164–78; Philip Dixon, 'Nice and Hot Disputes': The Doctrine of the Trinity in the Seventeenth Century (London: T&T Clark, 2003). The quote is from Dixon, 'Nice and Hot Disputes,' 212.
[11] G. L. Bray, "Trinity," in *New Dictionary of Theology*, ed. Sinclair B. Ferguson, David F. Wright, and J. I. Packer (Downers Grove, IL: InterVarsity, 1988), 694.

The Particular Baptists: A Trinitarian Community

Through the seventeenth and eighteenth centuries the Particular Baptists in the British Isles tenaciously confessed a Trinitarian understanding of the Godhead. And so, while other communities, such as the Presbyterians and General Baptists largely ceased to be Trinitarian,[12] the Particular Baptists continued to regard themselves, and that rightly, as a Trinitarian community. Their earliest confessional document, the First London Confession of Faith (1644/1646), had declared this about God:

> In [the] . . . Godhead, there is the Father, the Son, and the Spirit; being every one of them one and the same God; and therefore not divided, but distinguished one from another by their several properties; the Father being from himself, the Son of the Father from everlasting, the Holy Spirit proceeding from the Father and the Son.[13]

B. R. White has argued that this confession gave these early Baptists an extremely clear and self-conscious sense of their community's distinct identity and *raison d'être*.[14] And yet, as this specific paragraph also reveals, these Baptists were desirous of declaring their complete solidarity with the mainstream of classical Christianity, which was rooted in the fourth-century Trinitarian creedal declarations and also included the medieval Western church's commitment to the filioque. The other major Particular Baptist confession of the seventeenth century, the Second London Confession of Faith (1677/1689), was equally forthright in its Trinitarianism—in the words of Curtis Freeman, its "words . . . resonate with Nicene orthodoxy"[15]—and firmly linked this core Christian doctrine to spirituality. The "doctrine of the Trinity," it affirmed, "is the foundation of all our communion with God, and comfortable dependence on him."[16]

Throughout the long eighteenth century this community unhesitat-

---

[12] For the loss of Trinitarianism among the General Baptists, see the very helpful discussion by Curtis W. Freeman, "God in Three Persons: Baptist Unitarianism and the Trinity," *Perspectives in Religious Studies* 33 (Fall 2006): 324–28.
[13] The First London Confession of Faith, 2, in William L. Lumpkin, *Baptist Confessions of Faith*, 2nd ed., ed. Bill J. Leonard (Valley Forge, PA: Judson, 2011), 144. The spelling has been modernized.
[14] See, in particular, the following publications by White: "The Organisation of the Particular Baptists, 1644–1660," *Journal of Ecclesiastical History* 17 (1966): 209–26; "The Doctrine of the Church in the Particular Baptist Confession of 1644," *JTS*, n.s., 19 (1968): 570–90; "Thomas Patient in Ireland," *Irish Baptist Historical Society Journal* 2 (1969–1970): 36–48, esp. 40–41; "The Origins and Convictions of the First Calvinistic Baptists," *Baptist History and Heritage* 25, no. 4 (1990): 39–47; and *The English Baptists of the Seventeenth Century*, rev. ed. (London: Baptist Historical Society, 1996), 59–94.
[15] Freeman, "God in Three Persons," 331.
[16] The Second London Confession of Faith, 2.3, in Lumpkin, *Baptist Confessions of Faith*, 237.

"To Devote Ourselves to the Blessed Trinity" 177

ingly maintained that this doctrine is, in the words of Benjamin Wallin (1711–1782), the "first and grand principle of revealed truth and the gospel."[17] In 1690, the London Baptist layman Isaac Marlow (1649–1719), for example, published a treatise on the Trinity in which he stated his conviction that of those elements of divine truth that redound most to the glory of God and best further the fellowship of believers, "the blessed doctrine of the holy Trin-unity is the chiefest."[18] Nearly fifty years later, the renowned preacher Joseph Stennett II (1692–1758) similarly affirmed that "the doctrine of the ever blessed Trinity, is of the greatest importance to his [i.e., God's] glory."[19]

Typical of the Particular Baptists' grip on the doctrine of the Trinity during this era was a major defense of this doctrine by the voluminous John Gill. His *Doctrine of the Trinity Stated and Vindicated*—first published in 1731 and then reissued in a second edition in 1752—proved to be an extremely effective defense of the fact that there is, as Gill put it, "but one God; that there is a plurality in the Godhead; that there are three divine Persons in it; that the Father is God, the Son God, and the Holy Spirit God; that these are distinct in Personality, the same in substance, equal in power and glory."[20] Gill was especially concerned in this treatise to affirm the eternal sonship of the second person of the Godhead. As he explained in a letter to John Davis (1702–1778), the Welsh pastor of the Baptist Church in the Great Valley, Devon, Pennsylvania, in March of 1745:

> Jesus Christ is the Son of God by nature and not office, . . . he is the eternal Son of God by ineffable filiation and not by constitution or as mediator in which respect he is a servant, and not a Son. And of this mind are all our churches of the particular Baptist persuasion nor will they admit to communion, nor continue in communion [with] such as are of a different judgment. . . . I have some years ago published a treatise upon the doctrine of the Trinity, in which I have particularly handled the point of Christ's sonship, have established

---

[17] *The Eternal Existence of the Lord Jesus Christ Considered and Improved* (London, 1766), iv–v.
[18] "To the Reader," in *A Treatise of the Holy Trinunity* [sic] (London, 1690), i–ii. For a brief discussion of this work, see Freeman, "God in Three Persons," 332–33.
[19] *The Christian Strife for the Faith of the Gospel* (London, 1738), 78, cited in Roger Hayden, "The Contribution of Bernard Foskett," in *Pilgrim Pathways: Essays in Baptist History in Honour of B. R. White*, ed. William H. Brackney and Paul S. Fiddes, with John H. Y. Briggs (Macon, GA: Mercer University Press, 1999), 197.
[20] *The Doctrine of the Trinity, Stated and Vindicated*, 2nd ed. (London, 1752), 166–67.

the orthodox sense of it, and refuted the other notion, which tho' it may be held by some, as not downright *Sabeleanism* [*sic*], yet it tends to it.[21]

The heart of this treatise was later incorporated into Gill's *Body of Doctrinal Divinity* (1769), which, for most Baptist pastors of that day, was their major theological reference work. As John Rippon (1751–1836), Gill's successor at Carter Lane, noted in a biographical sketch of his predecessor:

> The Doctor not only watched over his *people*, "with great affection, fidelity, and love"; but he also watched his *pulpit* also. He would not, if he knew it, admit any one to preach for him, who was either cold-hearted to the doctrine of the Trinity; or who *denied* the divine filiation of the Son of God; or who *objected* to conclude his prayers with the usual *doxology* to Father, Son, and Holy Spirit, as three equal Persons in the one Jehovah. Sabellians, Arians, and Socinians, he considered as real enemies of the cross of Christ. They *dared* not ask him to preach, nor *could* he in conscience, permit them to officiate for him. He conceived that, by this uniformity of conduct, he adorned the pastoral office.[22]

Gill's defense of the Trinity did far more than adorn the pastoral office; through it he played a key role in shepherding the English Particular Baptist community along the pathway of biblical orthodoxy.

Gill's concern to uphold the eternal sonship and reject Sabellianism was not misplaced. During the late 1740s and 1750s the influential Welsh Calvinistic Methodist leader Howel Harris (1714–1773) was pushing Patripassianism and seemed to be veering toward Sabellian heterodoxy,[23] while Gill's fellow Baptist Anne Dutton (1692–1765) was sure that she detected Sabellianism in a tract by the popular Anglican Evangelical William Romaine (1714–1795).[24] Among the Baptists, John

---

[21] Letter to John Davis, March 7, 1745 (transcribed by Gerald Priest; manuscript in The Baptist Church in the Great Valley, Devon, Pennsylvania; used by permission of the church). I am indebted to Dr. Priest, for many years professor of church history at the Detroit Baptist Theological Seminary, for access to this letter.
[22] John Rippon, *A Brief Memoir of the Life and Writings of the Late Rev. John Gill, D.D.* (1838; repr., Harrisonburg, VA: Gano, 1992), 127–28.
[23] Eifion Evans, *Daniel Rowland and the Great Evangelical Awakening in Wales* (Edinburgh: Banner of Truth, 1985), 273–74.
[24] For Dutton's concern about Romaine, see *A Letter on the Divine Eternal Sonship of Jesus Christ* (London, 1757), now in *Selected Spiritual Writings of Anne Dutton: Eighteenth-Century, British-Baptist, Woman Theologian*, ed. JoAnn Ford Watson, vol. 5 (Mercer, GA: Mercer University Press, 2008), 1–13.

Allen (fl. 1740s–1780s)—"a prickly and polemic character,"[25] and also something of a loner who emigrated to America, where he helped inflame politically radical sentiments prior to the Revolution—publicly accused Gill in 1770 of undermining the salvific work of Christ in his affirmation of the eternal generation of the Son. As Allen put it in his own peculiar style:

> I wonder for my part how the Doctor [Gill] dares to die with such an idea in his heart, that he who is the glory of God, the glory of heaven, the glory of the saints, has only his personal glory and existence by generation: does the Doctor think such stuff as this will pass in Israel? . . . The Doctor teaches, that a first, second, and a third person existeth [in the Godhead], the one by nature, the other by being begotten,—and the other by procession; such an idea as this of the existence of God, we think is unworthy his name, his nature, and perfection, and contrary to the declaration of the truth of Christ, who says, "I am, I am the first" [Rev. 1:17b]; as tho' he had said, "I am of myself, and derive neither essential nor personal glory from none"—therefore it is that we believe according to the sweet simplicity of the Scriptures, that the Father, Son, and Holy Ghost, the sacred three that bare record in heaven [see 1 John 5:7], self-exist in every glory and perfection of the divine nature, whether essential or personal as the Triune God. . . . [So] if he [i.e., Christ] is not self-existent in all the glories of his divine person, my soul, I think, can never be saved; for can that being (or to come close to the point) that divine person that has its highest existence by generation save another? And does not this idea cut through (as it were with the Arian and Socinian sword) all the glories of Christ's person, the merit of his blood, the conquest of his resurrection, and power of his intercession?[26]

In other words, Gill's promotion of the eternal generation of the Son ultimately achieved what the Arians or Socinians aimed at—it fatally undermined the confession of the Son's essential deity!

---

[25] The words of Hywel M. Davies, *Transatlantic Brethren: Rev. Samuel Jones (1735–1814) and His Friends: Baptists in Wales, Pennsylvania, and Beyond* (Bethlehem, PA: Lehigh University Press; London: Associated University Presses, 1995), 116. See Davies's account of Allen's career in *Transatlantic Brethren*, 115–19. See also Jim Benedict, "Allen, John (*d.* 1783x8)," *Oxford Dictionary of National Biography* (Oxford: Oxford University Press, 2004); online ed., May 2007, accessed December 18, 2013, http://www.oxforddnb.com /libaccess.lib.mcmaster.ca/view/article/380.

[26] *The Spirit of Liberty: or, Junius's Loyal Address* ([London ?], 1770), 91–92, 95. The capitals in this text have been altered to lowercase in accord with modern practice.

Although the particular piece in which this critique of Gill appeared also contained drubbings of numerous other English Baptists,[27] Allen's rejection of the eternal generation of the Son gained a hearing in more than one Baptist quarter. Andrew Fuller, for instance, was given one of Allen's publications on this subject to read when he was a relatively young Christian in 1775. True to a lifelong "determination to take up no principle at second-hand; but to search for everything at the pure fountain of [God's] word,"[28] Fuller tested Allen's views by Scripture and came to see that a number of biblical texts—namely, John 5:18; Galatians 4:4; Hebrews 1:8; 5:8–9; and 1 John 3:8—provided clear evidence that Allen was mistaken and that Christ was indeed "the Son of God antecedently to his being born of a woman, and that in calling God his own Father, he made himself equal with God."[29] In the long run, Fuller was glad that he wrestled with this issue among others early on in his Christian life. It gave him the deep conviction that "everything pertaining to the person of Christ is of more than ordinary importance." And it also provided a kind of test run for his polemical responses to Socinianism in the 1790s.[30]

Socinianism

The leading form of heterodoxy within English Dissent in the last quarter of the eighteenth century was Socinianism.[31] In large part, this was due to the vigorous campaigning of Joseph Priestley (1733–1804), whom Michael R. Watts, in his study of the early history of British nonconformity, has dubbed the "Leonardo da Vinci of Dissent."[32] By his early twenties, Priestley was proficient in physics, philosophy, and

---

[27] See ibid., 95–104.
[28] Cited in Andrew Gunton Fuller, "Memoir," in *WAF* 1:20.
[29] Cited in John Ryland, *The Work of Faith, the Labour of Love, and the Patience of Hope Illustrated; in the Life and Death of the Reverend Andrew Fuller* (London: Button & Son, 1816), 62–63, 54.
[30] Ibid., 52, 54. See also John W. Eddins Jr., "Andrew Fuller's Theology of Grace" (ThD diss., The Southern Baptist Theological Seminary, Louisville, Kentucky, 1957), 123–30.
[31] H. L. Short, "Presbyterians under a New Name," in C. G. Bolam et al., *The English Presbyterians from Elizabethan Puritanism to Modern Unitarianism* (London: George Allen & Unwin, 1968), 229–33.
[32] *The Dissenters*, vol. 1 (Oxford: Clarendon, 1978), 472. For the biographical details of Priestley's career, I am especially indebted to *The Memoirs of Dr. Joseph Priestley*, ed. John T. Boyer (Washington, DC: Barcroft, 1964); Robert D. Fiala, "Priestley, Joseph (1733–1804)," in *Biographical Dictionary of Modern British Radicals*, ed. Joseph O. Baylen and Norbert J. Gossman, vol. 1 (Hassocks, Sussex: Harvester; Atlantic Highlands, NJ: Humanities, 1979), 396–401; Erwin N. Hiebert, "The Integration of Revealed Religion and Scientific Materialism in the Thought of Joseph Priestley," in *Joseph Priestley: Scientist, Theologian, and Metaphysician*, ed. Lester Kieft and Bennett R. Willeford Jr. (Lewisburg, PA: Bucknell University Press, 1980), 27–61.

mathematics, as well as a variety of modern and ancient Near Eastern languages. During the 1760s and 1770s his reputation as England's foremost experimental scientist was established by his publication of a weighty history of electrical experimentation and his discovery of ten new gases, including oxygen, ammonia, and sulfur dioxide. Alongside this illustrious career as a scientist Priestley was also a prolific and profound theological author. In fact, he regarded his work as a theologian to be his true vocation.

After his conversion to the Socinian cause, which probably took place in 1769,[33] Priestley devoted much of his time to theological writing "with no other view," he baldly stated on one occasion, "than to make proselytes."[34] "An unflagging and often pugnacious controversialist," Priestley sought to establish his position not on nature and human reason, as did the deists, but on a serious and rational investigation of the Scriptures and history.[35] As a Dissenter he had inherited the Protestant commitment to the Scriptures as a sufficient source of religious truth. "Revelation," Martin Fitzpatrick has noted, "lay at the core of his religion."[36] This attachment to the Scriptures, though, was yoked to a deep-rooted conviction that the "plainest and most obvious sense of the Scriptures is in favour of those doctrines which are most agreeable to reason."[37] In other words, the Scriptures do indeed contain divine revelation, but their interpretation is to be determined by what accords with sound reason. Priestley did not deny that certain affirmations of Scripture are beyond the grasp of human reason. He admitted, for example, the historicity of many miracles of

---

[33] Robert E. Schofield, "Priestley, Joseph (1733–1804)," in *Oxford Dictionary of National Biography*, accessed April 1, 2013, http://www.oxforddnb.com.libaccess.lib.mcmaster.ca/view/article/22788.

[34] *Defences of Unitarianism, for the Year 1786* (1787), in *The Theological and Miscellaneous Works of Joseph Priestley* (hereafter *WJP*), ed. J. T. Rutt, 25 vols. (London, 1817–1832; repr., New York: Klaus, 1972), 18:372.

In a lecture "On the Spirit of Socinianism," which Fuller's friend Robert Hall Jr. (1764–1831) gave in 1823, the Baptist preacher took note of the Socinians' "zeal for proselytism" (*The Works of the Rev. Robert Hall*, ed. Olinthus Gregory and Joseph Belcher, vol. 3 [New York: Harper & Bros., 1854], 24).

[35] For Priestley's threefold appeal to reason, Scripture, and history, see his *Defences of Unitarianism, for the Year 1786*, in *WJP* 18:350; *An History of Early Opinions concerning Jesus Christ* (1786), in *WJP* 6:7. The description of Priestley is that of Martin Fitzpatrick, "Toleration and Truth," *Enlightenment and Dissent* 1 (1982): 25.

[36] "Toleration and Truth," 29n119. On the commitment of Socinianism in general to Scripture, see Klaus Scholder, *The Birth of Modern Critical Theology: Origins and Problems of Biblical Criticism in the Seventeenth Century*, trans. John Bowden (London: SCM; Philadelphia: Trinity, 1990), 32–38.

[37] *An Appeal to the Serious and Candid Professors of Christianity* (1770), in *WJP* 2:385. See also J. G. McEvoy and J. E. McGuire, "God and Nature: Priestley's Way of Rational Dissent," *Historical Studies in the Physical Sciences* 6 (1975): 325–26; Fitzpatrick, "Toleration and Truth," 4–5.

the apostolic era, including the bodily resurrection of Christ.[38] What he refused to countenance, though, were interpretations of Scripture that, to his mind, entailed a logical contradiction. This explains why orthodox Trinitarianism bore the brunt of Priestley's theological polemic.[39] Priestley was convinced that the doctrine of the Trinity not only had no scriptural foundation, but also was a mathematical impossibility, "since three cannot be one, or one, three."[40] From Priestley's perspective, if there is one divine being, there must perforce be one person and thus one God; if there are three divine persons, then there must be three divine beings and so three gods.

In the *Institutes of Natural and Revealed Religion*, Priestley's earliest major theological work, Priestley thus maintained that God had instructed "the first parents of mankind" in the truth of his oneness and the fact that he alone is to be worshiped. "History," Priestley told his readers, "informs us that the worship of one God, without images, was in all nations prior to polytheism."[41] This "primitive religion of mankind," however, soon became corrupted, and idolatry gradually superseded the worship of the one true God. In order to free men and women from their idolatry, God gave to human beings the Scriptures, a fact that Priestley regards as self-evident when one considers "how strongly this great article, the worship of one God only, is guarded in all the books of Scripture."[42] Yet, because of the human bent toward idolatry, this article was subject to corruption both during the time of the Old Testament dispensation and after that of the New. Priestley was especially concerned with the latter period, for it was then that there was introduced into the life of the church not only the worship of Mary and "innumerable other saints," but also what he bluntly described as the "idolatrous worship of Jesus Christ."[43]

The Reformation had only partially rectified this state of affairs,

---

[38] *An History of the Corruptions of Christianity*, vol. 2 (1782; repr., New York; London: Garland, 1974), 440.
[39] Cf. Scholder, *Modern Critical Theology*, 40; Geoffrey Gorham, "Seventeenth- and Eighteenth-Century Intellectual Life," in *The Routledge Companion to Theism*, ed. Charles Taliaferro, Victoria S. Harrison, and Stewart Goetz (New York; London: Routledge, 2013), 129–30.
[40] *Defences of Unitarianism, for the Years 1788 and 1789* (1790), in *WJP* 19:108. See also his *Appeal to the Serious and Candid Professors of Christianity*, in *WJP* 2:395; *History of Early Opinions concerning Jesus Christ*, in *WJP* 6:33–37; *Letters to the Members of the New Jerusalem Church* (Birmingham, 1791), 2.
[41] *WJP* 2:74.
[42] Ibid., 2:280.
[43] Ibid.

for while it had rejected prayers to the Virgin Mary and to the saints, "prayers to Christ, who is no more a proper object of worship than his mother, . . . were retained."[44] In arguing against the propriety of praying to Christ, Priestley envisaged himself as completing, therefore, one aspect of the rediscovery of New Testament Christianity that had been left undone by the sixteenth-century Reformers. In fact, Alexander Gordon has pointed out that the major difference between the Socinianism promoted by Priestley, along with friends like Theophilus Lindsey (1723–1808), and earlier English versions of this heterodoxy is that while Priestley and company condemned the worship of Christ as idolatrous, the earlier English versions merely sought to keep it within due moderation. In Gordon's words, Priestley and Lindsey made "reduction of worship to a strict Patrolatry . . . central and distinguishing."[45]

From what he called "the general tenour of Scripture," Priestley argued that the early church knew nothing of Christ as "a proper object of worship" or prayer.[46] He found proof for this assertion in the fact, for instance, that Christ and his followers in the early church were in the habit of directing their prayers to God alone. As Priestley put it:

> Our Saviour himself always prayed to his Father, and with as much humility and resignation as the most dependent being in the universe could possibly do; always addressing him as his Father, or the author of his being; and he directs his disciples to the same great Being, whom only, he says, we ought to serve.[47]

Priestley appears to have in mind here such incidents in the life of Christ as his prayers in the garden of Gethsemane (e.g., Luke 22:42) and his response to his disciples' request to teach them how to pray (Luke 11:1–2). The life of the early church as it is described in Acts provided Priestley with further examples. In Acts 4:24–30 there is recorded a "prayer of some length," which is addressed solely to God. Later, when James the brother of John was martyred and Peter imprisoned, supplication was made on Peter's behalf to God without any mention of Christ (Acts 12:5).

---

[44] *Familiar Letters, Addressed to the Inhabitants of Birmingham* (1790), in *WJP* 19:250.
[45] *Addresses Biographical and Historical* (London: Lindsey, 1922), 276.
[46] *History of Early Opinions concerning Jesus Christ*, in *WJP* 6:31–33.
[47] Ibid., 6:28–29. See also 6:30; *Letters to Dr. Horsley* (1783), in *WJP* 18:95; *Familiar Letters, Addressed to the Inhabitants of Birmingham*, in *WJP* 19:249.

Likewise, the apostle Paul, in passages such as Ephesians 3:14, "speaks of himself as praying to God, and not to Christ."[48]

Not only did Priestley find no clear examples in the New Testament that provided a precedent for praying to Christ; he was also confident that the New Testament commands us to pray to none but God alone. James, for instance, directs those of his readers who lacked wisdom to ask God for it (James 1:5). He does not, Priestley emphasizes, advise "them to apply to Christ or to the Trinity for direction in these circumstances."[49] The same is true with regard to the apostle Paul. In Priestley's *Notes on All the Books of Scripture* (1804), he quotes with evident approval a comment by a fellow Socinian, Paul Cardale (1705–1775), on the apostle's instruction in Philippians 4:6 ("Let your requests be made known unto God"—KJV): "Had it been possible for St. Paul to entertain the doctrine of a Trinity, he would no doubt have directed his own prayers, and [those of] the Philippians, to the Sacred Three, as is the common language of the present age."[50] As Stephen Ford has pointed out, the final clause of this quote obviously has in view the language of the Church of England's Book of Common Prayer, in which prayers and collects are regularly concluded with a reference to the Trinity.[51] An open letter that Priestley wrote to a Swedenborgian congregation in 1791 made a similar point regarding Christ's instructions about prayer in John 16:23 ("In that day ye shall ask me nothing. Verily, verily, I say unto you, whatsoever ye shall ask the Father in my name, he will give it you"—KJV). According to Priestley's reading of the text, Christ "plainly distinguishes between praying to the Father, and asking any thing of himself."[52] His comments on this verse and its context in the *Notes on All the Books of Scripture* reiterate that "Christ is not to be the object of worship or prayer in any respect," and that, contrary to what Christ appears to teach by the phrase "whatsoever ye shall ask the Father in my name," "the intercession of Christ with God for us is needless. We are to address our prayers to God himself

---

[48] *Letters to Dr. Horsley*, Part II (1784), in *WJP* 18:243–44; *Notes on All the Books of Scripture*, in *WJP* 14:274.
[49] *Letters to Dr. Horsley*, Part II, in *WJP* 18:243.
[50] *Notes on All the Books of Scripture*, in *WJP* 14:320.
[51] "Coleridge and Priestley on Prayer," *Anglican Theological Review* 70 (1988): 353. Cf. Priestley, *Familiar Letters, Addressed to the Inhabitants of Birmingham*, in *WJP* 19:249–50.
[52] *Letters to the Members of the New Jerusalem Church*, 21. See also *Notes on All the Books of Scripture*, in *WJP* 13:315.

immediately; and his affection for us is such as will always induce him to grant whatever is proper for us, without the intercession, or mediation, of any being whatever for us."[53]

In his scientific enquiries Priestley was regularly guided by utilitarian considerations, since he believed that the "immediate use of natural science is the power it gives us over nature, by means of the knowledge we acquire of its laws; whereby human life is . . . made more comfortable and happy."[54] Similarly, "the sound knowledge of Christianity is not of importance as a matter of speculation merely"; the theological convictions for which Priestley contended could not be believed without an impact on the "sentiments of our hearts, and our conduct in life."[55] In the case of his belief regarding the nature of God there were at least two practical consequences. First, God the Father alone should be the recipient of prayer and he alone worshiped. Then, Socinians must separate themselves from those who disagreed with them, and they needed to form their own congregations. Addressing men and women of like mind, Priestley therefore raised the question that if

> it was a sufficient justification of the first Reformers, that they considered the church from which they separated as worshipping saints and angels; will it not justify your separation from their partial reformations, that you consider them as praying to and worshipping one whom you consider as a man like yourselves, though honoured and distinguished by God above all other men? To join habitually in public worship with Trinitarians, is countenancing that worship, which you must consider as idolatrous; and which, however innocent in them, is highly criminal in you.[56]

The society in which Priestley was seeking to propagate his viewpoint and establish Socinian congregations was, however, to a great extent still dominated by a powerful *ancien régime* whose political ideology and religious convictions were firmly interwoven.[57] Consequently,

---

[53] *Notes on All the Books of Scripture*, in *WJP* 13:328.
[54] Quoted in John G. McEvoy, "Joseph Priestley, 'Aerial Philosopher': Metaphysics and Methodology in Priestley's Chemical Thought, from 1762–1781. Part 1," *Ambix* 25, no. 1 (1978): 18.
[55] *Appeal to the Serious and Candid Professors of Christianity*, in *WJP* 2:402.
[56] Ibid., 2:414.
[57] On this *ancien régime*, see especially J. C. D. Clark, *English Society 1688–1832: Ideology, Social Structure and Political Practice during the Ancien Regime* (Cambridge: Cambridge University Press, 1985); Clark, "England's Ancien Regime as a Confessional State," *Albion* 21 (1989): 450–74.

it is not at all surprising that his assertions regarding the person of Christ involved Priestley in a variety of heated and prolific debates during the 1780s and early 1790s, which fostered a widespread public perception of Priestley as an enemy to both church and state. Indeed this perception was the key factor in the violent Birmingham "Church and King" riots of 1791, which witnessed the destruction of Priestley's home, library, and laboratory, as well as the meetinghouse in which he regularly preached, and which eventually led to his emigration to the United States in 1794.[58]

"Ardent Love to Christ": Fuller's Response to Socinianism

Among Priestley's fellow Dissenters who publicly deplored these riots was Andrew Fuller. From Fuller's point of view the riots were an "iniquitous business," contrived and executed by "men of no principle."[59] Fuller's profound disapproval of the riots did not deter him, however, from publishing in 1793 an extensive critique of Priestley's position in *The Calvinistic and Socinian Systems Examined and Compared, as to Their Moral Tendency*.[60] Fuller was well aware that there had been numerous replies to the Socinian position by orthodox authors. What made his response unique was that it sought to determine which one of these two rival perspectives on the Christian faith was most "aretegenic," that is, most conducive to the development of moral transformation and the creation of virtuous character.[61]

As has been noted, Socinians such as Priestley argued that the first-century church refused to venerate Christ and thus worshiped God aright. Yet, Fuller asks, if this be so, how does one explain the fact that

---

[58] On these riots, see Arthur Sheps, "Public Perception of Joseph Priestley, the Birmingham Dissenters, and the Church-and-King Riots of 1791," *Eighteenth Century Life* 13 (1989): 46–64.
[59] *Calvinistic and Socinian Systems Examined and Compared*, in WAF 2:111. See also the comments by Fuller in his *Memoirs of the Rev. Samuel Pearce*, in WAF 3:433.
[60] WAF 2:108–242. Fuller received advice from both Abraham Booth (1734–1806) and John Fawcett (1740–1817), fellow Baptist ministers, in drawing up this treatise. See J. W. Morris, *Memoirs of the Life and Writings of the Rev. Andrew Fuller* (London, 1816), 330–31.
[61] *Calvinistic and Socinian Systems*, in WAF 2:112. The term "aretegenic" is a neologism coined by Ellen T. Charry. See her important work *By the Renewing of Your Minds: The Pastoral Function of Christian Doctrine* (New York: Oxford University Press, 1997). See also the study of this area of Fuller's response to Priestley by Ryan Patrick Hoselton, "'The Love of God Holds Creation Together': Andrew Fuller's Theology of Virtue" (ThM thesis, The Southern Baptist Theological Seminary, Louisville, Kentucky, 2013).

the primitive Christians . . . worshipped Jesus Christ. Not only did the martyr Stephen close his life by committing his departing spirit into the hands of Jesus, but it was the common practice, in primitive times, to invoke his name. "He hath authority," said Ananias concerning Saul, to bind "all that call on thy name" [Acts 9:14]. One part of the Christian mission was to declare that "whosoever should call on the name of the Lord should be saved" [cf. Rom. 10:13], even of that Lord of whom the Gentiles had not heard. Paul addressed himself "to all that in every place called upon the name of the Lord Jesus Christ" [cf. 1 Cor. 1:2]. These modes of expression (which, if I be not greatly mistaken, always signify Divine worship) plainly inform us that it was not merely the practice of a few individuals, but of the great body of the primitive Christians, to invoke the name of Christ; nay, and that this was a mark by which they were distinguished as Christians.[62]

In order to demonstrate that the worship of Christ was not unknown during the period covered by the New Testament, Fuller began with Acts 7:59, a text frequently raised during this controversy over the person of Christ. The Baptist author saw in Stephen's "calling upon" Christ an act of invocation and prayer, and thus worship.[63] Fuller observed that the verb "to call upon" is used in a variety of contexts in the New Testament to designate Christians. Ananias, for instance, described the believers in Damascus as "all that call on thy name" (Acts 9:14). This description is found in the midst of an address to the "Lord" (Acts 9:10, 13), who, from the context, can be none other than Jesus (Acts 9:17; see also 9:5). A similar phrase was used by the apostle Paul when he characterized his ministry as a proclamation of God's desire to save "whosoever shall call upon the name of the Lord" (Rom. 10:13) and when he designated Christians as all those who "call upon the name of Jesus Christ our Lord" (1 Cor. 1:2). Since this phrase clearly depicts prayer in Acts 7:59, Fuller reasoned that it must have a similar meaning in the other New Testament texts where it appears. Thus, he stated that "these modes of expression . . . always signify Divine worship."[64]

[62] *Calvinistic and Socinian Systems*, in WAF 2:160.
[63] See also his interpretation of Acts 7:59 in *Socinianism Indefensible on the Ground of Its Moral Tendency*, in WAF 2:260; "Defence of the Deity of Christ," in WAF 3:698.
[64] *Calvinistic and Socinian Systems*, in WAF 2:160.

Moreover, the early Christian writers, Fuller maintained, made the dignity and glory of Christ's person "their darling theme," for they "considered Christ as the All in All of their religion; and, as such, they loved him with their whole hearts."[65] Among the examples he adduced in support of this observation is Paul's depiction of Christ in Ephesians 1–3.

> Feeling in himself an ardent love to Christ, he vehemently desired that others might love him too. For this cause he bowed his knees to the Father of our Lord Jesus Christ [cf. Eph. 3:14], in behalf of the Ephesians; praying that Christ might dwell in their hearts by faith. He represented him to them as the medium of all spiritual blessings; of election, adoption, acceptance with God, redemption, and the forgiveness of sins; of a future inheritance, and of a present earnest of it; as Head over all things to the church, and as him that filleth all in all. He described him as the only way of access to God, and as the sole foundation of a sinner's hope; whose riches were unsearchable, and the dimensions of his love passing knowledge.[66]

Priestley, as has been noted, regarded the fact that Paul directs his prayer in Ephesians 3:14 to God the Father, and not to Christ, to be a significant indication of the apostle's convictions about the impropriety of prayer to Christ. Fuller, though, sought to relate this prayer to its immediate and larger context in the letter to the Ephesians. Central to the prayer in Ephesians 3 is Paul's request of the Father that Christ might indwell the hearts of his readers by faith. Who is this Christ, though, about whom Paul makes such a request? Well, in what precedes his prayer Paul has described Christ, to use the words of Fuller, as "the medium of all spiritual blessings" (cf. Eph. 1:3), the "only way of access to God" (cf. Eph. 2:18), and the One "whose riches were unsearchable" (cf. Eph. 3:8). Moreover, the apostle finishes his prayer by stating that "the dimensions of his [i.e., Christ's] love" surpass knowledge (Eph. 3:18–19). Could the love that is evident in such descriptions as these, Fuller justly asked, ever be bestowed on "a fellow creature"—"a fallible and peccable man" in Priestley's perspective[67]—without it being

---
[65] Ibid., 2:189, 192.
[66] Ibid., 2:192.
[67] Ibid., 2:193.

considered anything but "the height of extravagance, and essence of idolatry"? In other words, while Paul's prayer may not actually be addressed to Christ, its content and that which it presupposes all point to a conviction of Christ's deity.

The Socinians' rejection of the propriety of praying to Christ or worshiping him led in turn to Fuller's refusal to recognize them as Christian brothers and sisters.[68] As the Baptist theologian pointed out in an article entitled "The Deity of Christ":

> Calling on the name of the Lord Jesus is considered, in the New Testament, as of equal importance with believing in him, having the same promise of salvation annexed to it.—"Whosoever shall call upon the name of the Lord shall be saved" [Rom. 10:13]. And seeing it is asked, "How shall they call on him in whom they have not believed?" [Rom. 10:14], it is strongly intimated that all who truly believe in Christ do call upon him. This is one of the distinguishing characteristics of the primitive Christians. Paul's Epistle to the Corinthians was addressed to them, in connexion with "all who in every place call upon the name of Jesus Christ our Lord" [1 Cor. 1:2]. Now as a rejection of the Divinity of Christ renders it idolatry to worship him, or call upon his name; so it must involve a rejection of that by which primitive Christians were distinguished, and which has the promise of salvation.... We have no warrant to acknowledge those as fellow Christians who come not under the description given of such in the New Testament; that is, who call not upon the name of Jesus Christ our Lord.[69]

Romans 10:13–15a outlines the chain of events by which a person is saved. It begins with God's sending forth someone to preach the gospel and concludes with a person responding in faith by calling upon the name of the Lord. Fuller noted how vital is the final link in this chain, the calling upon the name of the Lord, for this action is determinant of the status of Christian. Unless a person has called upon the name of the Lord for salvation, he or she cannot consider himself or herself a Christian. This conclusion is further supported by 1 Corinthians 1:2, which describes Christians by means of the verb "to call upon" and

---
[68] "Agreement in Sentiment the Bond of Christian Union," in *WAF* 3:490, 491.
[69] "The Deity of Christ," in *WAF* 3:696, 697.

where this verb is used in a similar fashion to Romans 10, namely, the invoking of the risen Christ in prayer. The Socinians, however, rejected the propriety of prayer to Christ on any occasion and for any reason. By so doing, Fuller could only conclude, they should not be regarded as Christians in the New Testament sense of the term.

Fuller thus was in full accord with Priestley that Socinians and Trinitarians should not worship together and that the former ought to have their own "separate communion"[70] or community.

> Some of the grand ends of Christian society are, unitedly to worship God—to devote ourselves to the blessed Trinity by Christian baptism—and to acknowledge the atonement made by the Redeemer, by a participation of the ordinance of the Lord's supper. But what union could there be in worship where the object worshipped is not the same—where one party believes the other to be an idolater, and the other believes him to be a degrader of Him who is "over all, God, blessed for ever" [Rom. 9:5]? . . . Either we are a company of idolaters, or they are enemies to the gospel—rendering the cross of Christ of none effect. Either they are unbelievers, or we are at least as bad—rendering to a creature that homage which is due only to the Creator; and, in either case, a union is the last degree of absurdity.[71]

Fuller's Trinitarianism

Foundational to Fuller's response to Priestley was the former's deep conviction that Jesus is fully divine. For Fuller, Socinianism's denial of Christ's deity made it akin to deism, and this could only lead to the total ruination of the virtuous life.[72] As he put it in a sermon he preached in 1801, "The person and work of Christ have ever been the corner-stone of the Christian fabric: take away his Divinity and atonement, and all will go to ruins."[73] Christ's deity and his atoning work are "the life-blood of Christianity"; deny them and there is only death.[74] Fuller thus frequently insisted that without the confession of the deity of Christ,

---

[70] "Decline of the Dissenting Interest," in *WAF* 3:487.
[71] *Leading Sentiments of Mr. R. Robinson*, in *WAF* 3:601.
[72] *Calvinistic and Socinian Systems*, in *WAF* 2:220–33.
[73] *God's Approbation of Our Labours Necessary to the Hope of Success*, in *WAF* 1:190. See also *Calvinistic and Socinian Systems*, in *WAF* 2:183; *The Backslider*, in *WAF* 3:637.
[74] *Christian Steadfastness*, in *WAF* 1:527. See also *Calvinistic and Socinian Systems*, in *WAF* 2:183, 191–92.

one simply cannot be counted as a Christian, for "the proper Deity of Christ... is a great and fundamental truth in Christianity."[75]

Given this insistence about Christ's deity, it is noteworthy that when it came to the divinity of the Holy Spirit, Fuller was nowhere near as emphatic, though he did believe that the Scriptures "expressly call... the Holy Spirit God" in Acts 5:3–4, and he did not hesitate to assert that "every perfection of Godhead" has been ascribed to the Spirit.[76] This lacuna is somewhat surprising since Fuller, like others impacted by the evangelical revivals of the eighteenth century, had a robust understanding of the Spirit's work and ministry.[77] In part, this is because Priestley and the other apostles of Socinianism focused their attention overwhelmingly upon Christ and not the Holy Spirit. When Fuller on one occasion referred to the first principles of Christianity he believed were the focus of the Socinian controversy, he listed the doctrine of the Trinity, the deity of Christ, and the atoning death of the Lord Jesus,[78] not the distinct deity of the Spirit. Fuller's defense of the deity of Christ and the propriety of worshiping him is therefore akin to the way Athanasius argued in the fourth century. The church father also spent most of his time and energy defending the full and essential divinity of Christ in the face of the Arian onslaught against Christ's person. Only near the end of his life did Athanasius turn his attention to the Spirit.[79] However, Fuller was also aware that the Spirit's overarching new covenant ministry is the glorification of the Lord Jesus—the "Holy Spirit is not the grand object of ministerial exhibition; but Christ, in his person, work and offices"—and this is a key reason why "much less is said in the Sacred Scriptures on the Divinity and personality of the Holy Spirit."[80] And here Fuller seems to have followed Scripture.

---

[75] *Calvinistic and Socinian Systems*, in *WAF* 2:180; *Justification*, in *WAF* 1:284; *Calvinistic and Socinian Systems*, in *WAF* 2:183, 191–92; *Defence of a Treatise Entitled The Gospel of Christ*, in *WAF* 2:458; "Decline of the Dissenting Interest," in *WAF* 3:487; "The Deity of Christ," in *WAF* 3:693–97; *Calvinistic and Socinian Systems*, in *WAF* 2:180.
[76] "Defence of the Deity of Christ," in *WAF* 3:698; "Remarks on the Indwelling Scheme," in *WAF* 3:700. See also *Letters on Systematic Divinity*, in *WAF* 1:711; "Mr. Bevan's Defence of the Christian Doctrines of the Society of Friends," in *WAF* 3:758.
[77] See, for example, his *Causes of Declension in Religion, and Means of Revival*, in *WAF* 3:319–20, 324, and *The Promise of the Spirit the Grand Encouragement in Promoting the Gospel*, in *WAF* 3:359–63.
[78] *Socinianism Indefensible*, in *WAF* 2:249.
[79] See his *Letters to Serapion*, written in the late 350s. Athanasius died in 373. See further my *The Spirit of God: The Exegesis of 1 and 2 Corinthians in the Pneumatomachian Controversy of the Fourth Century* (Leiden: Brill, 1994).
[80] *Letters on Systematic Divinity*, in *WAF* 1:711.

Finally, with regard to statements about the Trinity, Fuller is certain that the Scriptures affirm the existence of three divine persons—the Father and the Son and the Holy Spirit.[81] These three are never to be considered three separate beings, but one God. As Fuller put it, "In a mysterious manner, far above our comprehension, there are in the Divine unity three subsistences."[82] How they are one has not been revealed—and so to believe it steadfastly requires faith and humility.[83] Moreover, this is a truth that must be regarded as above reason, not against it or a contradiction. As long as Christian theology does not make the mistake of the Socinians, which is to regard God as unipersonal, it can affirm this truth without fear of being irrational. In this, Christians need to "regulate [their] ideas of the Divine Unity by what is taught us in the Scriptures of the Trinity; and not those of the Trinity by what we know, or think we know . . . of the Unity."[84]

In addition to the experience of worship, discussed at length above and which for Fuller was determinative for his understanding of the Godhead, Fuller's reflections upon baptism served to reinforce his Trinitarianism. His main piece on this ordinance is *The Practical Uses of Christian Baptism*, a highly significant tract on the meaning of baptism. Fuller argued that since baptism is to be carried out, according to Matthew 28:19, "in the name of the Father and of the Son and of the Holy Spirit," submission to the ordinance entails an avowal of the fact that God is a triune being. Well acquainted with the history of the early church at this point, Fuller rightly stated that this baptismal formula was widely used in that era to argue for the doctrine of the Trinity.[85]

---

[81] See *Jesus the True Messiah* (1809), in *WAF* 1:219; "Passages Apparently Contradictory," in *WAF* 1:668; "Remarks on the Indwelling Scheme," in *WAF* 3:700; "The Doctrine of the Trinity," in *WAF* 1:707–8. In the last of these passages Fuller cites a catena of Trinitarian texts, including Matt. 28:19; Rom. 15:30; 2 Cor. 13:14; Eph. 2:18; 2 Thess. 3:5; 1 John 5:7; and Jude 20–21.

[82] "The Doctrine of the Trinity," in *WAF* 1:708.

[83] *Nature and Importance of an Intimate Knowledge of Divine Truth*, in *WAF* 1:163–64.

[84] *Letters on Systematic Divinity*, in *WAF* 1:708; "Remarks on the Indwelling Scheme," in *WAF* 3:700. Cf. *Walking by Faith* (1784), in *WAF* 1:124–25: "It is one thing to say that Scripture is contrary to right reason, and another thing to say that it may exhibit truths too great for our reason to grasp." "Trial of Spirits," in *WAF* 1:654.

[85] *The Practical Uses of Christian Baptism*, in *WAF* 3:340. The very same point had been made a quarter of a century earlier by John Collett Ryland (1723–1792), the eccentric Baptist largely remembered today for his dampening rebuke of William Carey's zeal for overseas missions. Also writing in a circular letter for the Northamptonshire Association, Ryland had observed that "the true doctrine of the Trinity" had been "kept up in the Christian church" by the ordinance of baptism "more than by any other means whatsoever" (*The Beauty of Social Religion; or, The Nature and Glory of a Gospel Church* [Northampton: T. Dicey, 1777], 10n).

To relinquish the doctrine of the Trinity is thus tantamount to the renunciation of one's baptism.[86]

Fuller tied baptism to the Trinity again, and also to worship, in a small piece entitled "The Manner in Which Divine Truth Is Communicated in the Holy Scriptures." He wrote:

> The doctrine of the Trinity is never proposed to us as an object of speculation, but as a truth affecting our dearest interests. John introduces the sacred Three as witnesses to the truth of the gospel of Christ, as objects of instituted worship, into whose name we are baptized; and Paul exhibits them as the source of all spiritual good: "The grace of the Lord Jesus Christ, the love of God, and the communion of the Holy Spirit be with you all. Amen." [2 Cor. 13:14] Again, "The Lord direct your hearts into the love of God, and into the patient waiting for Christ." [2 Thess. 3:5][87]

What is noteworthy about this text is the refusal to see the Trinity as merely a "metaphysical mystery," or as Fuller put it, "an object of speculation."[88] Rather, Fuller emphasized that the doctrine has a bearing on our "dearest interests," namely, the truth as it is in the gospel, worship, and "all spiritual good." The first item, the truth of the gospel, is supported by an allusion to 1 John 5:7, the famous *Comma Johanneum*, which Fuller evidently regarded as genuine.[89] For the third point, "all spiritual good," Fuller has recourse to 2 Corinthians 13:14 and 2 Thessalonians 3:5. The use of the latter Pauline text is fascinating. Fuller's Trinitarian reading of it ultimately goes back to Basil of Caesarea (c. 329–379), who employs it in his argument for the Spirit's deity in his classic work *On the Holy Spirit*.[90] Fuller most likely found this reading of the Pauline verse, however, in John Gill's commentary on 2 Thessalonians 3:5, where Gill follows Basil's interpretation.[91]

---

[86] *The Practical Uses of Christian Baptism*, in *WAF* 3:340. For other instances of Fuller's Trinitarian exegesis of Matt. 28:19, see *Calvinistic and Socinian Systems* in *WAF* 2:236; "On the Sonship of Christ," in *WAF* 3:705–6.
[87] "The Manner in Which Divine Truth Is Communicated in the Holy Scriptures," in *WAF* 3:539.
[88] For the phrase "metaphysical mystery," I am indebted to Stephen Holmes. See "The Quest for the Trinity: An Interview with Stephen R. Holmes," *Credo Magazine* 3, no. 2 (2013): 49.
[89] See his extended argument in *Letters on Systematic Divinity*, in *WAF* 1:708–9.
[90] See Basil of Caesarea, *On the Holy Spirit* 21.52.
[91] Here is the relevant section of Gill's comments on this verse: "The phrase of directing the heart to God . . . is not to be done by a believer himself, nor by the ministers of the Gospel: the apostle could not do it, and therefore he prays 'the Lord' to do it; by whom is meant the Spirit of God, since he is distinguished from God the Father, into whose love the heart is to be directed, and from Christ, a patient waiting for whom

It is with regard to the second point, the Trinity as the object of adoration, that Fuller mentions baptism: "the sacred Three" are described "as objects of instituted worship, into whose name we are baptized." Fuller was presumably thinking of Matthew 28:19. The reason why doctrinal confession of the triunity of God is vital is that it lies at the heart of Christian worship. Fuller clearly saw baptism into the name of the triune God as not only the initiatory rite of the church—what made it a "Trinitarian community"—but also the beginning of a life of worshiping the Trinity. Fuller made the same point in yet another text that has already been cited: some from among "the grand ends of Christian society are unitedly to worship God," and this meant nothing less than "to devote ourselves to the blessed Trinity by Christian baptism—and to acknowledge the atonement made by the Redeemer, by a participation of the ordinance of the Lord's supper."[92] Fuller's choice of the verb "devote" here is noteworthy. Christian baptism is an act of dedicating oneself to the triune God—an act that surely is to continue throughout the Christian life till it culminates in the beatific vision of the Trinity.

'tis also desired the heart may be directed into; and since it is his work to shed abroad the love of God in the heart, and to lead unto it, and make application of it; and which is a proof of his deity, for none has the direction, management, and government of the heart, but God, . . . and in this passage of Scripture appear all the three Persons [of the Godhead]; for here is the love of the Father, patient waiting for Christ, and the Lord the Spirit" (*An Exposition of the New Testament*, vol. 3 [1809; repr., Paris, AR: Baptist Standard Bearer, 1989], 3:265). See also John Gill, *The Doctrine of the Trinity, Stated and Vindicated* (London: Aaron Ward, 1731), 198–99.

[92] *Leading Sentiments of Mr. R. Robinson*, in WAF 3:601.

9

An Examination of Three Recent Philosophical Arguments against Hierarchy in the Immanent Trinity

PHILIP R. GONS AND ANDREW DAVID NASELLI

The notion of hierarchy in the immanent Trinity evokes no small controversy among evangelicals today.[1] Both sides of the debate accuse their opponents of heresy, tampering with the Trinity, and rejecting historic, orthodox Trinitarianism.[2] But the reason runs deeper than a

---

[1] *Immanent Trinity* refers to what God eternally and necessarily is in himself (*ad intra*) and how he relates to himself. Synonymous terms include *ontological Trinity*, *essential Trinity*, *absolute Trinity*, and *eternal Trinity*. *Economic Trinity* refers to God as he reveals himself in time in relationship to his creation (*ad extra*). Synonymous terms include *revelational Trinity*, *mediatorial Trinity*, *historical Trinity*, and *functional Trinity*. Theologians differ on the degree to which the economic Trinity reveals the immanent Trinity.
[2] Robert Letham sounded the alarm in "The Man-Woman Debate: Theological Comment," *WTJ* 52 (1990): 65–78 (esp. 67–69, 77–78) by calling attention to evangelical feminism's "dangerous path" heading toward "abandon[ing] an orthodox view of God" (78). Thomas Schreiner followed with "Head Coverings, Prophecies, and the Trinity: 1 Corinthians 11:2–16," in *Recovering Biblical Manhood and Womanhood: A Response to Evangelical Feminism*, ed. John Piper and Wayne Grudem (Wheaton, IL: Crossway, 1991), 124–39, calling attention to egalitarianism's "serious misunderstanding of . . . the doctrine of the Trinity" (129). Gilbert Bilezikian responded in "Hermeneutical Bungee-Jumping: Subordination in the Godhead," *JETS* 40 (1997): 57–68, which he originally presented at ETS in 1994, and called the subordination view "theological innovation" (56). Stephen Kovach retorted in "Egalitarians Revamp Doctrine of the Trinity: Bilezikian, Grenz, and the Kroegers Deny Eternal Subordination of the Son," *Council on Biblical Manhood and Womanhood News* 2, no. 1 (1996): 1–5. Bruce Ware followed with "Tampering with the Trinity: Does the Son Submit to His Father?," *JBMW* 6, no. 1 (2001): 4–11. Kevin Giles replied in *The Trinity and Subordinationism: The Doctrine of God and the Contemporary Gender Debate* (Downers Grove, IL: InterVarsity, 2002), accusing complementarian Trinitarians of rejecting the traditional view, heading off on their own, and being dangerously close to Arianism. In *Jesus and the Father: Modern Evangelicals Reinvent the Doctrine of the Trinity* (Grand Rapids: Zondervan: 2006), Giles charged complementarians with reinvent-

concern to defend orthodox Trinitarianism. Behind the Trinity debate, complementarians and egalitarians clash about the roles of men and women in the church and the home. What started as an exegetical debate over biblical texts about the relationship between men and women has turned into a theological and philosophical debate about the inner life of the eternal Trinity.

The heart of the gender debate has become the heart of the Trinity debate: can a person (human or divine) be equal in essence and necessarily subordinate in role to another person?[3] Complementarians insist that women are necessarily subordinate to men in their roles (in the contexts of marriage and the church) while being equal to men in essence. Egalitarians argue that such a claim defies simple logic.[4] Complementarians turn to the relationship between the Father and the Son, in which they find an analogy that seems to refute the egalitarians' objection: the Son is eternally and necessarily under the authority of the Father and will apparently remain so even after the Father restores all things (1 Cor. 15:28), yet the Son is equally God and shares with the Father the one divine essence. If in the Trinity full equality and necessary subordination can coexist in complete harmony, why not also in human gender relations?

Like the gender debate, the Trinity debate has gone through various stages. It too began as an exegetical debate, turned into a theological debate, and from there became a historical debate.[5] Recently some have tried to end the debate on philosophical grounds.[6] This chapter evaluates the successfulness of this most recent move.

---

ing the doctrine of the Trinity. In a 2008 Trinity debate over the question "Do relations of authority and submission exist eternally among the Persons of the Godhead?" Tom McCall and Keith Yandell compared the affirmative position to Arianism, and Bruce Ware and Wayne Grudem compared the negative position to modalism (http://henrycenter.tiu.edu/resource/do-relations-of-authority-and-submission-exist-eternally-among-the-persons-of-the-godhead/). Cf. Millard J. Erickson, *Who's Tampering with the Trinity? An Assessment of the Subordination Debate* (Grand Rapids: Kregel, 2009), who essentially sides with the egalitarian Trinitarians.

[3] *Necessity* is a philosophical term indicating that something could not be different from what it is, that it must be that way in all possible worlds.

[4] E.g., Rebecca Merrill Groothuis, "'Equal in Being, Unequal in Role': Exploring the Logic of Woman's Subordination," in *Discovering Biblical Equality: Complementarity without Hierarchy*, ed. Ronald W. Pierce and Rebecca Merrill Groothuis (Downers Grove, IL: InterVarsity, 2004), 301–33.

[5] Both sides appeal to church history to support their views and argue that their opponents depart from historical Trinitarianism. E.g., Giles, *The Trinity and Subordinationism*, 21–117; Ware, McCall, and Yandell in the 2008 Trinity debate. Cf. Erickson, *Who's Tampering with the Trinity?*, 139–68.

[6] See the 2008 Trinity debate; Thomas McCall and Keith E. Yandell, "On Trinitarian Subordinationism," *Philosophia Christi* 11 (2009): 339–58; Erickson, *Who's Tampering with the Trinity?*, 169–93; Thomas H. McCall, *Which Trinity? Whose Monotheism? Philosophical and Systematic Theologians on the Metaphysics of Trinitarian Theology* (Grand Rapids: Eerdmans, 2010), 175–88.

Identifying the Sides

There are two main viewpoints in the current Trinity debate:

1. *Eternal functional subordination* (EFS) holds that the Son is eternally and necessarily subordinate to the Father, not in terms of his deity, but in his role in relationship to the Father.[7]
2. *Eternal functional equality* (EFE) holds that the Father and Son are completely equal in all noncontingent ways: all subordination is voluntary, arbitrary, and temporary.[8]

Both acknowledge a relationship of authority and subordination between the Father and the Son. The differences concern its nature, duration, and application. Three overlapping questions show the divide:

1. *Nature*. Is the Son necessarily or contingently subordinate to the Father?
2. *Duration*. Is this subordination eternal or temporary?
3. *Application*. Does this subordination describe the immanent or economic Trinity?

Table 2 summarizes how the two positions answer these questions.

Table 2. Two positions on the Son's subordination

	Nature	*Duration*	*Application*
EFS	necessary	eternal	immanent and economic
EFE	contingent	temporary	economic only

Thesis

This chapter argues that EFE's philosophical arguments against hierarchy in the immanent Trinity do not succeed. While they sound compelling on the surface, they oversimplify complex issues, equivocate nuanced terminology, and gloss over crucial distinctions. Our goal is

---

[7] Proponents of EFS include Wayne Grudem, Bruce Ware, D. A. Carson, John Frame, Thomas Schreiner, Andreas Köstenberger, Stephen Kovach, John Piper, and Tim Keller. Roger Olson represents another version of EFS, which avoids the language of authority and submission. Charles Hodge and A. H. Strong may fall into this category. Robert Letham affirms order, which includes relations of authority and submission, but he rejects subordination and hierarchy terminology (*The Holy Trinity: In Scripture, History, Theology, and Worship* [Phillipsburg, NJ: P&R, 2004], 480, 484, 489).
[8] Proponents of EFE include Tom McCall, Keith Yandell, Millard Erickson, Kevin Giles, Rebecca Groothuis, and Gilbert Bilezikian.

not to make a case for EFS. Others have already done that.[9] Rather, we intend to demonstrate that the philosophical arguments against EFS do not stand up to careful scrutiny and fail to prove that hierarchy cannot exist in the immanent Trinity without compromising the Nicene doctrine of *homoousion*.

Proponents of EFE have made numerous attempts to demonstrate that EFS is philosophically indefensible.[10] This article focuses on three of the most common and seemingly devastating.

Argument 1. The Eternal Subordination of the Son to the Father Entails the Denial of Homoousion

Argument

Tom McCall and Keith Yandell argue that if EFS is true, then the Son possesses a property from eternity that the Father lacks (i.e., being subordinate to the Father). Consequently, the Father and the Son are not of the same essence (*homoousios*), but of different essences (*heteroousioi*), and historic, orthodox Trinitarianism is lost. McCall asserts unambiguously, "Hard EFS entails the denial of the *homoousion*."[11] He argues:

(1) If Hard EFS is true, then the Son has the property *being functionally subordinate in all time segments in all possible worlds*.
(2) If the Son has this property in every possible world, then the Son has this property necessarily. Furthermore, the Son has this property with *de re* rather than *de dicto* necessity.
(3) If the Son has this property necessarily (*de re*), then the Son has it essentially.
(4) If Hard EFS is true, then the Son has this property essentially while the Father does not.
(5) If the Son has this property essentially and the Father does not, then the Son is of a different essence than the Father. Thus the Son is *heteroousios* rather than *homoousios*.[12]

---
[9] E.g., see the essays in this volume by Wayne Grudem, Chris Cowan, and Jim Hamilton.
[10] Cf. note 6.
[11] McCall, *Which Trinity?*, 179. McCall strangely distinguishes between "Soft EFS" and "Hard EFS." His "Soft EFS" is not EFS at all; rather, it is equivalent to EFE. His "Hard EFS" is EFS as we define it in the previous section.
[12] Ibid., 179–80.

Millard Erickson states the same argument with less philosophical precision,[13] and others similarly argue that EFS must also entail eternal ontological subordination.[14]

Response

On the surface this argument seems devastating to EFS. If metaphysics requires that eternal differences be necessary differences, and if necessary differences must find their grounding in ontological differences, then we are left with an inescapable ontological difference between the Father and the Son. If the Father and the Son are ontologically different (i.e., different in their being, nature, or essence), then they cannot be *homoousios* (i.e., of the same being, nature, or essence).

At the outset, it is important to understand the ramifications of this argument. If it is indeed sound, not only does it prove that the authority-submission distinction cannot coexist with full equality of essence between the Father and the Son in the immanent Trinity, but it also eliminates *any* necessary property distinctions.[15]

In the same way, then, the historic doctrines of the eternal generation of the Son and the eternal procession of the Spirit, which the majority of the church has embraced in the East and the West since at least the Council of Nicaea in 325 and arguably much earlier,[16] would entail the denial of *homoousion*. We could restate McCall's argument this way:

---

[13] Erickson, *Who's Tampering with the Trinity?*, 172.
[14] Groothuis asserts, "The idea that Christ's subordination is eternal yet merely functional (and thereby compatible with ontological equality) is incongruent. An eternal subordination of Christ would seem logically to entail his ontological subordination" ("Equal in Being, Unequal in Role," 332). Bilezikian claims, "If Christ's subordination is eternal . . . it is also ontological" ("Hermeneutical Bungee-Jumping," 64). Adam Omelianchuk argues: "Subordination that extends into eternity cannot be merely functional, but must also be ontological. . . . If the Son is eternally subordinate to the Father, then the Father has a divine attribute that the Son does not have. And since eternity is an intrinsic quality of God's existence, it logically follows that what the Son *is* eternally, he *is* in being. If the Son is eternally subordinate in function, then he is eternally subordinate in being" ("The Logic of Equality," *Priscilla Papers* 22, no. 4 [2008]: 27).
[15] Yandell seems to recognize this and argues that the Father, Son, and Spirit possess identical properties. There is no property that one person possesses that the others do not also possess. What differentiates the Father, Son, and Spirit is not one or more properties. Rather, it is that they are distinct property bearers and centers of self-consciousness. Yandell does acknowledge the distinction of the existence-entailed properties *being the Father, being the Son*, and *being the Spirit* (2008 Trinity debate, 2:20:30–21:30; McCall and Yandell, "On Trinitarian Subordination," 354). However, these do not amount to real differences among the persons. Rather, they merely identify the persons as distinct property bearers (of identical properties). For his definition and discussion of existence-entailed properties, see Keith A. Yandell, "A Defense of Dualism," in *Philosophy of Religion: A Reader and Guide*, ed. William Lane Craig (New Brunswick, NJ: Rutgers University Press, 2002), 482–83.
[16] See the essays in this volume by Robert Letham, John Starke, and Michael Ovey.

1. If the Nicene doctrine of the Trinity is true, then the Son has the property *generate* in all time segments in all possible worlds.
2. If the Son has this property in every possible world, then the Son has this property necessarily. Furthermore, the Son has this property with *de re* rather than *de dicto* necessity.
3. If the Son has this property necessarily (*de re*), then the Son has it essentially.
4. If the historic doctrine of the Trinity is true, then the Son has this property essentially while the Father does not.
5. If the Son has this property essentially and the Father does not, then the Son is of a different essence than the Father. Thus the Son is *heteroousios* rather than *homoousios*.[17]

If this argument is valid, not only does it refute EFS's proposal that the distinction between the Father and the Son is best understood in terms of authority and submission, but it also refutes the view held by the vast majority of the church for at least the last seventeen hundred years, namely, that the Father, Son, and Spirit possess unique personal properties that distinguish them from one another.[18]

If what McCall and Yandell argue is true, then the church's best theologians, the very ones who defined and defended *homoousion*, unknowingly denied it and differed only slightly from Arians. The entire history of orthodox Trinitarianism was unknowingly heterodox for the simple reason that its view of the Trinity entails a denial of *homoousion*. That is a weighty charge.[19]

---

[17] Strangely, McCall ignores the implications of his argument and even suggests that believing in eternal generation might allow one to escape the force of his argument (*Which Trinity?*, 180–81). However, in a later publication, McCall and Yandell seem aware of this extension, but oddly speak of it only in terms of possibility: "The doctrine of eternal generation . . . perhaps even entails ontological subordinationism" ("On Trinitarian Subordinationism," 350). Why they are not as confident of their argument's force against eternal generation as they are with the authority-submission properties is not clear. Perhaps it is the audacity of the claim and its ramifications.

[18] A growing number of theologians reject the historic doctrines of eternal generation and procession (e.g., Loraine Boettner, J. Oliver Buswell, William Lane Craig, Millard Erickson, John Feinberg, Paul Helm, Robert Reymond, Keith Yandell), but most still retain the eternal identity of Father, Son, and Spirit and the eternal distinctions they entail. This argument, if successful, would charge those who maintain any eternal (non-existence-entailing) property distinctions, even if not eternal generation and eternal procession, of implicitly denying *homoousion* as well.

[19] It is beyond the scope of this chapter to prove that the church has historically affirmed that the Father, Son, and Spirit each possesses one or more personal properties that make them distinct from one another. But we point to John Calvin as a representative example. Calvin defines *person* this way: "a subsistence in the Divine essence,—a subsistence which, while related to the other two, *is distinguished from them by incommunicable properties*." Each subsistence, "though connected with the essence by an indissoluble tie, being incapable of separation, yet has a special mark by which it is distinguished from it." Calvin refers to "the peculiar property of each [that] distinguishes the one from the other" and maintains that "each of the three subsistences while related to the others is distinguished by its own properties" (*Institutes of*

Fortunately, escaping the force of this argument does not require abandoning the historic teaching that the Father, Son, and Spirit each have one or more unique personal properties that the others do not possess. The argument sounds compelling on the surface, but it fails to prove its conclusion.

The terms "essentially" and "essence" in the conclusion of McCall's argument need clarification. That they share the same root (*esse*) causes confusion. Substituting synonyms for these terms (*fundamentally* for "essentially" and *substance* for "essence") helps bring clarity. We could restate the conclusion this way: "If the Son has this property *fundamentally* and the Father does not, then the Son is of a different *substance* than the Father. Thus the Son is *heteroousios* rather than *homoousios*." In this version the conclusion is not as obvious as it was in the original. Does a fundamental property difference necessarily entail that the Father and the Son are not consubstantial? It depends. The syllogism lacks sufficient information to draw a reliable conclusion.

An eternal function is a necessary function, and a necessary function does indeed find its grounding in one or more essential or fundamental properties. So the Son's eternal subordination to the Father in terms of his role or function in the Godhead derives from a fundamental difference between him and the Father.

However, the Trinity has more than one referent to which *essential* or *fundamental* may rightly apply. The Trinity is more than essence; the Trinity is one essence *and* three persons, each of which may have fundamental properties. Properties of the essence are just as essential or fundamental to the essence as properties of the persons are to the persons.[20] McCall's argument leaves no room for this fundamental

---

the *Christian Religion*, trans. Henry Beveridge [Edinburgh: Calvin Translation Society, 1845], 1.13.6 [emphasis added]). Elsewhere Calvin asserts, "The Father differs in some special property from the Son, and the Son from the Spirit" (1.13.22). Calvin's view of personal properties is not unique. Rather, at its heart it represents historic Trinitarianism. According to Yandell, McCall, and Erickson, however, it necessarily entails a denial of *homoousion*.

[20] Cf. John M. Frame, *The Doctrine of God*, A Theology of Lordship (Phillipsburg, NJ: P&R, 2002), 720; Bruce A. Ware, "Alleging Heresy Where There Is None," a review of *Which Trinity? Whose Monotheism? Philosophical and Systemic Theologians on the Metaphysics of Trinitarian Theology*, by Thomas H. McCall, *JBMW* 16, no. 2 (2011): 45–46. John Dahms's discussion exemplifies this ambiguity (unhelpfully, in our view) when he argues for both "essential subordination" and "essential equality" ("The Subordination of the Son," *JETS* 37 [1994]: 351–64). Some attribute individual or personal essences to the persons, but to avoid confusion and adhere to the traditional terminology, we reserve *essence* for the one *substantia* or οὐσία. Cf. McCall, *Which Trinity?*, 180–81.

difference to be attributed to anything other than the one essence. But this shows merely the invalidity of the syllogism as it is currently stated.

The church has historically distinguished between (1) the one divine essence that the Father, the Son, and the Spirit hold in common and (2) the personal properties that differentiate each person from the others. Where the equivocation enters is that both the essence and the persons have essential or fundamental properties. Consequently, one must prove rather than assume the move from "essentially" to "essence."

The orthodox tradition has maintained that each person, each property bearer, has two sets of essential or fundamental properties:

1. The properties of the one *substantia* or οὐσία, which he shares equally with the other two persons
2. The properties of his unique *persona, subsistentia,* or ὑπόστασις, which belong to him alone

Consequently, there are four sets of essential or fundamental properties in the Trinity:

1. The properties of the one *substantia* or οὐσία
2. The properties of the Father's unique *persona, subsistentia,* or ὑπόστασις
3. The properties of the Son's unique *persona, subsistentia,* or ὑπόστασις
4. The properties of the Spirit's unique *persona, subsistentia,* or ὑπόστασις

All of the properties of the one *substantia* or οὐσία belong equally to all three persons. The properties of the three *personas, subsistentias,* or ὑποστάσεις belong to only one of the three persons. As Calvin describes them, they are unique incommunicable properties.[21] Vital to any discussion about properties in the Trinity is identifying whether the property belongs to the one *substantia* or οὐσία or to one of the three *personas, subsistentias,* or ὑποστάσεις.

Unfortunately, McCall and Yandell repeatedly gloss over this cru-

---

[21] See note 19.

cial distinction and ignore the proposal that the authority-submission property distinction belongs to the persons and not the essence.[22] It seems that in their view there is only one set of properties,[23] which clearly departs from historic Trinitarianism.[24] Unfortunately, they never defend this view or even acknowledge that it departs from historic Trinitarianism.[25] Once we remove the ambiguity in the argument and eliminate the equivocation of "essentially" and "essence," the conclusion becomes tautological. McCall's argument would be reformulated this way:

1. If Hard EFS is true, then the Son has the property *being functionally subordinate* in all time segments in all possible worlds, not *as God* in the one shared *substantia* or οὐσία but *as Son* in his unique *persona, subsistentia,* or ὑπόστασις.
2. If the Son has this property in every possible world, then the Son has this property necessarily. Furthermore, the Son has this property with *de re* rather than *de dicto* necessity.
3. If the Son has this property necessarily (*de re*), then the Son has it essentially not *as God* in the one shared *substantia* or οὐσία but *as Son* in his unique *persona, subsistentia,* or ὑπόστασις.
4. If Hard EFS is true, then the Son has this property essentially, not *as God* in the one shared *substantia* or οὐσία but *as Son* in his unique *persona, subsistentia,* or ὑπόστασις, while the Father does not have it in his unique *persona, subsistentia,* or ὑπόστασις.
5. If the Son has this property essentially in his unique *persona, subsistentia,* or ὑπόστασις and the Father does not have it in his unique *persona, subsistentia,* or ὑπόστασις, then the Son is a different person than the Father.

With the ambiguity and equivocation removed, the argument proves

---

[22] This is in spite of Ware's repeated attempts to make this point in the 2008 Trinity debate.
[23] As noted above, in the 2008 Trinity debate, Yandell repeatedly indicates that the three persons have no properties not held in common with the others. What makes the persons distinct is not their properties, but simply that they are unique bearers of properties. At one point, however, he acknowledges that they each have one unique property: *being the Father, being the Son,* and *being the Spirit.* For Yandell, however, these amount to existence-entailed properties, not essential properties. *Being the Father* means nothing more than being a distinct property bearer. There is no place for a property that is not a property of the one *substantia* or οὐσία. McCall's view, while not as clear, seems to be similar.
[24] See note 19.
[25] They do, however, admit to rejecting eternal generation and eternal procession. However, that does not entail rejecting any personal properties that differentiate the Father, Son, and Spirit, which we maintain is the historic view of the church.

nothing profound: the Father and the Son are not the same person—one of the basic tenets of Trinitarianism.

John Feinberg articulates this important distinction in a discussion on "each member of the Godhead's non-incarnational property":

> The church, as we noted, said that the Father is ungenerate and that he begets the Son. The Son's property is being eternally begotten by the Father, and the Holy Spirit's property is his procession from the Father (or Father and Son). Given these respective properties, if we are speaking about the sortal noun "deity" or the adjective "divine," we seem to have a problem, according to Bartel, for we can now write an argument like the following:
>
>> God the Son is eternally begotten of the Father *qua* divine.
>> God the Father is not eternally begotten of the Father *qua* divine;
>> Therefore, God the Son is not the same deity as God the Father.
>
> If Jesus and the Father are numerically the same God, this argument underscores the problem. As Bartel explains, "just as absolute identity will not tolerate divergence in properties exemplified *simpliciter*, so *being numerically the same f as* will not tolerate divergence in properties exemplified *qua f*."
>
> This may seem to be an insuperable dilemma, but Bartel thinks not, and I agree. . . . The reason is that *being eternally begotten and eternally proceeding are not properties the Son and Spirit have in virtue of being divine, but in virtue of being distinct subsistences of that divine essence* [emphasis added]. Hence, the premises of the above should read "*qua* subsistence or person," and the conclusion should say, "Therefore, God the Son is not the same person or subsistence as God the Father."[26]

According to EFS, *being in authority over the Son* inheres in what it means for the Father to be Father, not in what it means for the Father to be God; and *being in submission under the Father* inheres in what it means for the Son to be Son, not in what it means for the Son to be

---

[26] John S. Feinberg, *No One Like Him: The Doctrine of God*, Foundations of Evangelical Theology (Wheaton, IL: Crossway, 2001), 494–95.

God.[27] As such, these are not properties of the one essence, but unique incommunicable properties of the persons that define their intratrinitarian relationships.[28]

Properties that inhere in the persons and not in the essence do not entail a denial of *homoousion*.[29] Consequently, by affirming the eternal generation of the Son and the eternal procession of the Spirit, the church has not been unknowingly denying *homoousion* since Nicaea. Neither, then, do other properties inherent in the persons, like *authority over* and *submission under*, necessarily entail the denial of *homoousion*.[30]

For this EFE argument to succeed, its proponents must demonstrate one of the following two propositions:

1. The historic position of properties of the persons as distinct from properties of the one essence is flawed; all properties are properties of the one essence.
2. The authority-submission properties must be properties of the essence rather than the persons.

To our knowledge, they have done neither. Consequently, this argument fails to prove that the properties of authority and submission entail the denial of *homoousion*.

---

[27] Cf. Ware, "Alleging Heresy Where There Is None," 42–46: "The property of 'eternal functional subordination' that the Son possesses and the Father does not possess is indeed a personal property. That is, this is a property of the person of the Son, and it is a property that only could exist in relation to another person" (45).

[28] Erickson, aware of this counterargument, maintains that differentiating between properties of the essence and properties of the persons does not solve the problem "because if these are necessary properties of the persons, then the persons have different essences" (*Who's Tampering with the Trinity?*, 173). Erickson's astounding statement is sloppy and dismissive. It is sloppy because it confuses the properties of the essence with properties of the persons. It is dismissive because it entails a rejection of a key component of at least seventeen hundred years of orthodox Trinitarianism. While the church has affirmed that the three persons possess one or more unique incommunicable properties not proper to the others, Erickson makes it sound as if this view originated with Bruce Ware and Wayne Grudem.

McCall comes close to anticipating this counterargument when he says that Ware and Grudem "might want to hold both to a generic divine essence (the attributes of omniscience, omnipotence, etc.) and to individual or personal essences that are functional (i.e., the Father's individual essence is made up of properties such as *having authority over*, while the Son's individual essence is made up of such properties as *being subordinate*), but it is not obvious that they can do even this" (*Which Trinity?*, 181; cf. 184, 200). But McCall never gives any reasons that this will not work.

[29] So Bartel and Feinberg (see above) and Bruce Ware, who made this argument in his counterstatement in the 2008 Trinity debate and then again in "Alleging Heresy Where There Is None," 42–46.

[30] Of course, we have not proved that the properties *being in authority over* and *being in submission under* are properties of the persons rather than the essence. But we have proved that this argument fails without first establishing that such is not the case.

For an alternate response to the essence of this argument, see Arthur Pohle, *The Divine Trinity: A Dogmatic Treatise*, trans. Arthur Preuss, 2nd ed. (St. Louis: B. Herder, 1915), 238–40, who resolves the tension with the doctrine of perichoresis (i.e., the interpenetration or mutual indwelling of the three persons).

Argument 2. If Only the Son Could Have Become Incarnate, the Father Could Not Be Omnipotent

Argument

Another argument against EFS concerns which of the persons of the Trinity could have become incarnate. Was it possible for the Father or the Spirit to take on a human nature and come instead of the Son? McCall maintains that the answer must be yes, that is, unless one is prepared to deny the attribute of omnipotence to both the Father and the Spirit:

> If only the Son has the property *possibly being incarnate* (and has it essentially), then the Son again has an essential property that the Father does not have. So once again we are faced with a Son who is not *homoousios* with the Father. In addition, it seems that the Father and Son are not even of the same generic divine essence on this account. For if the defense of Hard EFS goes in this direction, then the Father and Son do not share the property of *omnipotence*: on this account the Father would be limited in his abilities to perform actions that are logically possible (i.e., becoming incarnate), even actions that are possible for a morally perfect being—thus the Father would be less than omnipotent. And if the Father does not have the property or attribute of omnipotence, then surely the Father does not have the whole generic divine essence. Thus the Father and the Son are not *homoousios*—even with respect to a generic divine essence.[31]

McCall reasons that if the Father was incapable of being united to a human nature, then he necessarily lacks something that the Son possesses. And this constitutes, again, a Father and a Son who are not equally divine; the result is a sort of reverse Arianism, in which the Son has more power than the Father. In other words, maintaining that any of the three persons of the Trinity could become incarnate is necessary to preserve *homoousion*. McCall points to Aquinas as a theologian who insisted "that any of the divine persons could have become incarnate"[32] and cites Richard Cross that "this view is held by virtually everyone in medieval Christology."[33]

---

[31] McCall, *Which Trinity?*, 182.
[32] Ibid. McCall references Aquinas, *Summa Theologiae*, IIIa, qq. 1–3.
[33] Ibid. McCall points readers to Richard Cross, *The Metaphysics of the Incarnation: Thomas Aquinas to Duns Scotus* (Oxford: Oxford University Press, 2002), 179.

Response

Like the first argument, this second argument seems compelling on the surface: if only the Son could have become incarnate, then the Son indeed had an ability that the Father and Spirit lacked, resulting in ontological inequality.

But are proponents of EFS really saying that the Father and the Spirit lack a property that the Son possesses—that it is not even theoretically possible for the Father or the Spirit to be united to a human nature? And do they have in mind a theoretical incarnation or *the* incarnation with all that it entails? It does not seem that the view as stated by its proponents (e.g., Grudem,[34] Ware,[35] Letham,[36] Köstenberger and Swain,[37] Reymond,[38] Bird and Shillaker[39]) requires McCall's reading, that is, that the Father and the Spirit lack the property necessary for a theoretical incarnation.[40] We cannot find anyone who states the view the way McCall represents it. If that is not the view of hierarchical Trinitarians, then what is?

Aquinas's discussion points to the answer. For Aquinas there are two separate issues: (1) what is possible and (2) what is fitting.

First, Aquinas insists:

> Whatever the Son can do, so can the Father and the Holy Ghost, otherwise the power of the three Persons would not be one. But the Son was able to become incarnate. Therefore the Father and the

---

[34] Grudem maintains that the "roles [of the Father's sending and the Son's obeying] could not have been reversed or the Father would have ceased to be the Father and the Son would have ceased to be the Son" (*Systematic Theology: An Introduction to Biblical Doctrine* [Grand Rapids: Zondervan, 1994], 250).

[35] Bruce A. Ware, *Father, Son, and Holy Spirit: Relationships, Roles, and Relevance* (Wheaton, IL: Crossway, 2005), 81–82.

[36] Letham, *The Holy Trinity*, 491: "The Father sends the Son, and the Father and the Son send the Spirit. These relations are not reversible."

[37] Andreas J. Köstenberger and Scott R. Swain, *Father, Son and Spirit: The Trinity and John's Gospel*, New Studies in Biblical Theology (Downers Grove, IL: InterVarsity, 2008), 126n64: "To the perennial dogmatic question 'Could any person of the Trinity have become incarnate?' John's Gospel says 'No!': that is, *if* the incarnation entails fulfilling the role of 'Servant of Yahweh' at the climax of Israel's history. Only *the Son* could do that."

[38] Robert L. Reymond, *A New Systematic Theology of the Christian Faith*, 2nd ed. (Nashville: Nelson, 1998), 341: "We know also that his Sonship implies an order of relational (not essential) subordination to the Father (which is doubtless what dictated the divisions of labor in the eternal Covenant of Redemption) in that it is unthinkable that the Son would have sent the Father to do his will."

[39] Michael Bird and Robert Shillaker, "Subordination in the Trinity and Gender Roles: A Response to Recent Discussion," *TrinJ* 29 (2008): 272: "The Son, who by his very nature reflects the image and glory of the Father and who is eternally sent by the Father, was the only member in the God-head uniquely suited to doing what God did in the incarnation."

[40] Ware denied that position in the 2008 Trinity debate. Yet McCall continued to argue against the position his opponents denied holding.

Holy Ghost were able to become incarnate.... The Divine power could have united human nature to the Person of the Father or of the Holy Ghost, as It united it to the Person of the Son. And hence we must say that the Father or the Holy Ghost could have assumed flesh even as the Son.[41]

McCall thinks that this conflicts with the EFS position, and by itself it might appear to. But that conclusion is not warranted for two reasons: Aquinas's view is more sophisticated than this narrow reading suggests, and the EFS position agrees with Aquinas's conclusions.

Aquinas goes on to address "whether it was more fitting that the person of the Son rather than any other divine person should assume human nature." After a lengthy discussion with numerous reasons, he concludes emphatically that "it was most fitting that the Person of the Son should become incarnate."[42]

McCall glosses over this important distinction in his discussion and misunderstands the view of his opponents. But Aquinas's conclusion is precisely what EFS proponents affirm: the Son is uniquely fit for the work of the incarnation. All three persons of the Trinity have the *capacity* to be united to a human nature and therefore from a strictly theoretical standpoint *could* have become incarnate. They all equally possess the property of omnipotence. However, to acknowledge this is not inconsistent with maintaining that in all possible worlds in which one of the persons of the Trinity would have become incarnate for the work of the incarnation, the Son *must* be that person.[43] This conclusion is the necessary consequence of God's wisdom.[44]

The unique personal properties of the Son make him best suited to be united to human nature and fulfill the role of Mediator. It is a matter of fitness, not ability. We can safely conclude, however, that in all possible worlds that include the biblical incarnation, the Son rather than the Father or the Spirit would have become incarnate because God's

---

[41] Aquinas, *Summa Theologiae*, III, q. 3 art 5, ad.
[42] Ibid., III, q. 3 art 8, ad.
[43] Consequently, in a different sense, it was not possible for the Father or the Spirit to become incarnate in any possible world in which the incarnation would exist—not because of a lack of ability in the Father or the Son, but because of the Son's fitness and God's wisdom.
[44] Geerhardus Vos defines God's wisdom as "that perfection of God by which He uses His knowledge for the attainment of His ends in the way that glorifies Him most" (*Theology Proper*, vol. 1 of *Reformed Dogmatics*, ed. Richard B. Gaffin, trans. Annemie Godbehere [Bellingham, WA: Logos Bible Software, forthcoming], 18).

nature is such that he always does what is most fitting. The incarnation corresponds to something in the Son, making his incarnation a necessary consequence of divine wisdom.[45] So while any of the three persons could have become incarnate with reference to capacity or ability, only the Son could have with reference to God's commitment to choosing the most fitting means to accomplish his purposes for the incarnation.

We could state the argument in a syllogism this way:

1. Although all three persons of the Trinity possess the properties necessary to being united with a human nature, it was most fitting for the Son to become incarnate in all possible worlds containing the biblical incarnation.
2. The triune God is eternally, necessarily, and infinitely wise, and it is not possible for him to cease to be wise or to act in a fashion inconsistent with that wisdom.
3. God's wisdom entails his choosing the most fitting means to accomplish his purposes.
4. Therefore, it was not possible for any person but the Son to have become incarnate to accomplish the work of redemption planned for the biblical incarnation.

The view that only the Son would become incarnate to accomplish the work of redemption planned for the incarnation is consistent with the insistence that the Father and the Spirit have the ability to be united with a human nature. Thus, all three persons are *homoousios*, yet one of those persons, based on his personal properties and relationships to the other two, is best suited for the work of redemption in the incarnation.

Argument 3. If the Son's Submission to the Father Indicates an Eternal Relationship of Submission, Then the Son's Submission to the Spirit Does Also

ARGUMENT

To establish their view that the Son is eternally and necessarily subordinate to the Father from all eternity, Grudem and Ware point to the numerous places in Scripture where the Father sends the Son into the

---
[45] We are not claiming that the incarnation was necessary, but that, given the incarnation, the Son's (and not the Father's or Spirit's) incarnation was necessary.

world. This sending, they say, demonstrates an authority-submission relationship—one that existed prior to the incarnation and, by extension, from all eternity.

McCall and Yandell take issue with the presumption that such sending indicates an eternal and necessary relationship.[46] Though they consider the premise unproved, McCall and Yandell argue that if we grant the premise, the argument turns into "outright contradiction" or proof of "*mutual* submission within the Trinity."[47] They state the argument this way:

1. If one divine person sends another, then the divine person sent is eternally and necessarily subordinate to the divine person who sends (Grudem's premise);
2. The Son is sent by the Spirit (Matt. 4:1; Mark 1:12; Luke 4:1);
3. Therefore, the Son is eternally and necessarily subordinate to the Spirit.[48]

The minor premise is undisputed. If the major premise is true, it proves not only that the Son is eternally and necessarily subordinate to the Father, but also that the Son is likewise subordinate to the Spirit (and the Spirit is likewise subordinate to the Son). The problems are obvious. The argument breaks the order of Father, Son, Spirit and results in a contradiction where the Son and the Spirit are both under each other—whatever that might mean. As McCall and Yandell point out, one could resort to some notion of mutual subordination between the Son and the Spirit (much like the egalitarian interpretation of Eph. 5:21). But it is not clear whether such a move would be successful.

RESPONSE

On the surface this argument seems to pose a problem for EFS. At the very least, it requires reordering the persons of the Trinity so that the Father is first and the Son and the Spirit are equally subordinate to the Father and to each other.[49] The Father sends the Son and the Spirit; therefore, the Son and the Spirit are subordinate to the Father.

---

[46] McCall and Yandell, "On Trinitarian Subordinationism," 344–46.
[47] Ibid., 345.
[48] Ibid.
[49] It is unclear if this kind of mutual submission even works.

No one sends the Father; therefore, the Father is not subordinate to anyone. The Son and the Spirit send each other; therefore, the Son and the Spirit are subordinate to each other.

This reordering, even if it were to work, is not necessary. Evaluating the argument more carefully provides a simpler solution. McCall and Yandell gloss over important differences. The argument breaks down based on the differences between the Father's sending the Son and the Spirit's sending the Son. They are fundamentally different.

First, the Father and the Spirit send the Son *at different times*. The Father sends the Son *before the incarnation*. The Spirit sends him *during the incarnation*.

Second, the Father and the Spirit send the Son *to different places*. The Father sends the Son *into the world*. The Spirit sends the Son, who is already in the world, *into the wilderness*.

Third, and most importantly, there is a crucial difference between the one the Father sends and the one the Spirit sends. The Father sends the Son *qua* God, that is, *before he has taken on a human nature*. The Spirit sends Jesus *qua* the God-*man*, after he has been hypostatically united to his human nature. The Spirit does not send the preincarnate Son. He sends him in view of his taking on a human nature. It was in his role as Mediator, the second Adam, that Jesus was sent by and submitted to the Spirit. As the *God*-man, Jesus remained hierarchically over the Spirit throughout the incarnation.

Fourth, the sending language differs. The New Testament never describes the Father's sending and the Spirit's sending with the same word.[50]

In light of these qualifications, we would need to revise McCall and Yandell's argument and state it this way:

1. If one divine person sends another *with reference to his divine nature*, then the divine person sent is eternally and necessarily subordinate to the divine person who sends.

---

[50] The Father's sending the Son into the world is mentioned in the New Testament at least fifty times (with varying degrees of specificity), each time using a form of the word ἀποστέλλω or πέμπω. The only exception is Gal. 4:4, which uses ἐξαποστέλλω. Forty-three instances are in John's writings: his Gospel (40x) and his first letter (3x). The other seven are in Matthew (1x), Mark (1x), Luke (4x), and Galatians (1x). The New Testament mentions the Spirit's sending the Son three times, each a Synoptic account of the Spirit's sending Jesus into the wilderness (Matt. 4:1; Mark 1:12; Luke 4:1). The texts each use different Greek words: (1) ἀνάγω, *to lead or bring up*; (2) ἐκβάλλω, *to send or bring out or away*; and (3) ἄγω, *to lead or encourage (in the direction of)* (BDAG).

2. The Spirit sends the Son *with reference to his human nature*; he does not send him *with reference to his divine nature*.
3. Therefore, it does not follow that the Son is eternally and necessarily subordinate to the Spirit.[51]

We must conclude, then, that this third argument, like the others, fails to prove its conclusion.

Conclusion

These three prominent arguments attempt to demonstrate the philosophical incoherence of EFS. After careful examination, we find them unsuccessful because they lack appropriate nuance, blur crucial distinctions, oversimplify the issues, and misrepresent the opposing position.

At least some versions of EFE eliminate any real property distinctions among the persons of the Trinity. This clearly departs from what the church has believed since at least Nicaea. If that is indeed what EFE proponents wish to do, they should unambiguously acknowledge their departure from historic Trinitarianism. If it is not, they need to abandon their arguments or demonstrate how the arguments do not eliminate all property distinctions.

As we continue to debate these important matters, we think it wise to proceed with caution and heed the words of Calvin:

> The Scriptures demonstrate that there is some distinction between the Father and the Word, the Word and the Spirit; but the magnitude of the mystery reminds us of the great reverence and soberness which ought to be employed in discussing it. It seems to me, that nothing can be more admirable than the words of Gregory Nanzianzen: "'Ου φθάνω το ἓν νοῆσαι, καὶ τοῖς τρισὶ περιλάμπομαι οὐ φθάνω τὰ τρία διελεῖν καὶ εἰς τὸ ἓν ἀναφέρομαι," (Greg. Nanzian. in Serm. de Sacro Baptis.) "I cannot think of the unity without being irradiated by the Trinity: I cannot distinguish between the Trinity without being carried up to the unity." Therefore, let us beware of

---

[51] McCall and Yandell respond that if we explain the temporary subordination of the Son to the Spirit in light of the Son's human nature, why should we not also explain the subordination of the Son to the Father in the same light? The answer to this is simple: the Scriptural data demonstrates the order of Father, Son, and Spirit before and after the incarnation, so that the Son's subordination is consistent with it, while the Son's subordination to the Spirit is a deviation from it.

imagining such a Trinity of persons as will distract our thoughts, instead of bringing them instantly back to the unity. . . .

It is far safer to rest contented with the relation as taught by [Augustine], than get bewildered in vain speculation by subtle prying into a sublime mystery. . . .

Here, if any where, in considering the hidden mysteries of Scripture, we should speculate soberly and with great moderation, cautiously guarding against allowing either our mind or our tongue to go a step beyond the confines of God's word. . . . We must conceive of him as he has made himself known, and in our inquiries make application to no other quarter than his word. . . . [We must] bring more docility than acumen to the discussion of this question, never to attempt to search after God anywhere but in his sacred word, and never to speak or think of him farther than we have it for our guide. But if the distinction of Father, Son, and Spirit, subsisting in the one Godhead, (certainly a subject of great difficulty,) gives more trouble and annoyance to some intellects than is meet, let us remember that the human mind enters a labyrinth whenever it indulges its curiosity, and thus submit to be guided by the divine oracles, how much soever the mystery may be beyond our reach.[52]

---
[52] *Institutes*, 1.13.17, 19, 21.

10

Simplicity, Triunity, and the Incomprehensibility of God

K. SCOTT OLIPHINT

Simplicity[1] and triunity. These two characteristics of God are central and crucial to affirm if one is to uphold biblical, historic, Christian orthodoxy. What I hope to show in this chapter is the inextricable link between the affirmation of God's simplicity, on the one hand, and of his triunity, on the other. Given that link, we need to be careful to understand as well something of what it means when we confess that the triune God is incomprehensible.

Simplicity

Of these two central doctrines of Christianity, the doctrine of simplicity has fallen on hard times of late. For example, in their rejection of the notion of God's simplicity, Moreland and Craig describe it thus:

> Divine simplicity is a doctrine inspired by the neo-Platonic vision of the ultimate metaphysical reality as the absolute One. It holds that God, as the metaphysical ultimate, is an undifferentiated unity, that there is no complexity in his nature or being. As such, this is a

---

[1] "The simplicity of God . . . is his incommunicable attribute by which the divine nature is conceived by us not only as free from all composition and division, but also as incapable of composition and divisibility" (Francis Turretin, *Institutes of Elenctic Theology*, ed. James T. Dennison Jr., trans. George Musgrave Giger, vol. 1 [Phillipsburg, NJ: P&R, 1992], 191 [3.7.3]).

radical doctrine that enjoys no biblical support and even is at odds with the biblical conception of God in various ways. According to the doctrine of divine simplicity God has no distinct attributes, He stands in no real relations, his essence is not distinct from his existence, He just is the pure act of being subsisting. All such distinctions exist only in our minds, since we can form no conception of the absolutely simple divine being. While we can say what God is not like, we cannot say what He is like, except in an analogical sense. But these predications must in the end fail, since there is no univocal element in the predicates we assign to God, leaving us in a state of genuine agnosticism about the nature of God. Indeed, on this view God really has no nature; He is simply the inconceivable act of being.[2]

If Moreland and Craig are right in the above description of God's simplicity, then it should surely be rejected. If its impetus is Neoplatonic, if it has no biblical warrant, if it requires that God is not related to anything *ad extra*, if it destroys theological predication, then these fatal implications must be avoided and the doctrine of simplicity must be jettisoned for the sake of much that is central to Christian truth.

Another influential denial of God's simplicity comes from Alvin Plantinga. In 1980, Plantinga gave the Thomas Aquinas lecture at Marquette University, which he titled "Does God Have a Nature?" This, of course, is a provocative question. Plantinga notes that the answer historically has been yes. However, if one answers yes to this question, then it could very well be that the doctrine of divine simplicity is denied. Divine simplicity affirms not that God *has* a nature but that God *is* his essential nature. Plantinga wants to answer yes and to argue that God's nature is not identical with who he is. As with the quotation above, if the implications Plantinga perceives are indeed correct, then simplicity can be no part of Christian orthodoxy. Perhaps it will help to summarize Plantinga's concerns with (his notion of) the doctrine of simplicity.

In his lecture, Plantinga first notes that the doctrine of divine simplicity is "a dark saying indeed."[3] To his credit, he thinks it is a dark

---

[2] J. P. Moreland and William Lane Craig, *Philosophical Foundations for a Christian Worldview* (Downers Grove, IL: IVP Academic, 2003), 524.
[3] Alvin Plantinga, "Does God Have a Nature?," in *The Analytic Theist: An Alvin Plantinga Reader*, ed. James F. Sennett (Grand Rapids: Eerdmans, 1998), 228.

saying because if one affirms divine simplicity, one is forced to affirm all kinds of notions that imply the rejection of the Christian God—that God is personal, for example. So his reason for seeing simplicity as "dark" is the threat he sees it posing to (central aspects of) traditional Christianity. He then proceeds to argue against the notion of God's simplicity.

Plantinga's first argument can be stated fairly simply. If God is one and thus identical with his properties—the properties of goodness, wisdom, and holiness, for example—then each of his properties is identical with the other. And if all of God's properties are identical, then there is only one property. And if God is identical with that property, then God is a property. This is the first problem for those who hold to simplicity (at least Plantinga's understanding of simplicity). Since Plantinga rightly does not want to affirm that God is a property, but rather affirms God as a person, simplicity must be rejected. We'll get to a response to this shortly.

Plantinga's second problem with simplicity is a complex web of arguments centering on what he calls the "sovereignty-aseity intuition (SAI)."[4] The SAI basically affirms that God is sovereign over all things and is dependent on nothing at all.[5] Plantinga then goes on to argue that while the redness of a rose, for example, may be within God's control, the proposition "whatever is red is colored" is not. This latter proposition is a necessary truth, and necessary truths, according to Plantinga, are not up to God; they are true by virtue of what they are. If they were within God's control, according to Plantinga, then it must be the case that God could cause them to be false (in other words, they must be contingent, rather than necessary, truths). But God could not cause such things to be false, since they are true necessarily.

What does this have to do with simplicity? Simplicity affirms that there is nothing on which God is essentially dependent. If there were anything, then God would only be "potential" with respect to what

---

[4] Ibid., 249ff.
[5] It would have been helpful to be more theologically precise here. God's independence does not entail his sovereignty. God is, and always was, essentially independent. Sovereignty, on the other hand, presupposes creation and thus is a contingent attribute of his. Once he determines to create, he cannot but be sovereign over it, but he did not have to create in the first place. It may be that Plantinga's notion of necessary truths fails to make this critical distinction. For more on God's essential and contingent (covenantal) properties, see K. Scott Oliphint, *God with Us: Divine Condescension and the Attributes of God* (Wheaton, IL: Crossway, 2012).

he is, rather than essentially actual. In other words, he would not be who he is unless other, external things were true and applied to him; he would be, "potentially," something or someone else. If it can be shown that there are some things on which God is dependent necessarily, then it should not be difficult for us to affirm that there are other things, things that compose who God is, on which he is dependent as well. So (to oversimplify), Plantinga's argument here is that God is dependent on a number of things, so we should have no problem rejecting the notion of simplicity (note how Plantinga rightly sees that God's independence entails his simplicity).

There are other and much more detailed arguments offered by Plantinga, but this will have to do for now. In (brief) response to his discussion, first, is it really the case that if God is identical with his properties, then there is, in reality, only one property and, as a matter of fact, God is a property? Perhaps it can follow logically that such is the case, but there are other logical ways to structure the relationship between God and his properties.

To construe the argument differently, why could it not be that if God is identical with his properties, rather than God being a property, whatever "property" is attributed to God's essential character is, *first of all*, not a property at all, but a person, or person*al*, and only secondarily a property? Perhaps the main reason Plantinga wants to force the identity relation in the direction of properties rather than person is that he is convinced that at least some properties are necessarily what they are, whether or not God exists. So (at least) conceptual, or logical, priority is given to the existence of properties, rather than to the existence of a personal God, at the outset.

This priority, however, gets things backward. If we begin our reasoning with the aseity (i.e., absolute independence) of God—that is, with God as *a se*—then we should recognize that before God created, there was only God. There were no necessities along with God that were not themselves also identical to him. Thus, for example, there were no necessary propositions that had to obtain; there were no propositions at all. There was only God—Father, Son, and Holy Spirit—the one God. There was no "2 + 2 = 4," no "all things red are colored"; there was God and his triune, essential character—nothing else. And whatever

God *knows* essentially is just identical with him; this is what simplicity affirms. If that is the case, then whatever properties are identical to God are first of all identified with *God*, and they are only properties *ad extra* (that is, "outside" of God's essential character) at the point of God's condescension (to decree, to create, etc.).

This brings us to the second response, a response to the sovereignty-aseity intuition (SAI). Is it really the case, since the proposition "whatever is red is colored" is a necessary truth, that God has no control over it? Must acknowledging God's control over it mean that it must be possible for God to make such a proposition false? These questions are integrally related to current discussions of possible worlds and modal logic and cannot be dealt with in depth here. We can say, however, that the answers to these questions have everything to do with how we think of the modal notions of necessity and possibility.

How do we know, for example, that whatever is red is *necessarily* colored? One way is to look at the meaning of the terms. Red is a color, and if something is red, it is by definition colored. The proposition, therefore, is analytic. The subject is contained in the predicate. *Necessarily*, then, if the subject (whatever is red) obtains, so does the predicate (is colored). But what kind of *necessity* is this? Is it the same necessity that we apply to God's being, character, and existence?

No. We cannot affirm that God and creation, including the necessary laws of creation, are subject to the same, and same kind of, necessity. To think of the necessities of creation in the same way that we think of God's necessity is to think univocally (i.e., necessity applies to God and creation in an identical way). And to think univocally is to undermine, distort, subvert, and contravene the distinction between God as *a se* and everything else as essentially dependent.

What seems to be a better, biblical affirmation is that necessity and possibility are all determined by God himself. This means that there is no such thing as a possible world in which God does not exist. It also means that *nothing else* can partake of this kind of necessity. With respect to the notion of necessity, therefore, we must maintain a distinction between God's own necessity and the necessity of anything else that might also be necessary.

This means that in order to think correctly of necessity, we should see it as defined in one way for the creature and in another way for the triune God. Whatever is necessary for us is such because God has so ordered and determined the world in that way. He might have determined it in that way because such things more closely reflect something of who he is—like distinctions we necessarily make in our thinking, which reflect something of distinctions made in God himself (thus logic is a necessary part of creaturely thinking). So, to use Plantinga's example, the reason it is necessary that "whatever is red is colored" is not that God is subject to some necessity outside himself or constraining his character. The reason is that he ordained and determined that there would be colors and that one of them would be red; and because he ordained them that way, their necessity lies in his creative hand, not in something abstract in or above God. Since he made things that way, he does indeed have control over them, *including over the decision to make the proposition itself necessary*. But it is necessary *only given God's free decision to create*, not in and of itself. Only God is necessary in and of himself. Created necessity *reflects* God's necessity, but can in no way be identical with it.

So, must we affirm that if God is in control of something necessary, it must be possible for it not to be what it necessarily is? There seem to be no indications that we must. God is in control of, for example, the proposition that "everyone who calls on the name of the Lord will be saved," but that does not mean that God can now make it false that everyone who calls on the name of the Lord will be saved. The book of Hebrews (cf. Heb. 6:13–20) reminds us that God swore by himself that he would be true to his promises. The necessity of this truth (and others) lies in his faithful character, and not in some abstract modal notion to which he must be subject. The same is true of all he created. Some things may be changeable, but his creation reflects necessary elements that are the way they are because of his sovereign activity, and not because of some ultimate, metaphysical, eternal reality that is what it is by its nature, quite apart from God's creation, character, and control.[6]

---

[6] This necessity, a created necessity, is what the Reformed have called "hypothetical necessity." Turretin explains it this way (in the context of God's will): "On the state of the question observe: (1) that necessity is twofold; one absolute, which simply and by itself and its own nature cannot be otherwise, as that God is good, just, etc. The other hypothetical, which is not so of itself and simply such but that it could be otherwise, but yet on the positing of something it necessarily follows and could not be otherwise; as for example, if you posit that God predestinated Jacob to salvation, it is necessary that Jacob should be saved,

That which is necessary, therefore, must take its place either in terms of God's own essential character, in which case it is absolutely necessary, or in terms of creation, in which case the necessity is based on a prior contingency (i.e., God's free act to decree and create). So, because sovereignty cannot partake of absolute necessity, in the way that aseity can, it muddies the waters to argue for or against simplicity on the basis of the extent of God's control over creation.

It is true, however, that simplicity entails that God is *a se*. Plantinga rightly sees these terms as interdependent,[7] and it is incumbent on us to grasp the inextricable link between these aspects of God's character. To affirm one (aseity) is to affirm the other (simplicity). If we see that simplicity is predicated of God *as God*, quite apart from his creation (including those properties that accrue to him by virtue of his decision to create), then we can see that simplicity is just another way of affirming that God is who he is, and that prior to creation all that existed was one God—Father, Son, and Holy Spirit—and nothing else.

Simplicity, therefore, is a biblical doctrine; it follows from God's aseity. Historically speaking, the rejection of God's simplicity as a central truth of orthodox theology is an anomaly. According to Richard Muller:

> The doctrine of divine simplicity is among the normative assumptions of theology from the time of the church fathers, to the age of the great medieval scholastic systems, to the era of Reformation and post-Reformation theology, and indeed, on into the succeeding era of late orthodoxy and rationalism.[8]

So the doctrine of God's simplicity has been the norm for orthodox theology throughout its history. Setting aside the miscontruals of simplicity noted above (as well as others not noted), the doctrine says that the characteristics of God are not "parts" of God that come together

---

namely on the hypothesis of the decree. Otherwise he could have been not predestinated and not saved. When, therefore, the question is asked whether God wills some things necessarily, but others freely I refer not only to the hypothetical necessity (for thus those things which God wills freely, the decree being posited, he no more not wills), but concerning the absolute necessity" (Turretin, *Institutes*, 1:218–19 [3.14.2]).

[7] Turretin, as well, notes the entailment of simplicity and aseity: "[Simplicity] is proved to be a property of God . . . from his independence, because composition is of the formal reason of a being originated and dependent (since nothing can be composed by itself, but whatever is composed must necessarily be composed by another; now God is the first and independent being, recognizing no other prior to himself)" (Ibid., 1:191 [3.7.4]).

[8] Richard A. Muller, *Post-Reformation Reformed Dogmatics: The Rise and Development of Reformed Orthodoxy, ca. 1520 to ca. 1725*, vol. 3, *The Divine Essence and Attributes*, 2nd ed. (Grand Rapids: Baker Academic, 2003), 39.

to make him what he is, but are rather identical with his essence, and thus with him. The simplicity of God not only affirms that whatever God essentially is, he is necessarily, but it says even more than that. The simplicity of God holds that God's essential attributes are not characteristics or properties that exist (in the same way that he exists) in any way "outside" of God, such that his having such characteristics or properties entails his participation in something other than himself. God just is his essential characteristics, and his characteristics are identical to him.

Perhaps we can think of it by way of the contrary. What if God *were* composed of parts? Let's say that eternity is a "part" of God's character such that it is not identical to him, but it also in some way actually composes his essential character; perhaps eternity is just a "context" in which God lives and moves, much as time is for us. What, now, must be true with respect to this "eternity"? Since it is not identical to God, it must be something "other" than him. If it is something "other" than him, then it must be "outside" him, at least in some important ways. Not only so, but if God is essentially eternal, and eternity is not identical to him, then he depends, in some essential way, on eternity to be who he is *as God*. Thus, God is dependent on something besides himself in order to be who he is essentially. If this were true, then God would not be *a se*; dependent on eternity to be who he is, he could not be independent.

The fact that God is eternal, therefore, according to the Christian tradition, does not mean that God participates in a property of eternity that surrounds his existence or exists with or alongside him.[9] Rather, as God, he simply *is* eternal, and the eternity that he is just *is* himself. As eternal, God does not partake of an eternal context in a maximal way such that he has the most of it, or all of its eternal manifestations, or anything of the sort. Rather, God's eternity just is God himself; to separate him from that eternity would, *per impossibile*, destroy him entirely. So also for all of God's essential attributes.

Not only so, but when we think of the simplicity of God, we are also

---

[9] This seems to be the way "eternity" is discussed in William Lane Craig, *Time and Eternity: Exploring God's Relationship to Time* (Wheaton, IL: Crossway, 2001). This is both ironic and unfortunate: ironic, in that Craig argues that analytic philosophers, not theologians, are uniquely equipped to deal with such issues, and unfortunate in that Craig can then suppose that God somehow gives up his eternity at the point of creation. God giving up his eternity would be like God giving up his goodness; it simply is not possible, since it is essential to who he is as God.

committed to the notion that God's attribute of eternity and all of his other essential attributes themselves are, since they are God's, attributed to him essentially and thus just are his essence. God's truth is an eternal truth, and his eternity is immutable and infinite eternity, just because the one is included in and (in God) identical with, the other.

So perhaps the best way to think about the simplicity of God is in the fact that it demands a denial of any essential composition of parts in God. In this denial is an equally important affirmation. The affirmative aspect of simplicity says that whatever essential attributes, qualities, or properties inhere in God, they are all identical with him, in the sense that they are not something "other" than God himself.

Having established simplicity as essential to God, we must also see that this simplicity can only properly be understood by contextualizing and correlating it with the biblical doctrine of God's triunity.

Triunity

Contrary to much of the literature, the doctrine of simplicity, in its best formulations, has never affirmed that God is some sort of being in which no distinctions are or could be made. As we have seen, that kind of "simplicity" is more akin to philosophical speculation than to biblical truth. It is, however, a natural result of the *way* simplicity has been argued in some circles.

Rather, the distinctions that do reside in God, because they accrue to him essentially, are identical with him and thus are not parts of God, parts that would serve, in sum, to make up the whole of who he is. The Westminster Confession of Faith (2.1) is one of the best affirmations of God's simplicity: "There is but one only, living, and true God, who is infinite in being and perfection, a most pure spirit, invisible, *without body, parts, or passions*; immutable, immense, eternal, incomprehensible, almighty, most wise, most holy, most free, *most absolute*" (emphasis added). Notice that within the context of an affirmation that God is without parts is also an affirmation that God is eternal, infinite, immutable, and so on.[10] Affirming the simplicity of God does not deny,

---

[10] Many today want to dismiss the notion that God is "without passions." This comes often from fundamental misconceptions of what is meant. For a discussion and affirmation of the notion that God is

and never has denied, distinctions; the Westminster divines affirmed both the *one* and the *many* with respect to God's essential character.

It is this "one and many" aspect of God's character that moves a discussion of God's simplicity to an affirmation of his triunity.[11] That is, God's oneness is always and at the same time to be understood in terms of his threeness. Or, more specifically, the fact that God is not composed of parts in no way negates, subverts, or undermines the fact that the one God is three persons, and that the three are one; instead, the oneness *requires* the threeness, and vice versa. Important, therefore, to a biblical understanding of God is an affirmation of the doctrine of divine simplicity—an affirmation at the heart of any orthodox theology proper—that will also entail an affirmation of God as triune.[12] To quote Muller:

> The doctrine of God remains incomplete until the concept of the unity and simplicity of the divine essence is drawn into relation with the concept of the Trinity of persons. Contrary to the frequently noted caveat that the doctrine of the essence and attributes stands as a philosophical discussion of "what" God is over against the doctrine of the Trinity as a biblical and "personal" statement of "who" God is, it must be recognized that the lines between these two parts of the doctrine of God are not so easily or neatly drawn. Not only did the medieval scholastics, the Reformers, and the Protestant orthodox recognize the necessity of a profound interrelationship between these two parts of the *locus de Deo*, they also were aware of the biblical, traditionary, and philosophical dimensions both of the doctrine of God as one in essence and of the doctrine of God as three persons. . . . Like the Cappadocian fathers and Augustine, and in the tradition of the medieval doctors, the Reformed orthodox recognized that the doctrine of the Trinity could only be supported in the context of a carefully enunciated monotheism—as

---

"without passions," see K. Scott Oliphint, *Reasons for Faith: Philosophy in the Service of Theology* (Phillipsburg, NJ: P&R, 2006), 216–23.

[11] Note that the Westminster Confession of Faith, chapter 2, moves from God's essential character as simple (in sec. 1), to his aseity (in sec. 2), then to his triunity (in sec. 3).

[12] A notion of simplicity that *entails* the Trinity moves a discussion of simplicity into a Reformed context: "The locus [doctrine of God] does not segment Trinity off from the discussion of essence and attributes: the issue addressed by this order is not a movement from an extended philosophical or speculative discussion of 'what' God is to a biblicistic, Trinitarian definition of 'who' God is, but the movement from a statement of 'what' (or 'who') the existent One is, namely, God, to a lengthy discussion in terms of attributes and Trinity, of precisely 'what sort' of God has been revealed, namely, a triune God who is simple, infinite, omnipotent, gracious, merciful, and so forth" (Muller, *Post-Reformation Reformed Dogmatics*, 3:156).

argued in the doctrine of the divine essence and attributes and quite specifically in the doctrine of divine simplicity.[13]

God's simplicity and triunity have historically been seen to require each other. This connection was seen by Calvin as well:

> God also designates himself by another special mark to distinguish himself more precisely from idols. For he so proclaims himself the sole God as to offer himself to be contemplated clearly in three persons. Unless we grasp these, only the bare and empty name of God flits about in our brains, to the exclusion of the true God. Again, lest anyone imagine that God is threefold, or think God's simple essence to be torn into three persons, we must here seek a short and easy definition to free us from all error.[14]

For Calvin, to think or speak of God only as *one*, without reference to his triunity, is to think or speak of a "bare and empty" name of God, which itself excludes the true God. So Calvin goes on to exclaim that the statement from Gregory of Nazianzus "vastly delights" him: "I cannot think on the one without quickly being encircled by the splendor of the three; nor can I discern the three without being straightway carried back to the one."[15] This is the glory of the Christian God—our minds are commanded, when we think of him, incessantly to move from the one to the three to the one. This should "vastly delight" every true Christian.

But the notion of divine simplicity has not always been so explicitly, directly, and inextricably joined to God's triunity. Christopher Hughes has mounted a considerable and sophisticated argument concluding (in part) that Aquinas's notion of simplicity is logically inconsistent with his notion of God as triune. At the end of his analysis, Hughes says:

> What emerges is a tradeoff between holding on to various elements of Aquinas' account of God's simplicity, and holding on to various elements of (what Aquinas considers) Trinitarian orthodoxy. By weakening Aquinas' account of divine simplicity in one way, we

---

[13] Richard A. Muller, *Post-Reformation Reformed Dogmatics: The Rise and Development of Reformed Orthodoxy, ca. 1520 to ca. 1725*, vol. 4, *The Triunity of God* (Grand Rapids: Baker Academic, 2003), 199.
[14] John Calvin, *Institutes of the Christian Religion*, ed. John T. McNeill, trans. Ford Lewis Battles (Philadelphia: Westminster, 1960), 1.13.2.
[15] Ibid., 1.13.17.

can make room for a plurality of persons of God; by weakening it in another way, we can make room for a plurality of first substances in God. I won't examine here the difficult question of what sort of weakening is optimal; at present I want only to underscore that the full-strength account of divine simplicity . . . describes a God who could not possibly be triune.[16]

There are problems with Hughes's analysis of Thomas, not the least of which is his assumption of a univocal notion of being with respect to God and creation. Having said that, we should expect, given Thomas's own explicit and self-conscious nature/grace methodology, that there will be insurmountable difficulties in his development of simplicity (nature) and then of Trinity (grace).[17] As I noted above, because the doctrine of divine simplicity that Thomas develops is a product of "reason alone," whereas his doctrine of the Trinity derives only from special revelation, it should not surprise us that the twain shall meet only with great, perhaps insuperable, difficulty.

Thomas develops his notion of divine simplicity, initially, from the standpoint of reason alone, but then attempts to give that doctrine its full and clear meaning in his articulation of the doctrine of the Trinity, which doctrine cannot be a product of nature, but of Scripture. The problem, then, is that some, like Hughes, have approached Thomas's doctrine of the Trinity from the perspective of Thomas's notion of simplicity. More specifically, it seems to me that what Hughes is doing, at least in part, is using Thomas's own initial *method* (i.e., reason alone) of doctrinal development in order to ascertain whether or not his notion of simplicity can fit with his notion of Trinity. Hughes is asking with respect to Thomas's two doctrines, can simplicity logically fit with Trinity if each is judged according to the principles of reason alone? Accord-

---

[16] Christopher Hughes, *On a Complex Theory of a Simple God: An Investigation in Aquinas' Philosophical Theology*, Cornell Studies in the Philosophy of Religion (Ithaca, NY: Cornell University Press, 1989), 240.
[17] This is a serious charge, but cannot be pursued here. The following points, noted by Muller, with respect to Thomas's *analogia entis* (analogy of being) in light of Reformed orthodoxy will have to suffice for now: "Virtually all of the formulators of Protestant theology denied the Thomist *analogia entis* and declared that no proportion exists between the finite and the infinite (*finiti et infiniti nulla proportio*). Where the Thomistic line of thought continues into the Reformation—for example, in the writings of Vermigli, Zanchi, and, to a certain extent, Keckermann—it is modified by a more negative assessment of the powers of reason and by a sense of diastasis between the ways of God and the ways of man that virtually cancels a Thomistic use of the *analogia entis* in theology" (Richard A. Muller, *Post-Reformation Reformed Dogmatics: The Rise and Development of Reformed Orthodoxy, ca. 1520 to ca. 1725*, vol. 1, *Prolegomena to Theology*, 2nd ed. (Grand Rapids: Baker Academic, 2003), 234.

ing to Hughes, the two are contradictory or insuperably incompatible, and at least one of them must be significantly altered or weakened if they are ever to exist in harmony. What Hughes has not incorporated (perhaps because he recognizes the inherent and irresolvable tension) is Thomas's dialectical nature/grace methodology. Thus, Thomas's notion of simplicity, which is had by reason alone, cannot fit with a notion of Trinity, obtained by the same method.

Thomas's retort at this point would be obvious. Given that the doctrine of the Trinity exceeds the ability of reason to produce it, its consistency with simplicity cannot be adjudicated according to the principles of reason alone. Thomas recognized that there were significant and central truths in Scripture that had to be affirmed even though they could not be adduced by reason alone. And once you get to the doctrine of the Trinity in Thomas, he is clear that simplicity and Trinity must be seen together.

But in spite of his possible missteps, Hughes might be on to something in his discussion. On what basis, we might ask, *must* Thomas move from principles of reason alone to principles of revelation? More specifically, how exactly does his natural theology, with its foundation in reason and conclusion for God's simplicity, fit with the supernatural theology, with its foundation in Scripture and conclusion of God's triunity? It would be difficult to bring the two foundations together without some other foundation behind them both.

At the time of the Reformation, the dialectic of reason/revelation was rejected *in toto*. It was rejected for a number of reasons, but chief among them was the fact that reason *as a foundation* could never be brought into fruitful contact with any notion of *sola Scriptura*. The latter, as foundational, must rule over, guide, and define any use of reason. Given this Reformed rejection, what is the status of natural theology? Is it, along with Thomas's rational mode of reasoning, also rejected? No, it is only "reassigned" and given its proper place. Muller explains:

> What is more, as indicated by the Reformed orthodox paradigm of true and false, archetypal and ectypal theology, the true, ectypal *theologia naturalis* is founded not on the interaction of reason in general with the natural order (so that it is not to be equated with

natural sciences like astronomy or physics) but on the examination of natural revelation by faithful reason.

Indeed, as we have already noted, natural and supernatural theology are viewed as belonging to the same *genus* of discipline or study, *given that both are grounded in revelation*.[18]

In a Reformed context, natural and supernatural theology must begin from the foundation of God's revelation in Scripture.

So, how then are we to think biblically and in line with these Reformed corrections about the simplicity and triunity of God?[19] This is a marvelously rich and fascinating question, the answers to which would serve to revolutionize the way we think about all of theology. We can begin to approach an answer to this question with a quote from Cornelius Van Til:

> It is, of course, true that we must distinguish between God's knowledge and his being. This is as true as that we must distinguish between the various attributes of God. But if these distinctions are really to be maintained in their full significance, *they must be maintained as correlative to a principle of identity that is as basic as they are themselves*. To avoid the blank identity of pantheism, *we must insist on an identity that is exhaustively correlative to the differentiations within the Godhead*. So also to avoid the abstract differentiations and equivocations of deism, *we need a differentiation that is exhaustively correlative to the principle of identity in the Godhead*.[20]

What Van Til is saying here is fundamental to our thinking about God's simplicity and triunity. To put this in more familiar terms, we refer again to Calvin: "And that passage in Gregory of Nazianzus vastly delights me: 'I cannot think on the one without quickly being encircled by the splendor of the three; nor can I discern the three without being

---

[18] Muller, *Post-Reformation Reformed Dogmatics*, 4:282 (emphasis added). For more on natural theology in a Reformed context, see K. Scott Oliphint, "Is There a Reformed Objection to Natural Theology?," *WTJ* 74 (2012): 169–204.

[19] Note Muller's assessment of Calvin: "For Calvin, divine simplicity functions not as a philosophical ground for discussion of the divine essence and attributes, but as a biblically revealed divine attribute and as a basic rule of God language identifying God as non-composite, particularly for the sake of a right understanding of the doctrine of the Trinity and of the unity and consistency of the divine power and justice" (Muller, *Post-Reformation Reformed Dogmatics*, 1:254).

[20] Cornelius Van Til, *An Introduction to Systematic Theology*, ed. William Edgar (Phillipsburg, NJ: P&R, 2007), 372–73 (emphases added).

straightway carried back to the one.'"[21] In other words, given the reality of the Trinity, it is incumbent on the Christian to think of the one even as we are "quickly being encircled by the splendor of the three," and to discern the three even while we are "straightway carried back to the one."

But how is it possible for us, as human beings, to think of the one and of the three in any meaningful way? The only way to do that is to submit our thinking to Scripture. It is not coherent to establish or consider the one by way of reason (as foundational), and then to add to that the three by way of Scripture (as foundational). The one God is what he is by virtue of his threeness, and his threeness is three only as it is correlative and corresponds to the one. So simplicity is only properly understood in the light of the tri-personal distinctions which themselves are entailed by, and correlative to, that oneness. And this, of course, takes us immediately to God's incomprehensibility.

The Incomprehensible Absolute

In his monumental work of theology, Herman Bavinck says that "mystery is the lifeblood of theology."[22] In other words, because there is mystery *at every point* of our Christian thinking and living, it is important to give a proper, biblical account of that mystery as we think through the various truths of Scripture (cf. Rom. 11:33–36).[23]

Surely there is mystery in God's simplicity; perhaps nothing is more complex than God's simplicity! There is mystery, in other words, in God's triunity. These biblical truths, which we must affirm, go together. And yet, even as we affirm them, we have no laws of thinking or experience that show us exactly *how* these aspects of God's character actually cohere. They do cohere; there is no darkness or mystery in God. But we cannot see exactly *how*—not in this life, nor in the next.

As noted above, the Westminster Confession of Faith, 2.1, affirms, among other things, that God is "most absolute." That characteristic

---

[21] Calvin, *Institutes*, 1.13.17.
[22] Herman Bavinck, *Reformed Dogmatics*, ed. John Bolt, trans. John Vriend, vol. 2, *God and Creation* (Grand Rapids: Baker Academic, 2004), 29.
[23] It is important to note here that mystery is not something that comes at the end of our study, as if we can master some things but have to default to mystery in the end. Mystery, as Bavinck says, is the lifeblood of *all* theology. We begin with it, we study and think and learn in its context, and we conclude with the joyous affirmation of its exhaustive presence in all that we know.

is one that only God can have. It relates intrinsically to his simplicity, which means it relates to everything that God is *in and of himself.*

Because only the triune God is *a se*, only the triune God is absolute. In his essential character, he is related to (relative to) nothing outside himself. Whatever relations there are *in* God are identical with him. They can never refer to anything but himself. So, for example, orthodox theology affirms that the Father is related to the Son, who is related to the Spirit, who is related to the Father. But these personal distinctions and relations are all identical with him; they are not "added" to him from the "outside."

So also, God is infinite and eternal. His infinity is not his relationship to space, such that we are saying that he covers all of it. Nor is his eternity a relationship to time, such that he extends it without end. In both cases, we affirm that God is constrained neither by space nor by time. He transcends them both, and when there was no space and time, he simply *was*. Infinity and eternity are two ways of describing God's essential character. Because they are essential to him, he *cannot* give them up or compromise them in any way (see 2 Tim. 2:13; Heb. 6:18).

Yet as we affirm that, we also affirm that God *does*, really and truly, relate himself to creation. As eternal, he freely decided that he would commit himself to that which was other than himself. Not only so, but in his eternal decree, he freely determined to bring to pass and to control all that would happen in creation, from the beginning on into eternity future. Is it the case, we can ask, that once God determines to decree and create, he now becomes "most relative" and gives up his "most absolute" character? As we have said, God *could not* do such a thing, since it would mean that he was denying himself.

So how do we think about the triune God remaining "most absolute," with all of the distinctions and relations *ad intra* that that entails, while also relating himself to that which is outside himself (*ad extra*)? Various answers have been given to this question. One way to answer it is to think of a concrete example of God's relationship to creation and then ask if that relationship compromises or denies, by virtue of that relationship, anything that God essentially *is*. That concrete example is given to us in the person of Jesus Christ.

First, in order to clarify, and by way of contrast with historic orthodoxy, perhaps the most blatant abuse of these categories (of God's essential character as well as of his relationship to creation, in Christ) can be seen in Karl Barth's novel notion of the relationship of Trinity (with its focus in the Son) and creation. The problem with Calvin and historic Calvinism, according to Barth, was that they thought there to be a decision and a God (especially the Son of God) in back of, or prior to, the incarnate Christ. For Barth, this could not be the case. The error of Reformed orthodoxy, thought Barth, was that the eternal, triune God was thought to be who he was essentially, quite apart from his decree to create and also to accomplish redemption.

Bruce McCormack, a premier Barth scholar, argues Barth's case:

> We come back to Barth's question: what must God be if God can live a human life, suffer and die? How can God experience these things without undergoing some kind of fundamental change on the ontological level; without, in other words, ceasing to be God? What are the ontological conditions in the eternal God which allow for this possibility?[24]

Barth's answer to these questions will stun anyone familiar with orthodox theology/christology, whether Romanist or Protestant:

> Barth's answer to this series of question [sic] is, first, that God can be the Subject of the *assumptio carnis* [assumption of the flesh] without undergoing any fundamental ontological change because the *assumptio carnis is essential to him*. And, secondly, the *assumptio carnis is essential to God* because God has willed that it be so. . . . God is so much the Lord that he is sovereign even over his own being. *In a primal decision*, God assigned to himself the being he would have for all eternity. That which is truly "essential" to him . . . consists finally in a decision whose content is the covenant of grace. Against the essentialism of the ancient Church, which made the self-identical element in God to consist in a mode of being which is untouched, unaffected, by all that God does, Barth said: there are no heights and depths in the being of God in which God is not already a God "for us" in Jesus Christ. No wedge may be driven,

---

[24] Bruce McCormack, "Christ and the Decree: An Unsettled Question for the Reformed Churches Today," in *Reformed Theology in Contemporary Perspective*, ed. Lynn Quigley (Edinburgh: Rutherford House, 2006), 139.

therefore, between a being of God in and for himself and a being of God "for us." God "is" in himself (in eternity) what he is in the covenant of grace.[25]

Readers concerned with biblical orthodoxy will immediately recognize the serious, even deadly, consequences of this way of thinking . As McCormack makes clear, it is the will of God that *determines* God's essential being; it even determines, according to McCormack, *that God would be triune,* and it determines everything else that God would be. *All* that God determines to be and to do, Barth thinks, is essential to who he is.[26]

But if God's decision that the Son would assume a human nature is *essential* to him, then there is no possibility that he could be God without also relating himself to creation. If that is the case, then the triune God could never be "most absolute." He can only be who he essentially is as he relates himself to the contingencies of creation. Even if, as McCormack thinks, God's decision to be essentially related to creation is an initial *free* decision, such confusion undermines any biblical and historical doctrine of God.[27]

For good biblical reasons, orthodox theology has never held such a view of the triune God or of the Son of God. Moving no further than the Chalcedonian Creed (AD 451), the church has held that the Son of God, as God, is to be "acknowledged in two natures, inconfusedly [ἀσυγχύτως], unchangeably [ἀτρέπτως], indivisibly [ἀδιαιρέτως], and inseparably [ἀχωρίστως]." The creed goes on to affirm, concerning this personal union of two natures, that "the distinction of natures [is] by no means taken away by the union, but rather the property of each nature [is] preserved, and concurring in one Person and one Subsistence, not

---

[25] Ibid. (emphases added). We should note here, for any interested in Barth's discussion of these points, that McCormack substantiates his claims by referring to Barth's *Church Dogmatics*, IV/1, 193, 186–210; II/2, 6–7, 64, 77. It should also be apparent that Barth/McCormack exalt the free will of God to absolute status, such that it even determines what God would essentially *be*. See also Cornelius Van Til, *Christianity and Barthianism* (Philadelphia: Presbyterian and Reformed, 1962), 75f.

[26] A corollary of this that we cannot pursue here is Barth's locating *covenant* within the eternal being of God. It seems to me the only (personal) distinctions we are biblically allowed to make with respect to God *ad intra* are that the Father is unbegotten, the Son begotten, and the Spirit proceeding. The only point at which there was a covenant in eternity was when Father, Son, and Spirit decreed to create, redeem, and so forth. At that point, there is no *ad intra* distinction, only *ad extra* (given the decree). To import anything else into the ontological Trinity—such as the notion of obedience on the part of the Son—is to confuse the *ad intra* and *ad extra* aspects of God's character. Such a confusion moves in the direction of the now-popular denial of the immanent Trinity in favor of some kind of social Trinitarianism.

[27] McCormack, "Christ and the Decree," 141.

parted or divided into two persons, but one and the same Son, and only begotten, God the Word, the Lord Jesus Christ . . ."[28]

In other words, orthodox theology has always made a distinction—a distinction that has its roots in biblical exegesis—between God (including the Son of God) as he is essentially and God as related to creation. In Christ, both of these are affirmed in one person, the person of the Son of God, and they are affirmed in such a way that the two natures are never confused or changed, nor are they divided or separated. Since the incarnation, the Son of God continues to remain, eternally, as one person, with two natures.[29] His divine nature, however, is essential to him, such that he could not be otherwise; his human nature is *not* essential, but is dependent on the triune God's decision to condescend.

We could think of this more broadly, then, and affirm that at any point where God relates himself to creation, he, as with the Son of God,[30] remains who he is essentially, and he really and truly relates to creation. Thus, God's essential characteristics are maintained (as they must be, since he cannot deny himself), and his real (covenantal) interaction with all things outside himself is affirmed as well. Neither aspect of God's character—neither the essential nor the covenantal—compromises the other.

Conclusion

A concluding thought or two, given what we have said above, might be food for future thought in our discussions about the simplicity of the triune God and also his real relationship to us.

First, it is imperative that we affirm *both* the ontological triunity (which includes simplicity) *and* the economic triunity. That is, we must

---

[28] We should remember as well that the Chalcedonian Creed was not all that was said, or needed, for the church with respect to the incarnation of the Son. There were more statements needed, and given, through ecumenical councils. Specifically, there was a need to further clarify that Jesus Christ was one person (by way of anathemas in the Second Council of Constantinople, AD 553), and whether there were two wills or just one in Christ (clarified in Constantinople in AD 680). These matters need not detain us here.

[29] For a fuller working out of these notions, as well as some of what follows, see Oliphint, *God with Us*.

[30] In *God With Us*, I argue that the condescension of God *just is* the condescension of the Son of God. That condescension is an eternal state of the Son of God, once it begins. It has its climax, "when the time had fully come," in the incarnation and continues into eternity future. For an exposition of Christ's mediatorial activity *in his exaltation*, see Herman Bavinck, *Reformed Dogmatics*, ed. John Bolt, trans. John Vriend, vol. 3, *Sin and Salvation in Christ* (Grand Rapids: Baker Academic, 2006), 374–82. About that activity, says Bavinck, "Those who would deny this must also arrive at the doctrine that the Son will at some point in the future shed and destroy his human nature; and for this there is no scriptural ground whatever" (482).

affirm as our absolute ontological ground the confession that the triune God is who he is. He alone is the triune "I AM." If we ever, as with Barth, import that which is of the nature of creation into the essential Godhead, we have denied the simple, triune, incomprehensible character of God himself. This we must not do. The price we pay is too high, and whatever gains we may think we get are nothing but smoke and mirrors. They are illusions.

If that is the case—and here we can only broach the subject—we should also recognize that when Scripture enjoins us in any way to be like God, or to reflect his character, or to take on his characteristics, it is enjoining us to be like, to reflect, to take on those characteristics that are his *by virtue of creation*—that is, covenantally—and not those that are his essentially.[31] In other words, it is not possible for us to be, as he is essentially, infinite, eternal, or immutable. In the same way, whatever God is in his essential triunity is his alone. Those characteristics that are his relative to creation, however, are the ones able to be reflected or "imaged" by us in a creaturely way.[32]

So, for example, the *order* (*taxis*) of persons in the Godhead is an *ad intra* order. Though it is *reflected* in the economy of the triune God (and thus not identical to it), we cannot move from economy to ontology and project all characteristics of the economic Trinity onto the ontological Godhead.[33] So also, we are not to (because we could not) think that we are to image infinity or eternity. But those characteristics that the triune God takes on by virtue of his covenantal condescension, which includes the obedience of the Son, for example, are, with qualifiers, to be taken on by us as analogs and images of his covenantal character.[34]

As Christians, then, we affirm the essential triunity of God, which

---

[31] One historic way of distinguishing God's characteristics to make this same point is by affirming that God has both incommunicable and communicable attributes.

[32] For example, when we are converted, we are then being renewed unto knowledge, righteousness, and holiness (Eph. 4:24; Col. 3:10). These three aspects refer to covenantal characteristics of God. Knowledge refers to our requirement to think God's thoughts (revelation) after him; righteousness refers to our relationship to the law; and holiness, to our separation from the world. All three, as God's attributes, are what they are by virtue of their *relationship* to that which he has created (revelation, law, separation).

[33] We should not, therefore, affirm that there is an *ad intra* covenant with respect to the ontological Trinity. The *pactum salutis*, which is an eternal covenant, is a covenant *ad extra*, since it is the commitment of the triune God to bind himself to that which is outside of him.

[34] So, for example, the relationship, given in Scripture, of husband and wife is meant to image the *economic* relationship of the Godhead, given that (contra Barth) the Son's obedience is an economic, not an ontological, category. This principle, though, holds true of all aspects of God's character that are to be reflected in creatures; they all refer to God's covenantal characteristics.

includes his simplicity. We affirm this even though such affirmations bring clearly to the fore the necessary incomprehensibility of God. In our affirmations, however, we also recognize that our responsibility as creatures made in his image is to mirror those characteristics of God which *can* also be reflected in us. In that way, being "image of God" means mirroring his covenantal character, which character is what it is because he freely chooses to relate himself to his creation, generally, and to man, more specifically, so that in Christ we might be renewed unto knowledge, righteousness, and holiness.

11

Does Affirming an Eternal Authority-Submission Relationship in the Trinity Entail a Denial of *Homoousios*?

A Response to Millard Erickson and Tom McCall

BRUCE A. WARE

In recent publications, both Millard Erickson and Tom McCall have offered their respective critiques of what I will here refer to as the "eternal relational authority-submission" (ERAS) understanding of the Trinity (which Erickson labels "gradational authority," and McCall "eternal functional subordination"). This view holds that God reveals himself in Scripture as one God in three persons, such that the Father, Son, and Holy Spirit are fully equal in their deity as each possesses fully and eternally the one and undivided divine nature; yet the Father is revealed as having the highest authority among the Trinitarian persons, such that the Son, as agent of the Father, eternally implements the will of the Father and is under the Father's authority, and the Holy Spirit likewise serves to advance the Father's purposes fulfilled through the Son, under the authority of the Father and also of the Son.

Erickson's *Who's Tampering with the Trinity?*[1] proposes to describe and critique what he calls the gradational-authority and equivalent-authority understandings of the Trinity (the former of which roughly corresponds to the "eternal relational authority-submission" view mentioned above). While Erickson himself has long been an advocate of the equivalent-authority view, he nonetheless positions himself as offering to readers an impartial assessment of both positions, being far more critical throughout the book of the gradational-authority position, as one might have expected.

McCall's *Which Trinity? Whose Monotheism?*,[2] deals broadly with many issues of contemporary Trinitarian discussion, including one chapter[3] devoted to his critique of the "eternal functional subordination" view (which also roughly corresponds to the "eternal relational authority-submission" view mentioned above) defended by Wayne Grudem, me, and a number of others he references less frequently. McCall's overall assessment of eternal functional subordination is strongly negative, even expressing his warning that this view "should be resisted" by those who uphold creedal orthodoxy.

While both Erickson and McCall offer critiques of ERAS, Erickson's is much more wide-ranging than McCall's, focusing on biblical, historical, philosophical, theological, and practical considerations. To date, one of the finest brief responses to many of the main arguments Erickson raises is Grudem's essay "Biblical Evidence for the Eternal Submission of the Son to the Father," in *The New Evangelical Subordinationism?*, edited by Dennis Jowers and Wayne House.[4] McCall's main line of critique is much narrower and primarily philosophical in nature, but his main critique is one that Erickson also discusses, and one that is quite weighty in view of the gravity of its charge. This chapter, then, will focus on this common philosophical critique against ERAS brought

---

[1] Millard J. Erickson, *Who's Tampering with the Trinity? An Assessment of the Subordination Debate* (Grand Rapids: Kregel, 2009).
[2] Thomas H. McCall, *Which Trinity? Whose Monotheism? Philosophical and Systematic Theologians on the Metaphysics of Trinitarian Theology* (Grand Rapids: Eerdmans, 2010).
[3] "'Eternal Functional Subordination': Considering a Recent Evangelical Proposal," chap. 6 in ibid., 175–88.
[4] Wayne Grudem, "Biblical Evidence for the Eternal Submission of the Son to the Father," chap. 10 in *The New Evangelical Subordinationism? Perspectives on the Equality of God the Father and God the Son*, ed. Dennis W. Jowers and H. Wayne House (Eugene, OR: Pickwick, 2012), 223–61.

by both Erickson and McCall. I hope to show that this charge against ERAS is misguided and should be withdrawn.

Erickson's and McCall's Common Philosophical Objection

We begin by hearing the objection, common to both Erickson and McCall, in which both conclude that the ERAS Trinitarian position necessarily entails a denial of the *homoousios* of the Son with the Father. For his part, Erickson states this objection as follows:

> If authority over the Son is an essential, not an accidental, attribute of the Father, and subordination to the Father is an essential, not an accidental, attribute of the Son, then something significant follows. Authority is part of the Father's essence, and subordination is part of the Son's essence, and each attribute is not part of the essence of the other person. That means that the essence of the Son is different from the essence of the Father. The Father's essence includes omnipresence, omniscience, love, etc., and authority over the Son. The Son's essence includes omnipresence, omniscience, love, etc., and submission to the Father. But that is equivalent to saying that they are not *homoousious* with one another.[5]

In light of this, Erickson concludes that ERAS (what he calls the "gradational" view) "seems to entail some sort of Arian or Semi-Arian position."[6] Although Erickson does not charge the advocates of ERAS with heresy, it is clear that his critique would rightly be seen as amounting to just that.

Using different language, McCall makes a very similar charge for very similar reasons. He opens his discussion of ERAS (in his terminology, "eternal functional subordination") indicating that some (throughout chapter 6 he quotes mostly from writings by Grudem and me) evangelicals have wanted to deny "ontological" or "essential" subordination while also insisting on the Son's eternal "functional" subordination to the Father.[7] But McCall challenges the validity of this position.

---
[5] Erickson, *Who's Tampering with the Trinity?*, 172.
[6] Ibid.
[7] McCall, *Which Trinity?*, 175.

He claims that what he calls "Hard EFS"—the view that the Son's submission not only was incarnational (which would be "Soft EFS") but in fact marks his relation to the Father for all eternity—"entails the denial of the *homoousion*."[8] On what basis does he level this charge? Here is McCall's argument:

(1) If Hard EFS is true, then the Son has the property *being functionally subordinate in all time segments in all possible worlds*.
(2) If the Son has this property in every possible world, then the Son has this property necessarily. Furthermore, the Son has this property with *de re* rather than *de dicto* necessity.
(3) If the Son has this property necessarily (*de re*), then the Son has it essentially.
(4) If Hard EFS is true, then the Son has this property essentially while the Father does not.
(5) If the Son has this property essentially and the Father does not, then the Son is of a different essence than the Father. Thus the Son is *heteroousios* rather than *homoousios*.

While Erickson's and McCall's objections are formally different and use different language, their basic charge is the same. Granted, Erickson uses the language and conceptual tool of "essential attributes," whereas McCall uses possible-world language to speak of properties possessed with a *de re* necessity. Nevertheless, the force and point of their objections are the same. Here is a summary of the line of argument from Erickson and McCall, as I understand them both:

1. If one holds that the Son submits eternally to the Father while the Father has eternal authority over the Son, then it follows that the Son has a property that is essential to him (viz., the property of submitting eternally to the Father) that the Father does not also possess.
2. But if the Son has a property essential to him as Son which property the Father does not also possess, then it follows that the Son has an essence that is different from the essence of the Father.
3. And if the Son's essence is different from the Father's essence, it follows that the Son cannot be *homoousios* (i.e., of the identically same essence) with the Father.

---
[8] Ibid., 179; cf. 176, 180, 188.

4. Therefore, to hold that the Son submits eternally to the Father entails a denial of *homoousios*.

The key idea within this critique is the notion that attributing to the Son a property that is *essential* to him as Son, but one not also shared with the Father, entails that the Son has a *different essence* than the Father, and hence the Son cannot be *homoousios* with the Father. Is this argument valid? Have the advocates of ERAS wittingly or unwittingly proposed a position that should rightly be rejected as heretical? Consider some responses to the Erickson-McCall objection.

Responses to Erickson's and McCall's Common Philosophical Objection

First, if ERAS advocates succumb to *heteroousios* based on the logic of this argument, then Athanasius and the framers of the Nicene Creed succumb likewise. Why? Simply for this reason: Athanasius and Nicaea also held that the Son possesses a property that is his alone, a property that is essential to who he is as the Son, one that he possesses in all possible worlds, such that his possession of it is with a *de re* (in principle) and not merely a *de dicto* (in fact) necessity, one that he possesses necessarily and noncontingently; and yet it is a property that the Son possesses exclusively, such that Father does not and cannot possess it also. What property is this? The Son's unique property, necessary to him as Son yet not possessed by the Father, is that he is eternally begotten of the Father, begotten, not made.

After all, for Athanasius and most Nicene and post-Nicene fathers, *not* to affirm that the begottenness of the Son is essential to the person of the Son would be to say that the Son is not the true and eternal Son of the Father. That is, his being begotten is not merely contingent (*de dicto*) and hence not necessary; rather, his being begotten is eternal and is absolutely necessary (*de re*). Hence, the Son's being eternally begotten is essential to his being the eternal Son of the Father. Clearly Nicaea saw no contingency attached to its declaration that the Son was the only begotten of the Father. Instead, the Son alone is begotten of the Father, and his begottenness is from eternity and hence essential to who he is as the Son. The Father, on the other hand, is unbegotten while the Spirit proceeds from the Father (and the Son—Western addition). But the Son, *qua* Son, is begotten from eternity, such that his begottenness is absolutely necessary and hence essential to his identity as Son. This property is true of the Son in every possible world, since this is not a contingent or accidental property but is a necessary property. This property is possessed by the Son with a *de re* necessity; it is a property that the Son has essentially (i.e., absolutely necessarily and noncontingently). And the Father not only does not possess it; the Father indeed cannot possess it. But, given the logic and claims of the Erickson-McCall argument, the charge brought against ERAS should be just as applicable to Athanasius and Nicaea.

1. If one holds that the Son is eternally begotten by the Father while the Father is eternally unbegotten, then it follows that the Son has a property that is essential to him (viz., the property of being eternally begotten) that the Father does not also possess.
2. But if the Son has a property essential to him as Son which property the Father does not also possess, then it follows that the Son has an essence that is different from the essence of the Father.
3. And if the Son's essence is different from the Father's essence, it follows that the Son cannot be *homoousios* (i.e., of the identically same essence) with the Father.
4. Therefore, to hold that the Son is eternally begotten by the Father entails a denial of *homoousios*.

The irony here is thick. Athanasius and Nicaea proposed *homoousios* and succeeded in getting this word and its attending concept into the first ecumenical creed of the church. But this same creed also speaks of the Son as "begotten, not made," and it thus affirms a property of the Son unique to him as Son, essential to him in his personhood as Son, and one the Father does not possess. If Erickson and McCall are correct, Athanasius and Nicaea are deeply and irreconcilably contradictory. While they affirm *homoousios*, their insistence on an essential property unique to the Son entails their denial of *homoousios*.

This brings me to my second response. Why are Athanasius and Nicaea not guilty as charged? And why are proponents of ERAS likewise not guilty? The property in question for each—the property of eternal begottenness for Athanasius and Nicaea, and the property of the eternal-relational submission of the Son for advocates of ERAS—is in each case a property of the *person* of the Son, not a property of the *essence* or *nature* which the Son shares fully with the Father and the Spirit. Erickson is mistaken, then, to refer to this property as an "attribute," since all divine attributes are the common and full possession of each of the three Trinitarian persons. Yet, each also has distinctive person-specific properties that constitute the Father as Father (not as Son or Spirit), the Son as Son (not as Father or Spirit), and the Spirit as Spirit (not as Father or Son). Without these person-specific properties, there is no basis for distinction among the Trinitarian persons. Advocates of ERAS, in line with the structure of Trinitarian understanding proposed by Athanasius and Nicaea, distinguish between the one common divine nature possessed eternally and fully by each of the three persons of the Godhead, and person-specific properties that are not of the nature or essence of God but are distinguishing properties of each of the persons of the Godhead. The Son's property of eternally submitting to the Father is a relational property that pertains to his distinctive personhood and not to his essence, which (essence) is common to and fully possessed by each Trinitarian person.

Furthermore, it particularly puzzles me why McCall did not consider this solution to the argument he set forth against advocates of ERAS. One reason for my puzzlement is this: Wayne Grudem and I gave this very response to Tom McCall and Keith Yandell in a public debate we had with them on October 9, 2008. In our opening remarks, provided to them in a document prior to the debate and to all who attended the debate, we wrote and then said:

> While the Son has *properties of his personhood* that the Father in his personhood does not and cannot have, yet each and every property of the Son's divine essence is a property possessed also fully and eternally by the Father in his divine essence. The Son, then, is rightly distinguished *in his personhood* from the Father, but the Son cannot rightly be distinguished *in his essence* from the Father, since then the Father would be in essence different from the essence of the Son (and Spirit).[9]

---

[9] Wayne Grudem and Bruce A. Ware, "Opening Statement for the Affirmative," on the question, "Do relations of authority and submission exist eternally among the persons of the Godhead?" in a debate

Although McCall's book was published in 2010, he indicated to me in e-mail correspondence that he had already written his chapter prior to the debate.[10] Yet, it puzzles me on something of this importance (accusing an evangelical colleague with what amounts to heresy!), why not even a footnote could have been added expressing the lines of our response to his argument.

Also puzzling is this: McCall actually refers at one point to a possible appeal to "personal properties" as those which distinguish the Father, Son, and Spirit from one another. But when he writes of these, he says:

> Traditionally, properties such as "being generated," "being ingenerate," or "being spirated" belong to the distinct persons and are thus called "personal properties." These belong eternally to the divine persons, and each is possessed by only one of the divine persons. The Father, Son, and Spirit are personally distinct in their relations, and they are so eternally. Given this, why would we need to appeal to functional properties to account for genuine distinction?[11]

How very strange, indeed. The property of the "eternal functional subordination" of the Son, or of his eternal submission to the Father, surely is a property exclusively of the Son and one that the Father does not possess. But is not this property strictly and only a personal property? That is, this is a property of the person of the Son, and it is a property that could exist only in relation to another person. The Son could not possess this property were he a monad or a Unitarian deity. But as the person of the Son, he is under the authority of the Father, and as such his property of eternally submitting to the Father is a property of his personhood in relation (and only in relation) to the Father; hence it is nothing other than a "personal property." I cannot fathom how or why McCall would fail to see this property as a personal property of the Son in relationship with the Father in the ways in which advocates of ERAS have labored to describe.

---

with Tom McCall and Keith Yandell, held in the chapel of Trinity Evangelical Divinity School, Deerfield, Illinois, October 9, 2008, 17
[10] Tom McCall, e-mail message to author, December 2, 2011.
[11] McCall, *Which Trinity?*, 184.

And adding to the puzzlement is this. Later in McCall's book, he references this very line of thought in considering how Zizioulas might escape a problem McCall has noted of his view. In discussing this possible escape, McCall notes that one might

> take recourse to the venerable distinction offered by the Cappadocians against the assaults of "neo-Arianism." Recall that when pressed by Eunomius that the divine hypostases must be different in either essence or accidents (neither of which was palatable), the Cappadocians responded that the properties that distinguished the divine hypostases were neither essential (which would amount to a denial of the *homoousion*) nor accidental (which would make the divine hypostases contingent), but that the divine hypostases are distinguished by personal properties. In other words, the hypostases are distinguished by relational properties—properties had by virtue of the relations to the other divine persons.[12]

So, it appears that McCall confuses two sets of properties that are distinguished within the ERAS position: (1) properties possessed fully and eternally by the Father, by the Son, and by the Spirit, of the one and undivided divine *essence*—properties, then, that are the *essential attributes* of God comprising the eternal nature of God, which is the one and same divine nature possessed fully and eternally by the Father, and by the Son, and by the Spirit—and (2) properties possessed distinctly by the Father, and other properties possessed distinctly by the Son, and yet other properties possessed distinctly of the Spirit, as properties of each of their respective *persons*—distinctly *relational and personal properties*, which must not be confused with the essential attributes of the one common divine nature. When advocates of ERAS state that the Son possesses eternally the property of being under the authority of the Father, they also propose this as a relational property of the Son's personhood and not an attribute of the Son's essence. ERAS, then, appeals to the very same distinction to which the Cappadocians appealed in response to the neo-Arians.

This leads me to my third response. An equivocation of sorts has occurred in how McCall in particular frames his argument supporting

---
[12] Ibid., 200.

his charge that Hard EFS denies *homoousios*. When McCall states in his premise (5), "If the Son has this property essentially and the Father does not, then the Son is of a different essence than the Father," it is clear that McCall sees the possession of a unique property "essentially" as indicating a unique "essence." But this confuses the meaning of the adjective "essential" and the noun "essence." That "venerable distinction offered by the Cappadocians" surely had in mind properties of personhood that were "essential," that is, "necessary" to the Father's being the Father (e.g., unbegotten), to the Son's being the Son (e.g., eternally begotten), and to the Spirit's being the Spirit (e.g., proceeding from the Father—as stated in the 381 Constantinople addition to the Nicene Creed), while also affirming that every property of the "essence" of God was possessed fully by the Father, and by the Son, and by the Spirit. But the distinguishing properties of the unique personhood of each Trinitarian person, while essential to who each is as a distinct person, are not properties of the divine essence. No, they are properties (essential though they be) of the persons.

Can it be otherwise? Can we say of the Father (or Son, or Spirit) that he has no essential (i.e., noncontingent, absolutely necessary) distinguishing properties of his personhood? If we do, then what marks the Father as the Father, or the Son as the Son, or the Spirit as the Spirit? Clearly, the distinction of the persons requires that there are distinguishing properties of each person, such that these properties of their unique personhood are necessary to each person as opposed to being merely contingent or accidental, are true of them in every possible world, are held with a *de re* kind of necessity, and hence are essential to the distinctive personhood of each Trinitarian person in distinguishing each from the other Trinitarian persons. In short, it does not follow that because the Son has a distinguishing property, a property that he possesses in every possible world, one that he possesses with a *de re* necessity, and one that he possesses essentially—it does not follow from this that he therefore has a different essence from the Father, so long as that distinguishing property is one of his person and not a property of the common essence he possesses eternally and fully along with the Father and the Spirit.

Conclusion

I conclude, then, that the charge brought against ERAS by Erickson and McCall—that attributing to the Son a property that is *essential* to him as Son but not also shared with the Father entails that the Son has a *different essence* than the Father, and hence the Son cannot be *homoousios* with the Father—is misguided and should be withdrawn. Especially understanding the gravity of this charge—one that implicitly charges advocates of ERAS with heresy—I would humbly request both Millard Erickson and Tom McCall to retract this charge.

Permit me a few related comments in closing. First, Erickson addresses some of the biblical support advocates of ERAS have put forward, though he misses much, and some that he misses is among the strongest biblical argumentation.[13] For his part, McCall simply skirts past altogether the massive biblical and historical evidence that Grudem and I put forward in our debate. His discussion of our position, if the reader knew nothing else, would lead one to think that we have only passages that speak of the incarnational submission of the Son to the Father to base our view on. This description of our view is deceptively selective and misleading, to say the least. The reader who cares to may listen to and view the October 9, 2008, debate in which Grudem and I lay out a large summary of our evidence, along with the McCall-Yandell opening statements and our interaction.[14]

Second, one wonders whether our culture, including our evangelical subculture, has become, in the words of Edith Humphrey, "allergic to authority."[15] She expresses astonishment at Gilbert Bilezikian's claim that the ERAS position comprises a "weird heresy" in the contemporary evangelical movement. To the contrary, she says, Bilezikian's is the position that stands against most of those in the history of the church—East, West, Catholic, and Protestant. Reflecting on the early Trinitarian formulations, she comments:

---
[13] See Grudem's response to Erickson in Grudem, "Biblical Evidence for the Eternal Submission of the Son to the Father."
[14] The debate video can be found at http://henrycenter.tiu.edu/resource/do-relations-of-authority-and-submission-exist-eternally-among-the-persons-of-the-godhead/.
[15] Edith Humphrey, "The Gift of the Father: Looking at Salvation History Upside Down," chap. 3 in *Trinitarian Theology for the Church: Scripture, Community, and Worship*, ed. Daniel J. Treier and David Lauber (Downers Grove, IL: InterVarsity, 2009), 94.

> It was a while before the entire church understood the full mystery of the Trinity and agreed to call the Son "of one essence with the Father." But the ancient theologians never left behind the clear implications of the name "Father," nor did they ignore the intimations of Scripture that the Son is eternally obedient to the Father. . . . Here is God's own answer to our faltering and power-hungry relationships. We need God's own pattern in our day, which is experiencing both a crisis of authority and a disregard for the dignity of each person. In the wisdom of the Holy Spirit, we have come to understand that hierarchy and mutuality are not at odds in the triune God, but an ineffable mystery.[16]

Third and finally, advocates of ERAS have consistently affirmed the full, unqualified, and eternal *homoousios* of the Son with the Father and Spirit. To deny *homoousios* and the full deity of the Son is unthinkable for those who advance this position. So the charge that our position entails its denial is weighty, serious, and grave, but a charge that we reject altogether.

Also weighty to us, though, is the clear biblical teaching that the Father created the universe through the agency of the Son (1 Cor. 8:6; Heb. 1:1–2), that the Son came down from heaven not to do his own will but to do the will of the Father who sent him (John 6:38), that the Son became incarnate not on his own initiative but because the Father sent him (John 8:42), that the Son submits himself to the Father in his exaltation as he sits at the Father's right hand (1 Cor. 15:28), and that this relationship marked by the Father's authority and the Son's submission is never, never reversed.

Faithfulness to Scripture requires affirming both the full equality of essence of the Father, Son, and Spirit, and the eternal authority-submission relationship distinctions among those persons. Equality and distinction both must be upheld for Trinitarian monotheism to be true. Our proposal seeks to do just this, and to do it in a manner fully faithful to all of the Bible's teaching. In the end, God will judge us all. May our goal be to represent the self-revelation of God as accurately and completely as we are able, that we may truly know the glory of the unity and distinctiveness of the one God who is three.

---

[16] Ibid., 98–99.

Contributors

Kyle Claunch (PhD candidate, The Southern Baptist Theological Seminary) is the senior pastor of Highland Park First Baptist Church, Louisville, Kentucky.

Christopher W. Cowan (PhD, The Southern Baptist Theological Seminary) is an editor for Bibles and reference books at B&H Publishing.

Philip R. Gons (MA, Bob Jones University) is senior director of marketing at the Faithlife Corporation.

Wayne Grudem (PhD, University of Cambridge) is research professor of theology and biblical studies at Phoenix Seminary.

James M. Hamilton Jr. (PhD, The Southern Baptist Theological Seminary) is professor of biblical theology at The Southern Baptist Theological Seminary and preaching pastor at Kenwood Baptist Church, Louisville, Kentucky.

Michael A. G. Haykin (ThD, University of Toronto) is professor of church history and biblical spirituality at The Southern Baptist Theological Seminary and director of the Andrew Fuller Center for Baptist Studies.

Robert Letham (PhD, Aberdeen University) is director of research and senior lecturer in systematic and historical theology at Wales Evangelical School of Theology.

Andrew David Naselli (PhD, Trinity Evangelical Divinity School) is assistant professor of New Testament and biblical theology at Bethlehem College and Seminary.

K. Scott Oliphint (PhD, Westminster Theological Seminary) is professor of apologetics and systematic theology at Westminster Theological Seminary.

Michael J. Ovey (PhD, King's College, London) is principal of Oak Hill Theological College.

John Starke (MDiv candidate, The Southern Baptist Theological Seminary) is the preaching pastor of Apostles Church in Manhattan.

Bruce A. Ware (PhD, Fuller Theological Seminary) is professor of Christian theology at The Southern Baptist Theological Seminary.

General Index

Absalom, 144–45
Adam, Peter, 127, 128n9
Adam-Christ typology, 98
ad intra and *ad extra* relations, of Trinity, 78n37, 90, 230
Adonijah, 144
Aeneas, 143
agency (Jewish concept), 49, 53
Allen, John, 178–79
Allen, Michael, 165–66, 171n58
analogia entis, 226n17
analogical, revelation as, 85–86, 88
Anatolios, Khaled, 113
Anchises, 143
anhypostasia, 166
archetypal and ectypal theology, 227
aretegenic, 186
Arianism, 18n5, 66, 106, 115, 120, 122, 127–28, 132–33, 135, 137, 139, 140, 149, 150, 158, 191, 195n2, 196n2, 200, 206, 239
Arius, 132n29
assumptio carnis, 231
Athanasius, 117, 127, 129, 131, 139n63, 142–45, 151, 241–43
  on divine cosmic monarchy, 136
  on eternal generation, 112–14
  on Holy Spirit, 191
Augustine, 25n13, 83–85, 87, 90–91, 105n9, 117, 155, 224
  on eternal generation, 161–66, 171
  on inseparable operation, 167–71, 172
  on love, 154
authority, headship as, 69–75, 80

Ayres, Lewis, 83n44, 130n19, 133, 134, 139n62

Bakunin, Mikhail, 127
Balthasar, Hans Urs von, 91n54
baptism, and the Trinity, 192–94
Barnes, Michele René, 83n44
Barrett, C. K., 47, 54, 54–55n25, 63, 71n22, 72n24, 75
Bartel, Timothy, 204, 205n29
Barth, Karl, 231–32, 234
Basil of Ancyra, 129, 140–42
Basil of Caesarea, 83n44, 114–15
Bavinck, Herman, 113, 119, 121, 229
Bedale, Stephen, 70
Beeley, Christopher, 117
begotten, 18n5, 28, 114, 120, 121, 142, 241–42
Belleville, Linda, 17, 26–28, 30–31, 33–37
Bible
  authority of, 32–44
  good and necessary deductions from, 110
  inerrancy of, 73n27
Bilezikian, Gilbert, 17, 66n3, 195n2, 199n14, 247
Bird, Michael, 207
Blasphemia (357), 129, 139–40, 149, 150
Blomberg, Craig, 95
Boettner, Loraine, 200n18
Buswell, J. Oliver, 200n18

Calvin, John, 105n9, 106–7, 118–19, 124, 164
   on headship, 75–76
   on incommunicable properties, 202
   on mystery of the Trinity, 212–13
   on persons of the Trinity, 200–201n19
   on simplicity and triunity of God, 225, 228–29
Cappadocians, 117, 224, 245, 246
Cardale, Paul, 184
Carnley, Peter, 128n5, 130, 140, 153
Carson, D. A., 55, 62, 197n7
Cary, Phillip, 17
Chalcedonian Creed (451), 28–29, 89, 232, 233n28
Charry, Ellen T., 186n61
christology, paradox of, 64n58
Christou, Panayiotis, 114
"Church and King" riots, 186
circumincession, 25n13
Comma Johanneum, 193
complementarians, 12, 95, 196
   on Augustine, 156, 158
   as *homoousian*, 171
   misrepresentation of, 160–61
Constantius, Emperor, 131, 133
Council of Nicaea (325), 199
Council of Constantinople (381), 117, 246
covenant condescension, 234
Craig, William Lane, 200n18, 215–16, 222n9
creation, 234
   versus generation, 120
Creator-creature distinction, 123
Creator-creature relationship, 140–41, 150, 151
Cross, Richard, 206
Cullmann, Oscar, 64n58

Dahms, John, 122, 201n20
Davey, J. Ernst, 55n28
David, sons of, 144–45
Davis, John, 177
Dawes, Gregory, 71

Dedication Creed (341), 131–33, 134, 135, 137, 139
deism, 190
ditheism, 63n57
divine monarchy, 136–37, 139, 151
Dünzl, Franz, 131n22, 133nn32–33, 134, 135n43
Dutton, Anne, 178
dyothelitism, 89, 171n58

economic Trinity, 67, 78–81, 195n1
   reveals immanent Trinity, 84–87, 88
egalitarians, 13, 95, 171, 196
   on Augustine, 156
enhypostasia, 166
Enlightenment, 173, 174
Epiphanius of Salamis, 141n68
equivalent-authority position, 40, 156n1, 238. *See also* "temporary submission" position
equivocal thinking, 85–86
Erickson, Millard, 17, 18, 61, 96, 106, 156n1, 171, 200n18, 205n28, 237–47
   on act of persons of Trinity, 19–25
   on Augustine, 158
   and authority of Scripture, 32–33
   on creation, 42
   on eternal functional subordination, 199
   on eternal generation, 110
   on names "Father" and "Son" as not eternal, 29–30
   on sending of Son, 35n33
   on temporary submission of the Son, 40–41
eschatological subordination of the Son, 105
essence, 246
   and person, 114, 118, 120, 200n19
   versus property, 240–43
eternal functional equality (EFE), 197
eternal functional subordination (EFS), 159–60, 197, 199, 203, 237–38, 239–40, 244, 246
eternal generation, 178–80, 200n19
   Augustine on, 85, 161–66, 171

church fathers on, 109–17
  as immanent, 86
  and inseparable operation, 156, 158–59, 164–65, 170–72
eternal procession, 200n19
eternal relational authority-submission (ERAS), 237–48
eternal submission of the Son, 32, 37, 88, 90, 243
eternal subordination of the Son, 60–64, 82, 83, 198–205
evangelical egalitarians, 12
evangelical feminists, 17, 28, 37
evangelicals, on authority, 247

Father, 28
  authority over the Son, 18, 204–5
  as beginning of deity, 164, 170
  chooses and predestines, 37–39
  chose us in the Son, 37–39
  creates the world through the Son, 41–42
  delegates authority, 35
  as eternal name, 29
  as "from no one," 90
  as greater than the Son, 59–60
  hears prayers of Jesus Christ, 35
  possible incarnation of, 206–9
  sending of the Son, 22, 35, 60n47, 61–62, 84–85, 91, 156, 169, 211
  as source, 116
  suffering of, 23
  as unbegotten, 90
Father-Son relationship, 140–41, 148, 150–52
  in the Gospel of John, 47–64
  in the Old Testament, 52
  same or separate will in, 170–71
  as symmetrical, 60
Fee, Gordon D., 68, 72, 75n30, 79
Feinberg, John S., 110, 200n18, 204, 205n29
feminist theologians, 12
finite and the infinite, 228n17
Fiorenza, Elizabeth Schüssler, 12
First Creed of Antioch (341), 131n26, 133n32, 148

First Creed of Sirmium (351), 137–39, 146, 148
firstfruits, 98–101
First London Confession of Faith (1644/1646), 176
Fitzpatrick, Martin, 181
Ford, Stephen, 184
form of a servant, 26, 85, 87, 163
form of God, 163
Frame, John, 197n7
Fuller, Andrew, 173–75, 178, 186–94
functional order of the Father and Son, 163
functional subordination, as Arian, 66

Gathercole, Simon, 106
gender roles, 12, 68, 196
General Baptists, 176n12
generation, 90, 110, 111, 118. *See also* eternal generation
  as ineffable, 119–20
  as participation, 113
  versus creation, 120
Giles, Kevin, 17, 18, 48, 53, 55n22, 58n39, 61, 66n3, 96, 122, 130, 144, 153, 157, 162, 165, 171, 195n2
  on Augustine, 83, 87, 105n9, 158
  on eternal subordination of the Son, 82
  on "isolated texts," 44
  on obedience of Christ, 128
Gill, John, 173, 177–80, 193
Gnosticism, 110
God
  aseity of, 218, 221
  attributes of, 228, 243, 245
  communicable and incommunicable attributes of, 234n31
  and creation, 230–33
  essential and covenantal characteristics, 233, 234
  eternity of, 222–23
  as "the head of Christ," 66–67, 75, 77–78, 79–82, 84–87, 93
  incomprehensibility of, 119–20, 229–33

independence of, 217n5, 218
as personal, 217
properties of, 217–18
simplicity of, 215–23, 229
sovereignty of, 217n5
triunity of, 223–29
as without passions, 223–24n10
Gordon, Alexander, 183
gradational authority, 237–38, 239, 156n1
Gregory of Nazianzus, 116–17, 225
Gregory of Nyssa, 83n44, 115–16
Groothuis, Rebecca, 17, 95, 199n14
Grudem, Wayne, 70, 88, 89n52, 106, 157, 196n2, 197n7, 205n28, 207, 209, 238, 243, 247
on eternal generation, 160, 162
Gruenler, Royce Gordon, 54–55, 60
Gunton, Colin, 152n99

Haenchen, Ernst, 55
Hammond, Fred, 66n4
Hanson, R. P. C., 129, 139n61
Harris, Howel, 178
head, headship, 67, 69–75
four gradations of, 75–76
head coverings, 69, 75, 76–77
heaven, 14
Helm, Paul, 200n18
heresy, 128, 244, 247
heteroousios, 198, 201
hierarchicalism, 13
Hilary of Poitiers, 129, 131n23, 133n34, 134n42, 145–50, 151, 152–53
Hildebrand, Stephen M., 115
Hodge, Charles, 107–8, 197n7
holiness, 234n32, 235
Holy Spirit
divinity of, 191
possible incarnation of, 206–9
procession of, 90, 200n19
sending of the Son, 209–12
sent by Father and the Son, 92
suffering of, 23

homoousios, 112, 114, 149, 151, 168, 171, 198–201, 206, 209, 239–41, 242, 246, 247–48
House, Wayne, 44, 238
Hughes, Christopher, 225–27
human generation, 120
human relationships
equality within, 123–25
fellowship and diversity in, 152
Humphrey, Edith, 247–48
husbands, love for wives, 26
hypostasis, 115, 116, 133, 245
hypothetical necessity, 220–21n6

image of God, 123, 234–35
immanent Trinity, 78, 81, 195n1
complementarity grounded in, 78–82, 92–93
as ground of economic Trinity, 84–87
hierarchy in, 195, 197–98
not imitated in social institutions, 66
one divine will in, 88–89
relation with economic Trinity, 67
revealed in economic missions of Son and Spirit, 84
incarnation, 79–81, 87, 91–92, 144, 166–67
corresponds to something in the Son, 209
subordination in, 107–8
inseparable operation, 156, 158, 160, 163, 167–71, 172
Irenaeus, 111

Jehovah's Witness, 128n8
Jesus Christ
on authority and sovereignty, 57
baptism of, 22, 30, 169
chooses those to whom he reveals the Father, 20–21
deity of, 11, 190
died for our sins, 23
divine and human nature of, 233
exaltation of, 13, 63
as "head of every man," 76–77, 79
humility of, 13

intercession of, 42–43
obedience of, 57, 128
as object of prayer and worship, 184–85, 187–90
prayer in Gethsemane, 169
resurrection of, 30, 97–103, 118–19
rule over the church, 76
as Son of God, 34
transfiguration of, 30
unity of will with Father, 57–58
John, Gospel of, 47–64
Father-Son language of, 35
John of Damascus, 117–18
Johnson, Alan F., 69–70n13, 70
Johnson, Keith E., 66n4, 158–60, 161, 162–63, 165, 167, 171
on Augustine, 83, 90–91
on sending of the Son, 167–71
John the Baptist, 49, 54
Jowers, Dennis, 17, 44, 238
Julius, Pope, 131
Justin, 110–11

Keener, Craig, 49nn8–9, 64n59
Keller, Tim, 197n7
knowledge, 234n32, 235
Köstenberger, Andreas, 197n7, 207
Kovach, Stephen, 195n2, 197n7

LaCugna, Catherine, 12
Letham, Robert, 11n1, 157, 162, 166, 170, 195n2, 197n7, 207
"life-in-himself," 62
Lindsey, Theophilus, 183
Lofthouse, W. F., 52
Logos doctrine, 111
love, 154
intratrinitarian, 14

Macrostich Creed (345), 135–37, 148
man, as "the head of woman," 77–78, 79–80, 93
Marcellus of Ancyra, 130n18, 131–33, 135, 137n54, 149
Marlow, Isaac, 177
marriage relationship, 73

McCall, Thomas, 66n3, 196n2, 198, 199–203, 205n28, 206–8, 210–11, 212n51, 237–47
McCormack, Bruce, 231–32
men and women, ontologically equivalent and functionally distinct, 66
Mercer, Calvin, 49n7
Meyer, Paul, 55–56
missions and processions of Trinity, 121
modalism, 11, 24–25, 86, 111, 125, 130n18
Moltmann, Jürgen, 12, 153n103
monarchianism, 25n14
monothelitism, 89
Moreland, J. P., 215–16
Morris, Leon, 48n5, 105n10
Mortimer, Sarah, 175
Muller, Richard A., 221, 224, 227–28, 228n17
mutual deference and submission between Father and Son, 54
mutual submission within the Trinity, 210

nature/grace methodology (Thomas Aquinas), 226
necessity, 196n3, 217, 219–20
neo-Arians, 245
Neoplatonism, 110, 215–16
Nestorianism, 128n10, 166
new creation, 72
Newman, John Henry, 128n4
Nicaea, 205
Nicene Creed (325), 28–29, 83, 127n1, 154, 241–43
Niceno-Constantinopolitan Creed (381), 109
Noble, Thomas, 116
non-Nicenes, 139, 154

obedience, 56
in Christ's humanity, 128
of disciples, 57
and unity of will, 58
Old Testament
on father-son relationship, 52

monotheism of, 27
on submission, 58
Olson, Roger, 197n7
Omelianchuk, Adam, 199n14
omnipotence, and incarnation, 206
one and many, of God's character, 224
only begotten, 28, 109, 114–15, 118, 141, 146, 241
ontological equality, 124
and functional subordination, 95, 106, 108
Open Theism, 130n19
order (*taxis*) of persons in Godhead, 90–93, 121, 212n51, 234
order of authority and submission, 156–60, 161, 171, 172
Giles on, 165
and inseparable operation, 167–68
Owen on, 164–65
Origen, 111–12, 132n29
Owen, John, 164–65

pactum salutis, 234n33
participation, 113
Particular Baptists, 175, 176–78
passions, 223–24n10
paternity, Athanasius on, 142–43
patripassianism, 23–24, 125, 169
Paul
on Father-Son relation, 34, 36, 106
on the resurrection, 96–103
on social customs, 81
Payne, Philip B., 95
Pederson, Johannes, 52
perichoresis, 24, 25n13, 118, 205n30
personal properties, of the Trinity, 200n19, 245
Pharisees, emissaries of, 49–50, 54
Photinus of Sirmium, 130n18, 137
Pinnock, Clark, 130n19
Piper, John, 197n7
Plantinga, Alvin, 216–17
Pohle, Arthur, 205n30
postmodernism, 130n17
power, and substance, 163–64
Praxeas, 111
Priestley, Joseph, 180–86, 191

properties
of the essence, 202, 205n28, 245
of the person, 200n19, 202, 205, 245
property, and essence, 201–3, 205n28, 240–43

reason and revelation, 226–27
Reeves, Michael, 67n6, 74n29
religious pluralism, 83n45
resurrection, 97–104
revelation, as accommodated, 85
Reymond, Robert L., 110, 118, 200n18, 207
righteousness, 234n32, 235
Rippon, John, 178
Romaine, William, 178
Ryland, John Collett, 190n85

Sabellianism, 130, 132, 134, 149, 169
Schreiner, Thomas, 68, 73, 74, 195n2, 197n7
Second Antioch Creed. *See* Dedication Creed (341)
Second Council of Constantinople (553), 109, 166, 233n28
Second London Confession of Faith (1677/1689), 176
Second Sirmium Creed. *See* Blasphemia (357)
semi-Arianism, 158, 239
sending/sent language, 49n9, 86, 106, 121, 159, 162, 165, 168, 172, 210–12
Serdica Encyclical (343), 133–35, 137, 147, 148
servant, and sonship, 142–45
Servetus, Michael, 175
Shillaker, Robert, 207
slaves, submission to masters, 81
Smith, Jay, 98
social model of the Trinity, 67, 92
Socinianism, 175, 178–85, 189, 190
sola Scriptura, 227
Son. *See also* submission of the Son; subordination of the Son
as creature, 140, 150–51

deity and subjection of, 138, 147
delivers kingdom to the Father, 101
as dependent upon and obedient to the Father, 50–51
as eternally Son, 28–32
as eternal name, 29
as from the Father, 90
filial subjection of, 149, 152–53
as firstborn, 119
humiliation of, 60n47
obedience of, 36, 55–56, 234n34
sent by the Father, 48–49, 61–62, 84–85, 92, 156, 159
submission after completion of earthly ministry, 42–43
submission to the Spirit, 209–12
suffering of, 22–23
uniquely fitted to the work of the incarnation, 208–9
will be subject to the Father, 105, 108
will hand kingdom over to the Father, 105, 108
Son of God, 27, 32–33, 34, 233n30
Son of Man, 32–33
source, head as, 69–75
sovereign-aseity intuition (SAI), 217, 219
Sozzini, Fausto, 175
Sozzini, Lelio Francesco, 175
Stennett, Joseph, II, 177
Strong, A. H., 197n7
submission of the Son, 20, 101, 122–23, 144, 146–65, 204–5. *See also* eternal submission of the Son; "temporary submission" position
subordination of the Son, 111, 114, 122–23, 125, 139–40. *See also* eternal subordination of the Son
"of filial love," 147
in immanent or economic Trinity, 197
subsistence, 200n19, 202
Sumner, Sarah, 25–26
superordination/submission, 128, 130–35, 137, 142, 144, 146, 148, 150

Swain, Scott, 165–66, 171n58, 207
systematic theology, 175

taxis. *See* order (*taxis*) of persons in Godhead
"temporary submission" position, 33, 37, 40–42, 44, 48, 60
temporary subordination of Son to the Spirit, 212n51
Tertullian, 111, 134n39, 136
theology, as assemblage of explicit biblical texts, 110
Third Council of Constantinople (680), 223n28
Thiselton, Anthony, 65, 70–71, 72n25
Thomas, profession of faith of, 31
Thomas Aquinas, 170–71, 206–8, 225–27
Thompson, Marianne Meye, 56, 58–60
three-willed Trinity, 88–91, 92
Trinitarian community, 175, 176, 190, 194
Trinitarian relations, shed light on human relations, 13
Trinity
  and act of any person as act of all three persons, 19–28
  ad intra and *ad extra* relations, 78n37, 90, 230
  and baptism, 192–94
  differentiation of persons of, 18–19, 89–90, 120, 123, 212
  as inherently relational, 119
  love within, 14
  orthodox doctrine of, 18–32
  as three-willed, 88–91, 92
tritheism, 125, 153n103
triunity, ontological and economic, 233–34
Turretin, Francis, 220–21n6, 221n7

univocal thinking, 85–86, 219
univocal notion of being, 226

Van Til, Cornelius, 228
Vergil, 143n77

virgin birth, 26n18
virtue, 186, 190
Volf, Miroslav, 25n13
Vos, Geerhardus, 169–70, 208n44

Wallin, Benjamin, 177
Ware, Bruce, 30, 81–82, 87, 88, 195n2, 196n2, 197n7, 203n22, 205nn27–29, 207, 209
  on Augustine, 157, 167–68
  on eternal generation, 110, 160, 162
Watts, Michael R., 180
Weinandy, Thomas, 112
Wellum, Stephen, 162
Westminster Confession of Faith, 110, 223, 229
White, B. R., 176
will
  of Father and Son, 170–71
  as property of person not essence, 88
Williams, Rowan, 128n7
wives, submission to husbands, 26
worship, 73

Yandell, Keith, 196n2, 198, 199n15, 200, 200n18, 203n23, 210–11, 212n51, 243, 247

Zizioulas, John, 245

Scripture Index

Genesis
2:21–24   75n29
2:24   74
19   151
19:24   138, 138n58

Exodus
20:12   53

Leviticus
23:9–14   98

Judges
18:19   52

2 Samuel
15:13   144n79

1 Kings
1:11   144n80

2 Kings
2:12   52
5:13   52

Psalms
1:2   58
2   30
2:2   30
2:6   30
2:7   30, 118
2:8   30
2:12   30n24
8:6   100
40:8   38, 58
110:1   100, 138
119:14   58
119:16   58
119:24   58
119:35   58
119:70   58
119:77   58
119:111   58

Isaiah
42   13
53:8   111

Daniel
7:13   104, 106
17   106

Matthew
book of   211n
1:20   26n18
3:16   22
3:17   22
4:1   210, 211n
11:25   35
11:27   20, 21, 35
15:24   35n33
20:23   43
26:39   35, 169
28:19   27, 121, 132, 192, 192n81, 193n86, 194
28:19–20   121

260 Scripture Index

Mark
book of	211n
1:11	30
1:12	210, 211n
7:9ff.	145n84
9:7	30
9:37	35n33
12:6	49
13:32	35, 108

Luke
book of	211n
1:33	106
2:49	30
2:51	151, 151n96
3	169
3:22	169
4:1	210, 211n
4:18	35n33
4:43	35n33
9:48	35n33
10:16	35n33
10:17	151
10:21	35
10:22	36
11:1–2	183
22:42	183

John
book of	48, 51–52, 54, 55n25, 56, 61, 64, 153, 211n
1:1	30, 35, 39, 47, 60, 64, 114
1:1–3	41
1:6	49
1:14	29, 31
1:18	64
1:19	50
1:22	50
1:24	50
1:33	49
3:16	27, 29, 35, 64
3:16–17	48
3:17	48, 61, 62
3:18	62
3:34	50
3:35	50, 53, 153
3:36	62
4:34	35n33, 38, 48, 51, 56, 58
5:17	50
5:18	18, 50, 140n67, 180
5:19	50, 51, 53, 55, 162, 169
5:19–20	21
5:19–30	50, 54
5:20	51, 53, 64
5:21	20, 31
5:21–29	51
5:22	35, 50, 55, 62
5:23	32, 48, 49, 53
5:23–24	35n33
5:25	32
5:26	31, 32, 50, 58, 59, 60, 62, 151n97
5:26–27	35
5:27	50, 54, 55
5:27–29	62
5:29	62
5:30	21, 35n33, 36, 49, 50, 51, 54, 170
5:36	50
5:36–38	35n33
6:29	35n33, 49
6:37	21, 50
6:37–39	21
6:38	36, 48, 49, 51, 54, 56, 62, 80, 132, 144, 145, 145n83, 248
6:38–39	35n33
6:39	50
6:44	21, 35n33, 50
6:57	35n33, 58, 59
6:65	21, 50
7:16	35n33, 49

Scripture Index 261

7:17	56	14:16	63
7:18	35n33, 49	14:21	57n35
7:28	36, 48, 50	14:23	57n35
7:28–29	35n33, 48	14:23–24	57
7:32	50	14:24	35n33, 48, 49, 57n35
7:33	35n33, 49, 62		
7:45	50	14:26	63
8:16	35n33	14:28	52n13, 53, 55n25, 59, 60, 64n58, 134
8:18	35n33		
8:26	35n33, 49, 50, 51	14:31	51, 58, 64, 128, 147, 153
8:28	21, 50, 53		
8:29	35n33, 48, 51, 53	15:10	51, 57, 57n35, 153
8:38	50, 51, 53	15:20	57n35
8:40	50, 51	15:21	35n33
8:42	35n33, 48, 50, 62, 248	15:23	53
		15:26	63
8:49	53	16:5	35n33, 49, 59
8:51	57n35	16:23	184
8:52	57n35	16:28	62
8:55	53, 57	17:2	50, 153
9:31	56	17:3	35n33, 48
10:15	169	17:4	50, 51
10:17–18	165	17:5	39, 63
10:18	51, 55, 57	17:6	50, 57n35
10:29	50	17:8	35n33, 50, 62
10:30	64, 64n58	17:9	50
10:30–39	140n67	17:18	35n33, 62
10:33	140n67	17:21	35n33
10:36	35n33	17:21–23	14
11:41	35	17:23	35n33
11:42	35n33	17:24	39, 63
12:44	48	17:25	35n33
12:44–45	35n33, 53	18:8–9	57
12:49	35n33, 49, 50, 51	18:11	50
13:1	62	19:7	140n67
13:3	50, 62	19:11	57
13:16	49	19:24	57b
13:18–19	57	19:30	51
13:20	35n33, 49, 53	20:17	63
14:9	115, 157	20:21	35n33
14:10	50	20:22	63n55
14:12	59	20:28	31
14:15	57n35	20:29	31

262 Scripture Index

20:30–31	31	1:19	36
		5–7	96
Acts		8–10	96
1	32	8:6	35, 42, 248
1:9–11	104	11	81
2:1–4	63	11–14	96
2:32	35	11:2–16	65, 67, 68, 69, 70, 71, 72, 73, 75, 78, 81, 92, 93
2:33	32		
4:24–30	183		
5:3–4	191	11:3	13, 65, 66, 67, 67n6, 68, 69, 71, 72, 72n25, 73, 74, 74n29, 75, 75n30, 76, 77, 77n36, 78, 79, 80, 80n, 81, 82, 86, 87, 92, 93, 108, 137n51
7:59	187, 187n63		
9:5	187		
9:10	187		
9:13	187		
9:14	187		
9:17	187		
10:42	35		
12:5	183	11:3ff.	74
13:33	30, 118	11:3–5	71
17:31	35	11:4	72, 79
25:24	43	11:4–5	75
		11:7	68
Romans		11:8	71n22, 72, 74
1:4	36	11:10	68, 75
1:30	145n84	11:14–15	68
8:3	34, 164	11:17–34	102
8:29	29, 35, 38	12:4–6	121
8:32	34, 36	15	95, 96, 103, 107
8:34	43	15:1	96
9:5	190	15:1–4	96, 101, 103
10	190	15:2	96, 102
10:13	187, 189	15:3	96
10:13–15a	189	15:3b–4	96
10:14	189	15:5	97
11:33–36	229	15:5–11	97, 101, 103
13:1	151	15:7	97
15:6	34, 36	15:8–10	97
15:30	192n81	15:11	97
		15:12	96, 98
1 Corinthians		15:12–13	97
book of	96n	15:12–19	97, 101, 103
1–4	96	15:14	97, 102
1:2	187, 189	15:15	97

Scripture Index 263

15:16	97	15:57	104
15:17	97	15:58	102, 103
15:18	97		
15:19	97	*2 Corinthians*	
15:20	100	1:3	34, 36
15:20–28	96, 97, 98, 99, 101, 102, 103, 104, 106	5:17	72
		11:31	34
15:21–22	98, 100	13:14	121, 192n81, 193
15:22–28	63		
15:23	98, 99, 100, 101, 108	*Galatians*	
		book of	211n
15:23b	104	2:20	36
15:23–25	98	4:4	34, 35, 36, 80, 164, 180, 211n
15:23–26	99		
15:24	28, 99, 101, 104, 105, 106, 107, 108	*Ephesians*	
		1–3	188
15:24–25	99, 100	1:3	34, 36, 188
15:24–28	96, 103, 106, 107	1:3–5	35, 37, 38
15:25	99, 100, 101, 104	1:9–11	39
15:26	99, 100, 101, 104	1:22	79
15:27	100, 101, 105	2:18	121, 188, 192n81
15:27–28	99, 100	3:8	188
15:28	13, 27, 28, 80n, 100, 101, 104, 105, 106, 107, 108, 196, 248	3:9–11	35, 39
		3:14	184, 188
15:29	102	3:18–19	188
15:29–34	102, 103	4:4–6	121
15:30–32b	102	4:13	36
15:32c	102	4:24	234n32
15:33–34	102	5	108
15:35	102	5:21	122, 210
15:35–49	103	5:21–33	71
15:36	102	5:22	73
15:36–38	102	5:22–24	73
15:39	102	5:22–31	74
15:40–41	102	5:22–33	72, 73, 74, 77n36, 80
15:42–49	102		
15:45	98	5:23	73, 76, 77, 79
15:50	102	5:24	73, 151n96
15:50–57	100, 103, 104	5:28	26
15:51–52	104	5:31	74
15:51–57	102	6:1–3	145n84
15:54	104		

Philippians

2:1–5	123
2:1–11	13
2:5	27
2:5–6	27
2:5–8	81
2:5–9	83n47
2:6	13, 27
2:6–7	26, 27
2:7	13
2:8	128
2:9–11	13
4:6	184

Colossians

1:3	34
1:15	119
1:16	72
1:18	79
3:10	234n32
3:18	151n96
3:20	145n84

1 Thessalonians

3:13	104
4:13–18	104
4:16–17	104

2 Thessalonians

3:5	192n81, 193

1 Timothy

book of	73n27
2:5	79
2:11–13	73, 74
2:13	74
3:4	145n84

2 Timothy

1:2	35
1:9	38
1:9–10	35
2:13	230

3:16	34

Titus

1:2	78

Hebrews

book of	220
1:1–2	35, 41, 248
1:2	29
1:5	30
1:8	180
1:13	100
2:5–9	100
2:17	89
5:5	30
5:8–9	180
6:13–20	220
6:18	230
7:23–26	42
9:14	123
10:7–9	36

James

1:5	184
4:10	13

1 Peter

1:1–2	40
1:19–21	40
3:1	151n96
3:6	151n96

2 Peter

1:11	106
1:17	36

1 John

book of	211n
2:3f.	57n35
2:3ff.	57
2:17	56
3:8	180
3:22	57

3:24	57, 57n35	19	99
4:9–10	35	19–20	99
5:3	57, 57n35	19:20	104
5:7	84, 84n49, 179, 192n81, 193	20	99, 99n, 100, 107
		20:1–6	99
		20:1–15	99
Jude		20:4	104, 107
20–21	192n81	20:4–5	104
		20:4–6	98
Revelation		20:5–6	99
book of	104	20:7–10	99, 104
1:1	35	20:11–15	99, 101
1:4–5	121	20:12–14	104
1:17b	179	20:13	99
2:26	35	20:14	99
3:8	57n35	21	107
4	107	21–22	104
4–5	107	21:3	104
4:11	141n69	21:5	104
5:10	104	21:23	104
11:11	104	22	107
12:17	57n35	22:3	107
13:8	40	22:3–5	104
14:12	57n35		

Also Available from Bruce A. Ware

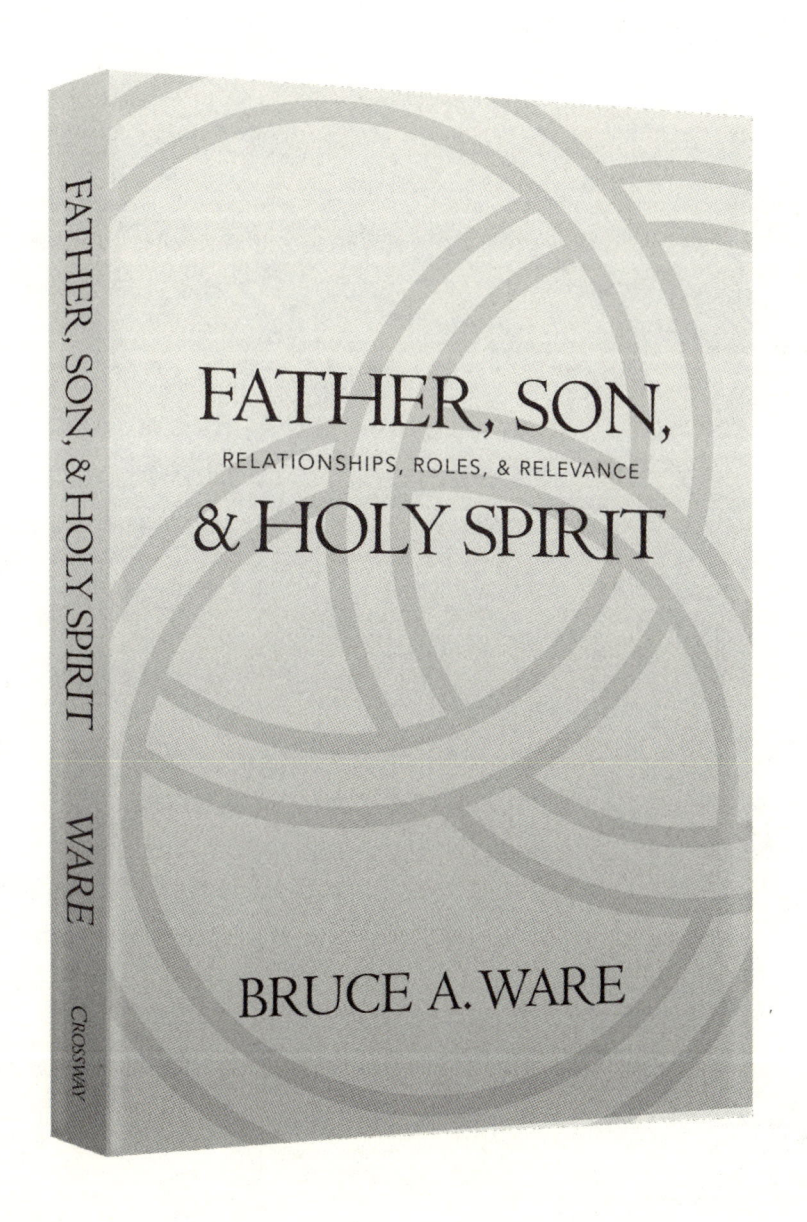

FATHER, SON, & HOLY SPIRIT

RELATIONSHIPS, ROLES, & RELEVANCE

BRUCE A. WARE

For more information, visit crossway.org.